ROD CRAFTING

A Full-Color Pictorial & Written History from 1843-1960

Jeffrey L. Hatton

Dad on his 79th birthday fishing the West Elk Wilderness with a Gnomish Rod Works Shedua mortised bamboo fly rod built by the author.

The Smith Age 1870 and earlier
The Expansion Era 1870 - 1900
The Classical Era 1900 - 1960

Featuring 150+ rods from over 50 makers and over 900 color photographs

Frank Amato
PORTLAND

Photo by Dave Shinn

The rod pictured with the author is a 100 plus year old example of what is most likely a one of a kind hollow-built quadrate rod. The rod butt section is made up of over 56 individual pieces of wood. Note how the rod is literally a see-through rod.

The author is a Colorado native horribly addicted from a very early age to anything having to do with fishing and especially fly fishing. It is all Dad's fault, and I dearly love him for it! He currently resides in the town of Paonia on the banks of the North Fork of the Gunnison River.

The author was raised on the Front Range north of Denver and graduated in 1979 from Longmont High School. After high school the author apprenticed himself to the local ironworkers union and attained his Journeyman's Card before the age of twenty-one. In the early 1980s, Hatton began to chase his dream of being a professional fly-fisherman. In the last 22 years this has consisted of a widely varied career path with the common thread of fly-fishing running through it, from tying flies for A.K. Best for three years, to working in fly shops, guiding in the Gunnison Gorge off and on over a 15-year period and even a 4-year stint as the production manager and harvest foreman for Whiting Farms. A three-year stint with the Scott Rod Company in the late 1990s convinced Hatton it was time to chase his dream of making split-bamboo fly rods under his own company name, Gnomish Rod Works. The author specializes in making mortised rods in the style of the late 1800s—when he's not chasing "old rods" or wild fish.

Interior design, lay-out, and editing supplied by author Jeffrey L. Hatton
Publishing (printing & distribution) supplied by Frank Amato Publications

All inquiries should be addressed to:
Frank Amato Publications, Inc. • P.O. Box 82112 • Portland, Oregon 97282
503-653-8108 • www.amatobooks.com

SB ISBN: 1-57188-356-8
SB UPC: 0-81127-00190-3
HB ISBN: 1-57188-357-6
HB UPC: 0-81127-00191-0
Limited HB ISBN: 1-57188-358-4
Limited HB UPC: 0-81127-00192-7
Printed in Hong Kong
1 3 5 7 9 10 8 6 4 2

Dedicated to

*M*y Brothers Bob and Dick, our time together in the woods and on the waters was way too short, but you on in my memories, When I am on the water or in the woods you are with me.

*A*nd secondly to all of the brothers and sister's of the Angle who admire a fishing rod not only for its function but also for the artwork and the abilities of the craftsmen who have created the tools that we fish with.

Jeffrey L. Hatton
Wading Along the Banks of Time, Stick in Hand

THE RIVER CRAY

The engravings and colored copper plates from the 1800s are examples of work by truly talented artisans.

Engraving from T.C. Hofland's British Anglers Manual 1839.

Pictured above and below are engravings from T.C. Hofland British Anglers Manual published in 1839 in London, England

Foreword
By Bob Corsetti

I have known Jeff Hatton for some years as one of my catalog customers and as an accomplished cane rod maker. As he built his cane rods, he wondered how the rod makers of yesteryear accomplished their tasks and this lead to a thirst for knowledge of the early rod makers. After much research, he told me that he intended to write a book on the history of cane rod making to supplement what was currently known and to do it from a different prospective.

*B*eing that Jeff lives in the great State of Colorado and didn't have access to the shows, museums and tackle meets that would exhibit the early, historical rods he realized he would have to overcome that obstacle. He then purchased antique rods to study, exchanged information and photos with other antique rod collectors, and extensively read existing reference books. I don't believe this book would have been possible without a deep appreciation of cane rod building and his desire for historical knowledge.

I, as a dealer and collector have always been fascinated by the history behind this wonderful sport of fishing. As I read the pre-published book I began to realize what a daunting task writing a book was, especially a book on antique fishing tackle. Not much is known about many of the early rod makers. One must realize that these craftsmen and entrepreneurs made fishing rods to make money! It was a business. Fishing has been a way for people to relax and feed themselves for centuries. With the advent of the industrial revolution and a "better way to build a mousetrap" attitude, early rod making became a large part of the then, new sporting goods business. It is no surprise that the earliest rod makers were located east of the Mississippi, as that was where the population and manufacturing centers were.

*T*here were many craftsmen and companies that ranged from poor to superb, just as there are today. The early rods were very labor intensive and as in any commercial market, you got what you paid for, at least most of the time. This is evident in the fact that some rods are being fished today that are over 100 years old, but some were relegated to the tomato garden for plant stakes years ago.

*A*ntique rod collecting is finally starting to come into it's own after many years of neglect by most cane rod collectors. The antique rod collectors were tolerated and their collections were "appreciated" but regarded as a bit esoteric. As one studies the making of cane rods thru the years it becomes evident the old axioms of "nothing new under the sun" is true and that "borrowing" or "adapting" someone else's ideas is not new either.

*T*his book compliments the few good reference books, most of which are out of print, and goes beyond most of them by offering a large amount of photographs and questions. Questions are very important in reference books, because some books take conjecture as fact and mislead the reader. It is pointed out in this book, there are many unanswered questions that will intrigue the reader and make a fascinating hobby even more fascinating.

*I*ntroduction

*G*reetings to those willing to tread their way along a path that is very addictive-that being the path of a collector of fishing rods. The different facets of fly-fishing and fly tying my whole life have fascinated me. As I have grown older my fascination with the history of rod making and the history of fly-fishing has grown as has my desire to learn more about this fascinating subject.

There are three books in particular that have fueled this fire in me and they are "Classic Rods and Rod Makers" by Martin Keane which was the first real work on the subject of collecting antique fishing rods and then the second book is "Classic & Antique Fly Fishing Tackle-a Guide for Collectors and Anglers" by A.J. Campbell which went into more depth of the early and odd makers scattered thru history and it also covered fly tackle in general. The third book was Michael Sinclair's "Bamboo Rod Restoration Handbook" which is an incredible wealth of information on the production class of Rodmakers from the classical era.

There are several other very well written works on individual rod makers and also on regional rod makers and I have listed these reference works in the bibliography at the back of the book.

My goal with this work is to show in full color as many of the Rodmakers mentioned in the above three books. Making this a color companion to those three works and also a small tribute to Martin Keane and A.J.Campbell for their efforts. This work came about do to my desire to have a book that showed how magnificent some of the rods made over the last 150 plus years are. Some of the rods pictured in this work are stunning examples of the art of rod making. From the snakewood rods by William Mitchell to the artistry of the "KOSMIC" crew to the Spartan clean lines of Everett Garrison. And we cannot forget the makers who delved into the mortised rods with the 12 strip butt sections.

This work does contain pictures of some of the truly rare rods known to exist today. For example, the unmarked Murphy 4 strip is most likely the earliest known rod by Charles F. Murphy. Another example is the unmarked Porter's General rod, which starts the book. This fifteen foot Conroy rod by either John Conroy or his Son J.C. Conroy is one of only two or three known to exist at this time. Or the blank by Merritt Hawes that was finished by Sam Carlson for Harmon Leonard who is the grand nephew of Hiram L. Leonard. I hope you enjoy this wade along the banks of time with all sorts of different sticks in your hand.

Humbly yours Jeff Hatton, Paonia Colorado 2004

A note about Footnotes.

*I*n this work I have not used footnotes due to the fact that every page would have a note to refer to one of the following works. Either A.J.Campbell's book "Classic and Antique Fly Fishing Tackle" or Martin Keane's book "Classic Rods And Rodmakers. Those two gentlemen covered the history very well and my main objective with this book is to show in color what those gentlemen so eloquently wrote about.

Note about the photography in this Book.

I guess you could also call it the *caveat emptor* on the photography. I am an amateur photographer at best and I have done my best with the photos contained herein. But you will notice some variation due to differences in cameras used by the different people who have shot pictures for this work. And you will see some variation in background colors due to camera angle and lighting.

Now the big *Caveat Emptor*.

I the author have done my best to accurately date and identify the rods contained within this work. But due to the fact that I am human, and I am sure that there are some mistakes contained within this book. I take full claim to the credit for any and all errors contained within this book. I have tried to arrange the book as chronologically correct as possible, using the research material available to me at this time. Any and all errors, historical or grammatical, are completely my own.

Jeff Hatton Paonia Co. 2004

Acknowledgements

*T*his work would not have been possible without the collaboration of a group of people. I must first off thank my mom and dad for not only putting up with my addiction to anything fishy but also encouraging it. And Mom passed on to me her nose for collecting. Little did they know what it would lead to. The times we shared on our family fishing and hunting trips were priceless and irreplaceable. Their support and faith in my efforts and me are second to none. I feel like I have the best parents in the world. Thanks Mom and Dad!!

*N*ow for the group of gentlemen who have helped with donations of time and photographs of their rods or have allowed me to invade their space on a frequent basis pestering them for more help in one of several different ways. I am not listing them in any sort of special order. It is a fairly small group starting with John Oppenlander, best friend and fishing partner for over 20 years. John has helped on this project with much encouragement and also John plays the devils advocate very well and he makes me think pretty hard sometimes. Tom Kerr, The best friend that I have that I have never met in person. We became acquainted over the Internet and the telephone. Tom is as fascinated by the smith age and expansion era tackle as I am {also thanks to Tom for the final edit of this work}. Dr. Richard Collar, D.D.S., fellow collecting fanatic and a true friend and compatriot. Richard is as fanatical about the rod collecting as anyone I know. Dr. Harmon Leonard, DVM. He is the grand nephew of H.L. Leonard and another of the group who is absolutely fascinated by the history of fly-fishing. It has been my great honor to meet and to get to know Harmon and his wife Joey. Dennis Nicks former guide client and now one of my best friends and he is my computer mentor. Without his help and patience this would have never happened. Brent Curtice, for his encouragement and advice and also for letting me pester him with new rods to test cast and the final edit. Don and Val Mundy for being a great sounding board and a place to retreat to, to have a single malt and relax. Also for there help from the Photographic end of the project. There are so many people who I should thank here and I know that I will miss some so please be assured If I have missed anyone it was completely unintentional.

*F*olks who have donated to this project with either rods or photographs of rods are, Bruce Handley and his wife Carla List-Handley, Sante Giuliani, Bob Carolan, Jerry Schaeffer, Dennis Nicks, Wayne Alfano, Craig Lynch, Russ and Erica Gooding, John Oppenlander, Tom Kerr, Richard Collar, Harmon Leonard.

*A*nd a special thanks to Dave Shin and Don and Val Mundy for helping keep me as sane as possible through out this experience.

Dad fishing the Gunnison 2003.

Jack and Lillian Hatton "Mom and Dad".

Dennis Nicks.

John Oppenlander.

Richard Collar.

Tom Kerr.

Contents

Contents continued

The Expansion era continued.

Contents continued

The Classical Era continued.

The smith age   1870 and older

The smith age is considered to be the time period up to 1870. Any and all tackle made previous to that was handmade and generally by gunsmiths and fletchers and bow makers and even going back as far as Waltonian times the fishing tackle was made by lance makers. Hallmarks of the smith age include seamed metal work, Generally the rods were made of hardwood sometimes even up to three or four different types were used.

They include Bethabara, greenheart, white ash, Cuban lancewood or lemonwood, hickory, Ironwood and even whalebone / baleen and in the early 1800s you start to see spliced tips of Calcutta cane, usually consisting of ¾ bamboo and ¼ hardwood. The rods were generally very large ranging from a short rod of 8 or 10 feet up to and exceeding 18 feet on occasion. The very first complete six-strip bamboo rod by Samuel Phillipe is made during this era. The guides on rods from this time frame were usually just a tube or a double ring soldered to a flat base or a hanging ring. Ferrules from the smith age were very plain usually not having a welt and if they did it was usually next to the wood not at the end of the ferrule. They were made of brass or the better ones were made of nickel silver. Most were doweled or spiked, in the later part of the smith age. Some very modern style ferrules were used by C.F. Orvis, Thaddeus Norris and a few others used what the modern Bamboo rod maker uses. You also see the appearance of complete rods of split bamboo by C.F. Murphy and several other makers. Reel seats in the later part of the smith age era usually consisted of a fixed band and a sliding ring. Usually very plain. The earliest reels from the smith age came not with a foot but with a clamp similar to a hose clamp to attach the reel or winch, as it was known then. Some of the rods from that time had hollow butts that you could carry your spare tips in, and one of the most unusual items that was sold with a fishing rod was the sandspike or spear it was used to plant your rod in an upright position allowing you both hands free to land your fish. It is extremely rare to find rods from the smith age in any degree of completeness. Rods from that time period came in as many pieces as a 5/5-rod that is a five-piece five-tip rod. And even a rod put up in the following configuration made by J.C. Conroy five piece three tips and a four-piece three-tip rod. The smith age was exemplified by the work of men Like Samuel Phillipe and his son Solon Phillipe of Eaton Pennsylvania. And C. F. Orvis and Hiram L. Leonard. Many of them built rods into the expansion era and beyond. You do see an overlap of the smith age and the expansion era. 1870-1885 is the gray area of the change from handmade by smiths to mass production of the expansion era.

John Conroy N.Y. "Porter's General Rod" Ash & Lancewood 1/3/3 circa 1843-1860

John Conroy was one of the earliest known American rod makers. He was located in New York City. The "Porter's General rod" pictured here is one of the least seen of American angling's earliest multi-purpose rods. This rod is capable of making different lengths and actions of rods. It consists of 1 butt, 3 mids and 3 tips. 2 of the tips are stored in the hollow butt section. The rod can be made up into a 15' salmon rod or a 12' heavier rod. A.J. Campbell in his book "Classic and Antique Fly Fishing Tackle" said he had seen one of these rods and he described the butt section as " Heavy enough to bludgeon a beaver to death with it. I would concur; the butt section is very stout. Some of the notable features of the rod are the 2-part rolled and seamed female ferrules; the female ferrules are also straight and not welted. The male ferrules are rolled and soldered and are open at the bottom. All of the hardware is nickel silver and hand made. I am basing my identification of this rod on its 2-part female ferrules and its classic smith age style of construction. This rod is from the Author's collection.

Opened butt cap showing the emergency inside tips stored in the hollow butt section {above left} and the pinned and seamed and soldered construction that is typical to the Smith Age {above right}.

Male doweled ferrules with exposed wood at the ends pictured {above left} and the female ferrules are {above right}, note the Prichard style guides.

Close up of the funnel style tiptops {above left}; note the difference in patina of the bright tiptop that has been stored in the butt section for 130 plus years. Above right are the Prichard style guides that have been in use well before Prichard patented that guide in 1859. The Tait lithograph from Currier & Ives of the mid 1850s shows a rod with that style of guide pre-dating Prichard's patent. Note the turning marks in the bright tiptop above left.

Pictured to the left is a close up of the two part Conroy female ferrules and above is the butchered reel seat.

Anonymous Lancewood Salmon Rod circa 1850's 1/2/3 15'

*T*his rod was pictured in the book "Classic and Antique Fly Fishing tackle" in the selection of vintage 2 handed Salmon rods in the color section on page #188. It is the first rod in the picture. It was originally most likely put up in a 1/2/3 configuration. It is missing one tip and both of the surviving tips are short. The rod is 15' long and has a turned wood butt cap and a rattan grip with the single strand of red silk wrapped up thru the rattan. All of the hardware is classical smith age workmanship, rolled and seamed nickel silver and all hand made. Chinese red silk wraps.

*N*otable features of the rod include its welted female ferrules and the massive NiS covered dowels and its standing soldered 2-ring guides. I acquired this rod from Bob Corsetti who had acquired it from A.J. Campbell. It is a massive rod. And is a typical example from that time period. This rod is from the author's private collection.

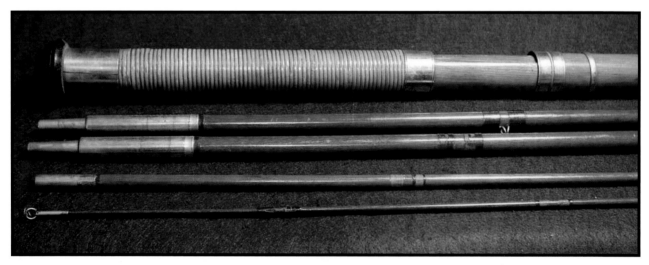

Wooden butt cap and rattan grip, massive covered doweled male ferrules, standing soldered two-ring NiS guides and the three ring tiptop. Note the modified male ferrule on the first tip. The covered dowel has been removed.

Male seamed and soldered heavy covered doweled ferrules.   *Female ferrules and tiptops.*

Reel seat, standing 2-ring guides and the 3-ring tiptop. Close up of the seamed and soldered slide band and pinned reel seat check ring above right.

Close up of the soldered standing 2-ring NiS guide and the 3-ring tiptops to the above left and a close up of the welts and seams and witness marks on the female ferrules above right.

Anonymous trout rod
Ash & Greenheart
14' or 10' 1/2/3
Circa 1850-1870

*F*rom its simple ferrules with the massive exposed wood dowels to its hand rolled and seamed NiS hardware, this unmarked Ash and greenheart rod shows its sign's of extreme age. The rod still has its original ferrule plugs. They are a 3-part plug consisting of a welted tube with a cork insert. This is another of the multi-purpose rods. It makes up into a 14' rod or a 10' rod.

*T*he configuration of this rod is 1/2/3. This rod originally had hanging ring guides on it. No guides have survived.

*N*ote the fairly intricate knurling on the reel seat slide band and on the ferrule plugs also. One of the odd things about this rod is that in the shorter and heavier length of 10' the tips are both ash and in the longer and lighter length the tip is greenheart. I am pretty positive there are parts of this rod missing. This rod is from the Author's collection.

Pictured above are the grip and reel seat and the exposed wood dowels with the seamed male ferrules.

Close up of the seamed straight male ferrule.

The female ferrules and tiptops.

Close up of the two-part funnel top on the green heart tip.

Ferrule plugs and tiptops.

Pictured above is a close up of where a hanging ring guide was wrapped on the green heart tip. To the left is a close up of the welts on the ferrule plugs.

Unmarked C.F.Murphy
4 Strip circa 1862
11' 3/2 Calcutta Cane

*T*his unmarked rod can be the work of only one person and that person is Charles F. Murphy of Newark New Jersey. This rod is one of the earliest known Murphy rods in existence. The rod was made prior to Murphy settling on 6-strip construction as the best in 1865 or 1866. The female ferrule on this rod is a match to the female ferrule on a marked Murphy, with the exception of the female ferrules being non-welted on this four-strip rod. That too points to an earlier date of manufacture of this rod. The rod is hollow built butt to tip. This rod has only come to light in the year 2004. It has obviously been well hidden for the last 140 years or so. The rod is wrapped in the deep red silk that Murphy used. It has hanging ring guides that have been soldered together to make the guide out of wire. The reel seat hardware is all NiS and is seamed and handmade. The tiptops are three ring tops. The grip is an undeterminable type of cord possibly over rattan then lacquered black.

*T*his rod is from the private collection of Tom Kerr.

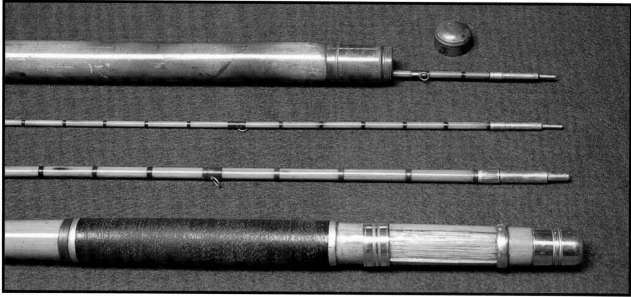

The early corded grip and male spiked ferrules and the Reel seat hardware used by Murphy.

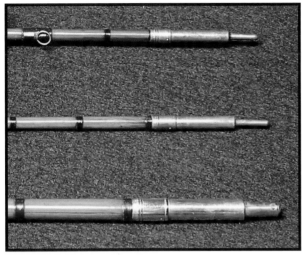

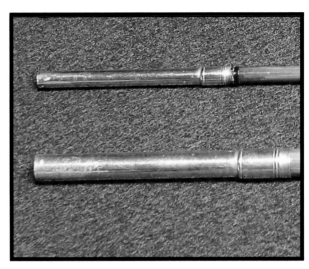

Close up of the male Murphy spiked ferrules.   *Close up of the straight Female ferrules.*

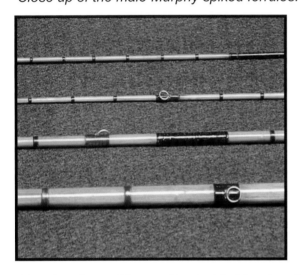

Hanging ring guides on the 4-strip Murphy above left. Female ferrule comparison above right, the top two ferrules are from a later circa 1864-65 signed Murphy. The bottom two ferrules are from the unmarked four-strip.

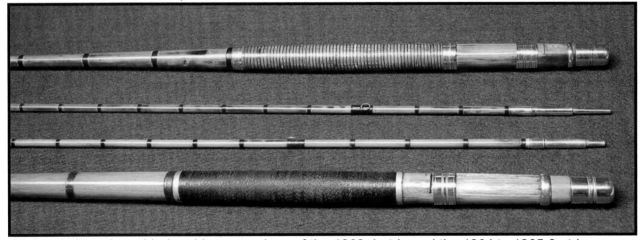

Pictured above is a side-by-side comparison of the 1862 4-strip and the 1864 to 1865 6-strip rod that has a 6-strip mid, and 4-strip tips showing the evolution of the work of Murphy.

Charles F. Murphy
Newark, New Jersey
circa 1862 to 1865 3/1
Calcutta Cane Fly Rod 12 ft.

Charles F. Murphy was one of the first men to make complete 6 strip bamboo rods for sale here in America. This rod is a fairly easy one to date due to some very unique features, such as, the black pinpricks in the butt section, the signature is just C.F. Murphy. It does not include the Newark N.J mark, which is a later marking. The most telling feature beyond the pinpricks is the fact that this one has a 4-strip tip.

The quality of workmanship on this rod is amazing when you consider the time frame of its manufacture {1862-65}. For example, the ferrules lack 3 things of being equal to a modern ferrule. #1 no serrations at the base of the ferrule. #2 it has a spike, which is unnecessary, and #3 No waterproofing in the ferrule due to the spike. Some of the truly modern features of the Rod are the ferrules welts and the reel seat, which is a very early up-locking style. This rod is very light for its length due to the fact that it is hollow built in the butt. The rod has a rattan grip and is wrapped in deep red silk and has hanging ring guides. The black pinpricks are actual holes in the bamboo where Murphy had affixed the cane enamel side down to a planning board with sharp brads. This rod is from the Author's private collection.

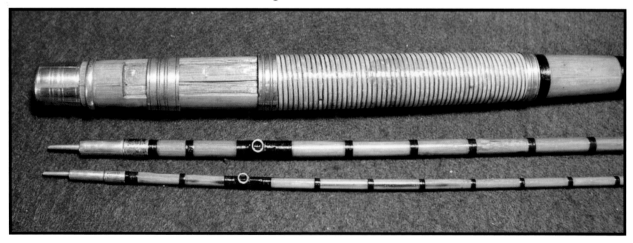

Pictured above are the rattan grip and up-locking slide band reel seat of the 1862-1865 Murphy rod.

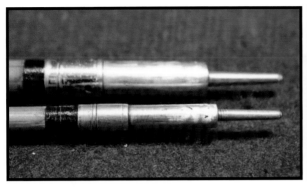 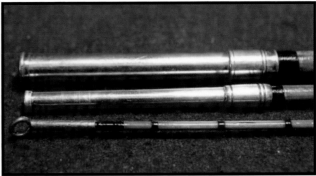

Pictured above are the Murphy ferrule, males to the left and females to the right.

Close ups of the Black pinpricks in the butt section, starting from the left they are just above the winding check then in the middle of the blank and then just below the ferrule station.

Close up of the slide band and check ring on the Murphy reel seat above left and above center is the "C.F.Murphy" marking on the upper reel seat check ring, and above right is a close up of the welt on the Murphy female ferrule.

*M*r. Murphy was well ahead of his time but he was a perfectionist and would have no help in his rod shop. He insisted on doing everything himself. His total production may have exceeded 400 but probably not by much.

At the left is a comparison of the 4-strip tip and the 6-strip mid section. Note the difference in widths of the cane strips in the two pieces. The strips in the tip are larger.

Charles F. Murphy, Fly rod Newark, N.J. circa 1863-65 Calcutta Cane 12' 3/2

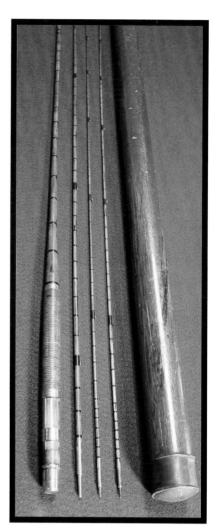

Charles F. Murphy was one of a group of four or five Rodmakers who were responsible for the revolution of bamboo as the preferred rodmaking material over hardwoods. He is also recognized as being the first rodmaker to actively sell complete six strip rods to the fishing tackle trade. This rod has the cup marks that Martin J. Keane wrote about in his book "Classic Rods and Rodmakers". The cup marks and the fact that this rod is a six strip butt and mid with four strip tips dates it to very early in Murphy's career as a rodmaker. Note the doubled intermediate wraps at the ferrule stations on the tips. That is a feature that is usually associated with John G. Landman rods. It is very possible that Landman copied this feature from Murphy. The rod is wrapped in a Chinese red silk and has hanging ring guides. The grip is rattan. All of the hardware is handmade out of NiS. The wood case is most likely original to the rod. It is a unique item in its style of build and most likely a one of a kind at this point in history. This rod is from the private collection of Tom Kerr.

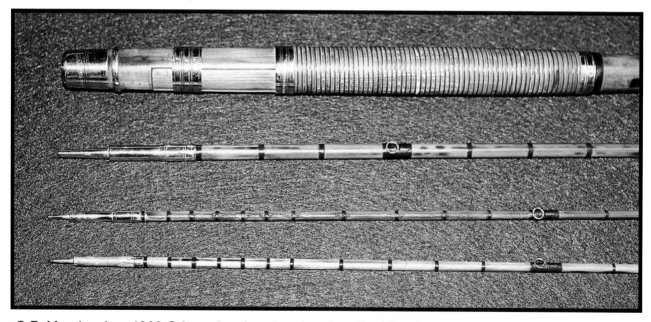

C.F. Murphy circa 1863 Grip and reel seat and male spiked ferrules, note the doubled intermediate wraps at the male ferrules on the tips.

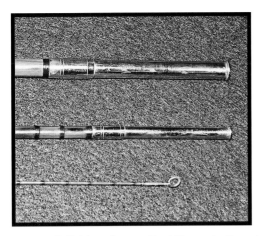

C.F.Murphy welted Female ferrule.

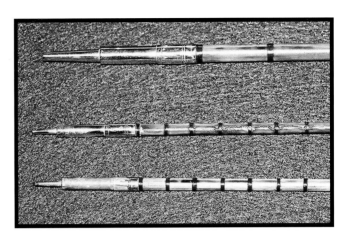

Spiked male ferrules.

Close up of the rod tube used by Murphy.

Cup mark in the cane.

Close up of the Murphy mortised reel seat and butt cap.

The lower grip check band or the fixed hood of the seat has the "C.F.Murphy, Newark, N.Y." stamping on it. Very few Murphy rods are known to exist but at least two Murphy rods have surfaced since the turn of the last century {2000}. The one pictured above is one of them. The other is the rod prior to this {The complete four strip} and it is one of the very earliest Murphys found to date.

Anonymous Hardwood Rod
10' 6" 3/2
circa 1860s

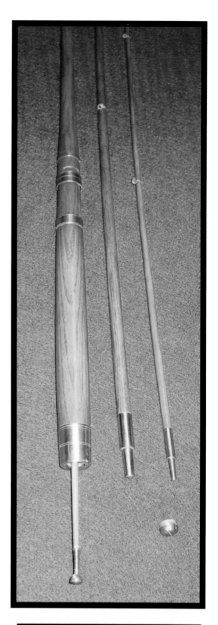

*T*his rod is an example of a very early hardwood rod that could have been made by any one of several makers. The Bartlett brothers or very early Chubb are two possibilities. Making an absolute identification of a rod like this is almost impossible unless there is a paper trail that goes with the rod or a hard and fast family history of an heirloom. This rod has the Pritchard patent guides dating it to later than 1859. The rod has a hollow butt that stores the short emergency fly tip inside. All hardware on this rod is soldered and handmade. The butt section is made out of white ash with a mid section and tip out of greenheart and the emergency tip is made of lancewood. The use of hollow butt sections to carry spare tips dates back to the 1830s or earlier. The ferrules and butt cap and reel seat hardware are made of brass. The guides are brass and are seamed showing they were handmade. Rods from the late smith age are a very rare find and are awe inspiring in the quality of the work at that time being pre 1870.

*T*his rod is from the private collection of Tom Kerr.

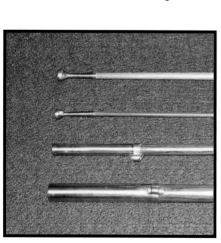

Female ferrules and Funnel tops.

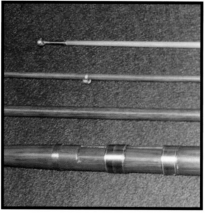

Reel seat hardware.

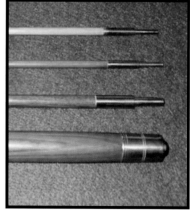

Butt cap and male ferrules.

GRAND FALLS ON THE NIPISSIGUIT.

First engraved plate from Thaddeus Norris's "American Anglers Book" 1865-second edition from the Authors personal library.

glued" tip. He also made the simple tool represented below, in which are united what may be called a " V tool" and a "draw-plate." It is made of thin steel, and tempered very hard.

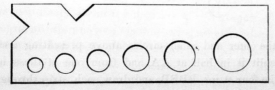

The notch in the end and top of the plate are true right angles, with a cutting or rather a scraping edge; the holes also have scraping edges. When this implement is screwed in a vice, by drawing a piece of split cane through the V,

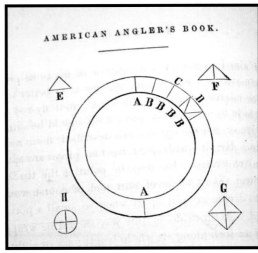

AMERICAN ANGLER'S BOOK.

The above two engravings which show a v-tool and a diagram of the end of a culm showing where the strips of cane come from are also from the American Anglers Book" by Norris.

The last engraving is a concurrent theme through Thaddeus Norris's book. Contemplating the world while relaxing and blowing the fish whistle.

Anonymous Trout Rod
Greenheart & Lancewood
10'2" 4/1 Circa 1865-80

*H*ere is an example of a rod from the mid to late 1800s that is in the condition that you are more used to seeing. The guides are gone and you probably have a tip or tips missing, and short pieces. The Ferrules on this rod are brass and have a covered dowel. The reel seat hardware and the butt cap are made of plated brass. The butt is of ash and the mids are greenheart and the remaining tip is made of lancewood. The remaining tiptop is a three-ring top made out of NiS.

*N*ote the hollowing of the shaft above the grip, which denotes a post late 1850's or later date of manufacture. The butt is hollow and unfortunately there was not a spare tip in this rod. This rod could have had guides of hanging rings or Pritchard patent guides or even possibly single standing rings but it was most likely originally built with the Pritchard patent guides.

This rod is from the private collection of Tom Kerr.

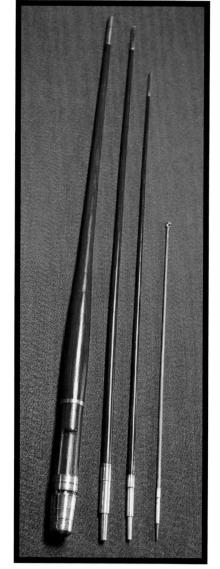

Mortised reel seat with butt cap off showing the hollow for the spare tip and the covered doweled male ferrules below left and the straight non-welted female ferrules below right.

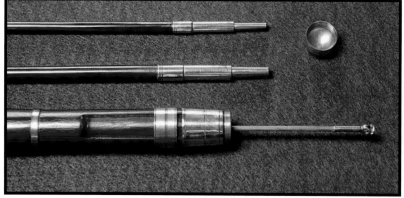

*T*he possible makers of this rod could have been Chubb or Bartlett. The unmarked rods from 100 plus years ago are a delightful puzzle to mull over at this point in time.

Anonymous Hardwood Trout rod 4/1 13' circa 1870s

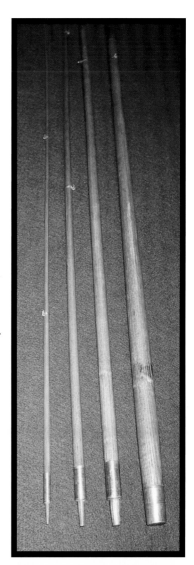

*T*his rod uses multiple types of hardwood to achieve the action the rodmaker was looking for. The butt and mid sections are made of ash and the tip is made of lancewood. The rod has the 1859 Pritchard patent guides. All metal fittings are made of brass. The exposed doweled ferrules were a feature of the smith age that could be found clear thru to the classic era. It is a rare find to discover a complete wood rod from the smith age. Usually by now they have ended up in pieces at best and or usually lost to the garden or the campfire. The beauty of these old wood rods is not truly done justice by the photos herein. They are outstanding examples of early to late 1800s craftsmanship at its best. Some of the possible makers of this rod would be the Bartlett brothers or possibly even a very early Chubb 1880 or earlier. Unmarked rods like this one will probably never be positively identified. But they are fun to speculate over and are works of art in their own right.

*T*his rod is from the private collection of Tom Kerr.

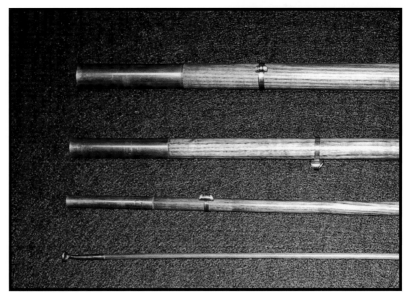

Brass male ferrules above left with the exposed wood dowel. Female ferrules and Pritchard guides above right.

J.C.Conroy Unmarked Ash & Lancewood 13'6" 4/1 circa 1870s

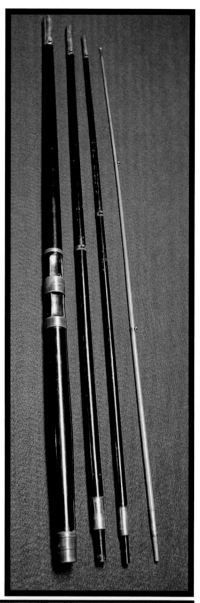

John C. Conroy was the son and partner of John Conroy whose tackle making efforts can be traced back to as early as 1810 – 1820. The guides can date this rod in particular, which are the Henry Pritchard standing adjustable single ring guide for which he was awarded patent #25,693 on Oct 4th 1859. The hardware on the rod is all of hand made seamed and soldered NiS. The tip is lancewood with the rest of the rod being black Japanned ash. All of the hardware is elaborately knurled. The reel seat is mortised into the wood of the butt section. The diameter of the guides is very small due to the diameter of the silk line used at that time being very small also. The male ferrules are exposed wood dowels with a simple straight NiS female ferrule with no welts or reinforcements. The rod is a fairly rare example of smith age work that is still basically complete to this day. The rod is most likely missing anywhere from one to possibly as many as four or five extra tips and possibly an additional upper mid section.

This rod is from the private collection of Tom Kerr.

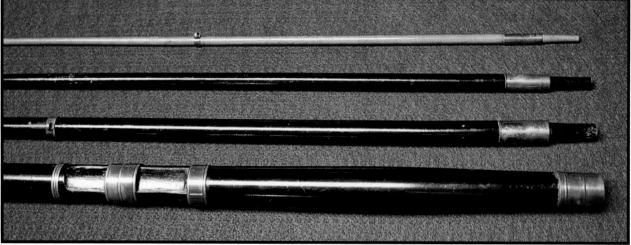

Lower grip reel seat and Pritchard patent guides and the male ferrules pictured above.

Close up of butt cap.

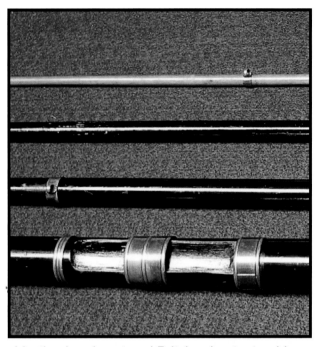

Mortised reel seat and Pritchard patent guides.

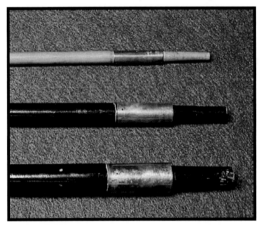

Male exposed dowel ferrules.

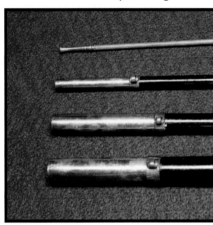

Female ferrules with guides attached.

Pictured to the left is a close up of the mortised reel seat.

Edward Vom Hofe 7-strip Bait caster circa 1870s 8'6" 3/2 Calcutta Cane

*T*his is an example of one of only three or four known seven-strip rods existing today. The grip is made of rattan and all of the NiS hardware is handmade. The bell guides that remained with the rod are stamped "E. Vom Hofe, NY" inside of the bell. The butt cap is stamped with the "Edward vom Hofe, Maker, Fulton St. NY" makers mark. The male ferrules are spiked and the females are a straight-welted ferrule. The rod was originally wrapped in Chinese red silk and had full intermediate wraps. The rod was in restoration when photographed thus the stripped mid and tip section in the photos. The rattan grip has the spiral of red silk wrapped up thru it. Edward vom Hofe was one of the innovators of the late smith age and into and thru the expansion era. Besides building rods like this rare seven strip he also made six-strip cane rods as well as eight-strip cane rods and even wooden rods for deep-sea use. The rods and reels by the Vom Hofe family are some of the most sought after early fishing tackle collectibles.

*T*his rod is from the private collection of Tom Kerr.

The removable rattan grip with its NiS reel seat and signed butt cap.

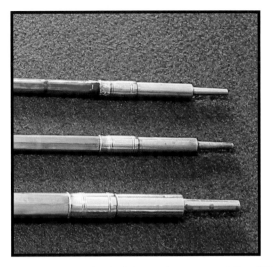
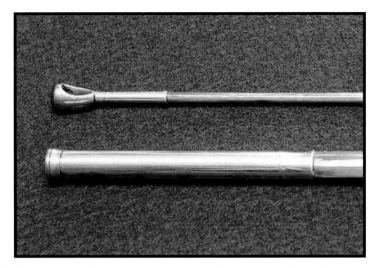

Pictured at the left is a close up of the EVH Male spiked ferrules and above right are the female ferrule and the agate stirrup tiptop.

Pictured above is a close up of the NiS reel seat used on the seven-strip EVH rod.

Pictured at left is the butt cap with the "Edward vom Hofe, Maker, Fulton St. NY" stamping.

Note the condition of the varnish on the rattan grip it necessitates that the rod be restored to maintain its integrity.

Anonymous 13'6" 4/2
Ash & Lancewood
Circa 1860-1880

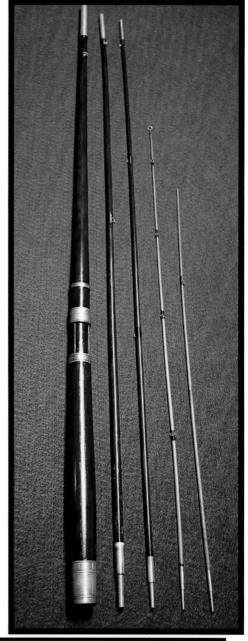

The most likely maker of this rod is John or John C. Conroy. The rolled fittings and the style of the two part female ferrule and the butt cap are all features that bespeak of the early work by the Conroy's. The seamed two part female ferrule in particular was a hallmark of the Conroys "Porter's General Rod" Please see page #2 and compare the two rods, reel seat hardware and the female ferrule close ups the two rods are obviously by the same maker. My best guess is J.C. Conroy and not his father. All hardware is hand made seamed and soldered NiS. The male ferrules are NiS covered dowels, which are seamed and soldered. The rod has a few remaining original hanging ring guides that were wrapped on with black silk. Rods from the late smith age 1860-1880 are the hardest rods to find in any degree of completeness as shown by this rod with the short tip. The longer of the two tips may or may not be the original length. This rod is from the private collection of Tom Kerr.

Grip, mortised reel seat and male doweled ferrules and hanging ring guides below.

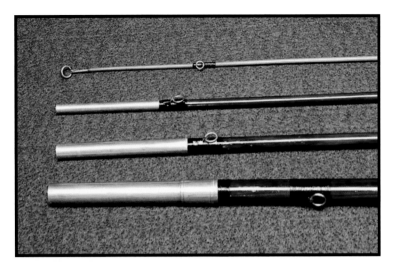 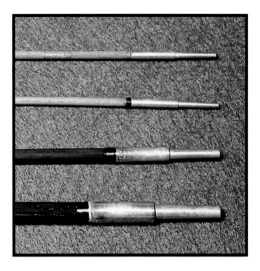

Female straight non-welted ferrules and hanging ring guides. *Male covered dowel ferrules.*

Close up of the mortised reel seat and the rolled and seamed and pinned hardware.

Close up of the butt cap at left.

Close up of the seamed slide band at right.

Anon. Ash & Lancewood 12' 6" 4/1 Trout Rod. circa 1860-1890.

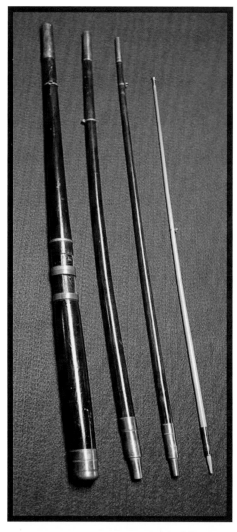

*E*ither The Bartletts or J.C. Conroy or T.H. Chubb could have made this rod. I am basing this on the style of build and a mid 1880s Eugene Bartlett catalog that has a cut of a rod that is almost identical to this rod. The reel seat is mortised into the butt in the traditional style used by the Conroys and the Bartletts on their wood rods. The guides are the 1859 Pritchard patent guides with the tiptop being a funnel type. The hardware is all of brass with the male ferrules having massive covered dowels and the females are straight and non-welted. The time frame when this rod was made would indicate that it originally would have had an additional upper mid and additional spare tips. The butt and the mid sections are made of light ash with the tips made out of lancewood.

*T*his rod is from the private collection of Tom Kerr.

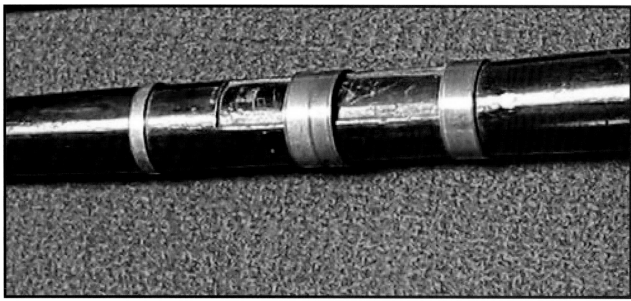

Close up of the Pinned brass reel seat hardware and the mortise for the reel foot.

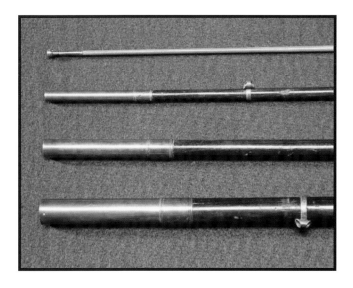

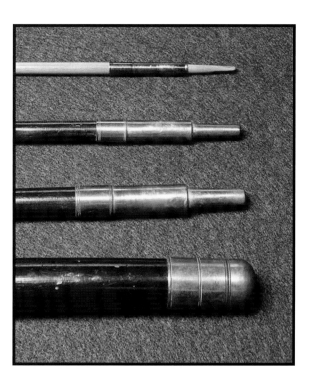

Female ferrules and the funnel tiptop above and the butt cap and heavy doweled male ferrules to the right.

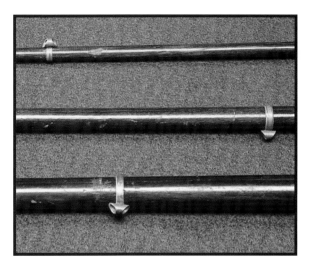

Pritchard 1859 patent guides.

Close up of the butt cap.

Lower grip and reel seat and butt cap pictured above.

The very early expansion era/late smith age rods that were unmarked by their maker are very hard to identify and will remain a mystery but we can make an educated guess as to the maker due to the 2-part ferrules and the style of build.

MAKING SPLIT-BAMBOO RODS.

Pictured to the left is an engraving of Hiram L. Leonard from the article "Notes on Salmon Fishing" from the October 1876 Scribner's monthly Vol. XII No. 6. From the Author's personal library.

And pictured below is the other set of engravings from the 1876 Scribner's article about salmon fishing by Dr. A.G. Wilkinson. Note that in fig.3 below the shaft has been rounded.

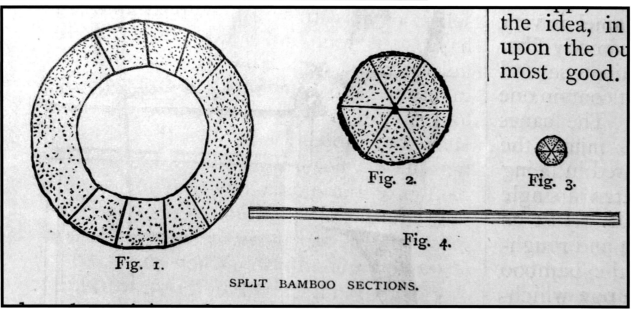

the idea, in
upon the ou
most good.

Fig. 1.

Fig. 2.

Fig. 3.

Fig. 4.

SPLIT BAMBOO SECTIONS.

The Expansion Era 1870 to 1900

The expansion era was symbolized by great growth in the manufacture of fishing tackle and it was brought about by a small handful of men. This group included Hiram L. Leonard, Thomas H. Chubb and Charles E. Wheeler. This group of men brought about the mass production of fishing rods and rod components. The availability of low cost, high quality rod components allowed a very large number of rod-makers to enter the market. During the expansion era we saw the addition of steel added to the inventory of the rod makers supplies. In bamboo the use of Calcutta cane from India was slowly changed over to the use of Tonkin cane by the end of the expansion era. There were many changes in those thirty-years and one of the more important ones was the invention of the modern snake guide in the mid 1870s to the mid 1880s. The hanging ring guides had a fairly short life, from the early 1800s to about 1900 to 1920. During the expansion era one group of rod makers formerly with the Leonard Rod Co. formed their own company. The men were F.E. Thomas, Eustis Edwards and Loman Hawes in 1891. They built what were to become some of the most coveted of fly rods and also set the modern standard for a fly rod. They were called the Kosmic Rod.

During the expansion era John G. Landman invented the screw lock reel seat. John G.Landman also happened to be one of the originator's of the American sweatshop. Long hours and low pay and he used women and children virtually as slaves. The head hardware man at Leonard left at the same time as Thomas and Edwards and Payne and Hiram Hawes, Hiram Leonard's Nephew. The hardware man was named George I Varney; he also started his own co. Some of the other changes during this era was in grips, in thirty years we saw the change from a wood grip to rattan to sheet cork to 1/8" rings of cork and up to ½" ring cork. During this time we also had grips out of cotton cord wrapped around a cedar core. The addition of agate and agatine guides and tiptops. It was an exciting time in the tackle Industry. It was at this time the giants of mass production started to appear, The Bartletts who started the Montague City Rod Works and Horrock`s & Ibbotsson`s were two of them. Fred Divine was also producing large quantities of tackle. We also see the invention of the automatic fly reel by the Loomis & Plumb. During the expansion era some of the most intricate rods ever made were produced they are called mortised rods, it was a 6 strip rod into 12 strips / what was done was an inclusion of 6 additional strips of a different type of wood giving a heavily swelled butt. The mortised rod was a very labor-intensive rod to build. Those thirty years saw more innovation than ever seen before. The fishing tackle industry bloomed at the same time as the Industrial Revolution. Thomas H. Chubb made a major contribution to the revolution of the tackle industry when he brought back to America the Nasmyth Steam hammer technology from Scotland.

John B. McHarg, Rome N.Y.
Ash, Greenheart & Lancewood
10'6" 3/1 circa 1873-1900

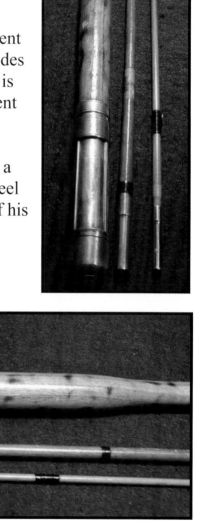

*T*his rod is an example of an unsigned rod by John B. McHarg of Rome, New York. The reel seat and the use of multiple different woods are the clues as to the maker of this rod. The butt section is of white ash that has been burned to look like Calcutta cane, which was the new and preferred material to build rods with at that time. The mid section is made of greenheart and the tip is made of lancewood. The reel seat, which is made of NiS plated brass has the Mar 18th 1873 patent on the reel seat also indicating a J.B.McHarg origin. The guides are hanging rings made of brass with brass keepers. The rod is wrapped in black silk. The ferrules are from at least 2 different makers and eras. J.B.McHarg was another of the very early makers who supplied his hardware to other makers, see the William H. Cruttenden rod on page # 48 which is marked as a Cruttenden rod but the reel seat is the 1873 patent McHarg reel seat. McHarg also used components from Chubb on many of his rods. In 1901 Horrocks & Ibbotson purchased The John B. McHarg Company.

*T*his rod is from the Author's private collection.

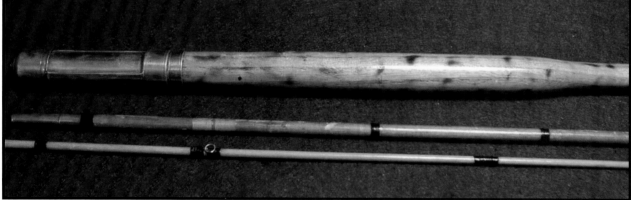

Pictured above is the John B. McHarg March 18th 1873 patent date reel seat and the ash butt section burned to look like Calcutta cane and the greenheart mid section and the lancewood tip with its hanging ring guides.

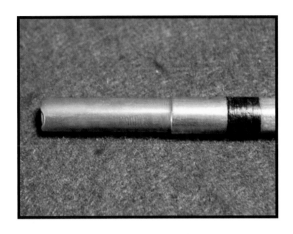

Male McHarg ferrule.

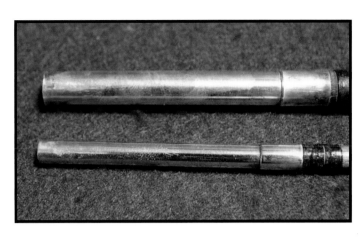

Female ferrules from the J.B. McHarg rod.

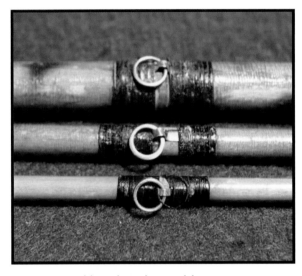

Hanging ring guides.

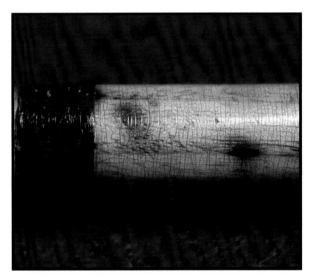

Burns to imitate Calcutta cane in the ash.

John B. McHarg " Pat Mar 18 1873" reel seat marks. Close up of the very distinctive McHarg butt cap.

H.L. Leonard, Fly Rod
Bangor, Me.
circa 1876-1878
3/2 Calcutta Cane

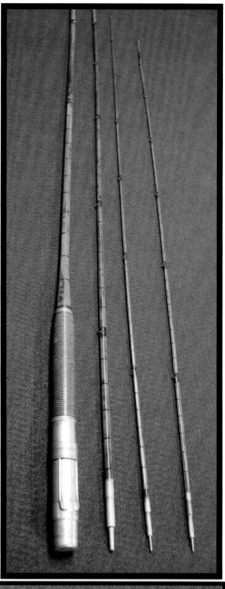

*T*his is a very early example of Hiram L. Leonard's work. The "H.L.Leonard, Maker, Bangor Me." marking denotes it was made before the William Mills & Sons association. Making it one of the earliest examples of a true hexagonal 6-strip cane rod. The rod is wrapped in Chinese red silk with full intermediates.

*A*ll of the hardware is handmade out of NiS. The guides are hanging rings and the grip is rattan with the red silk spiral in the rattan. The ferrules are spiked which in the case of a H.L. Leonard rod is another telling factor in age determination. This rod is one of the earliest rods made on a commercial beveller. The other makers using a commercial beveller at that time were C.E.Wheeler and T.H. Chubb.

*T*his rod is from the Private collection of Tom Kerr.

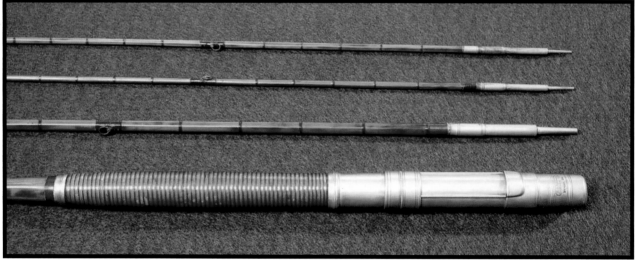

The rattan grip and reel seat on the very early Leonard rod. Note the similarity to the work of C.F. Murphy of Newark N.J.

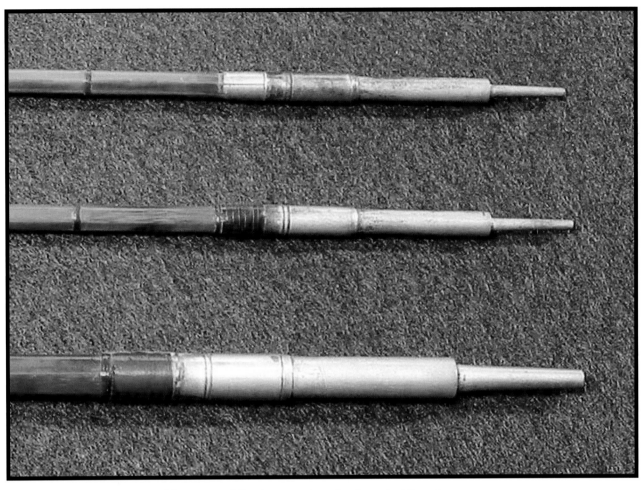

Close up of the Leonard male doweled ferrules.

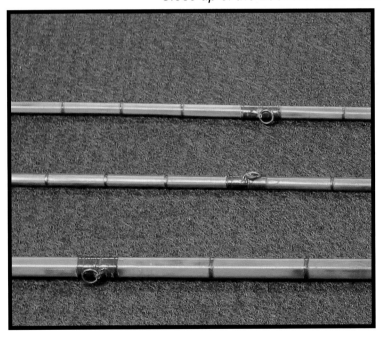

Close up of the hanging ring guides.   *The "H.L.Leonard, Maker, Bangor, Me." butt cap stamping.*

H.L. Leonard, Salmon Rod
Wm. Mills & Son
Sole Agents
3/2,10'6", Calcutta Cane.
circa 1879 to 1886

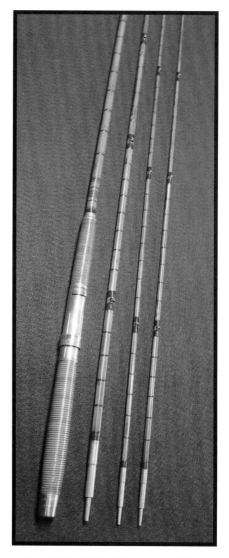

*T*his rod by H.L. Leonard is an example of one of his light salmon or grilse rods. Sold by the Mills firm between 1879 and 1886. That time frame determined by the "Wm Mills & Son, Sole agents" stamping in the butt cap. The rod is wrapped in Chinese red silk with full intermediate wraps and has all rolled and seamed NiS hardware. The guides are NiS trumpet guides. The two female ferrules are stamped with the Oct. 26th 1875 and Sep. 3rd 1878 Leonard patent dates. The rattan grips have the traditional wrap of red silk up thru the rattan. The early work of H.L. Leonard is not impossible to find, but it is fairly rare. This rod is in near mint-restored condition.

*T*his rod is from the collection of Tom Kerr.

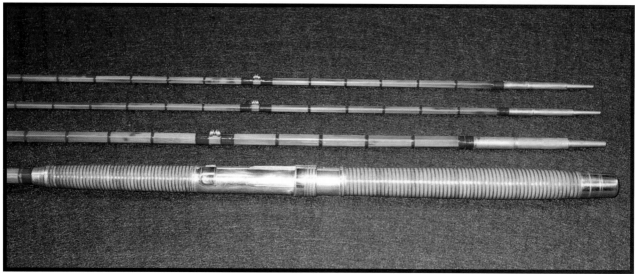

Pictured above are the two handed Leonard Rattan grip and male spiked ferrules and the NiS reel seat and trumpet guides.

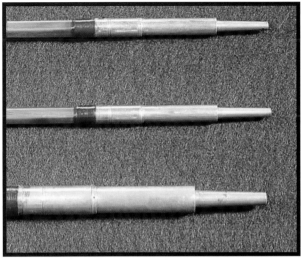

Male Leonard spiked ferrules.

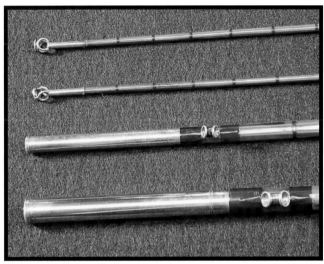

Female ferrules and the three ring tiptops.

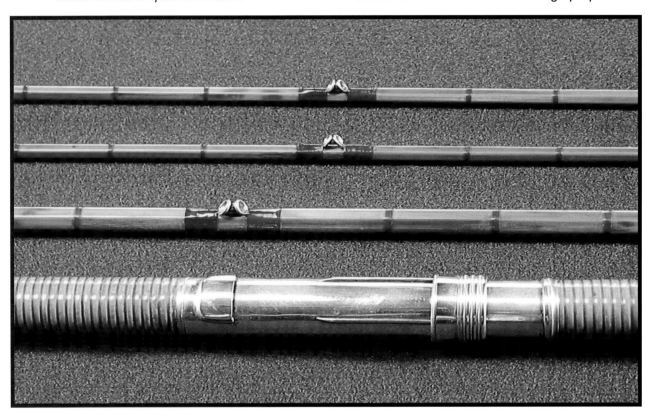

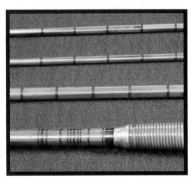

Pictured above is a close up of the full Nickel silver reel seat. Note the soldered hood and reel foot rails which are the work of George I. Varney who was the head hardware maker for Leonard at the time this rod was made.

To the left are the signature wrap and front grip check and the intermediate wraps.

H.L. Leonard,
Wm Mills & Son
Sole Agent 3/2 10'3"
circa 1879-1886

This rod by The H.L. Leonard Co. is a fairly easy one to date due to its butt cap stamping which reads "H.L. Leonard, Maker Wm Mills & Son N.Y. Sole Agents". This rod is in near mint condition and was most likely restored at the Leonard factory at some point in recent time. It is wrapped in green silk and has Chinese red silk trim wraps with the intermediates in the green silk. This rod has the H.L. Leonard patents on the female ferrules. The reel seat, guides and ferrules are NiS. Note the very early use of the soldered reel rails and the soldered hood in the George I. Varney style. The grip is out of 5/16th" cork rings (the grip was most likely changed from rattan when restored). The rod is made of Calcutta cane. This rod is very light for its length and could be an early predecessor of the Catskill model.

This rod is from the private collection of Tom Kerr.

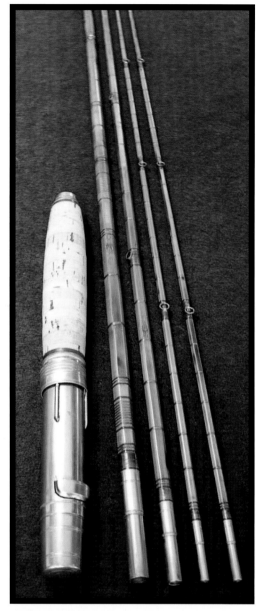

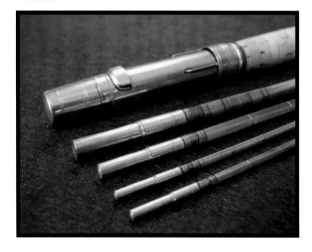

Reel seat and male ferrules pictured above left and a close up of the "H.L. Leonard Maker W. Mills & Son N'YORK Sole Agents" makers mark on the butt cap above right.

Leonard patent male ferrules at left, females at right.

Guides and tip-top. Ferrule showing the Oct. 26th 1875, Sep. 3rd 1878 patent dates.

Close-up of the guides and tip-top.   *Front grip check and butt ferrule.*

This rod is has the patented waterproof ferrules that were a big step forward from the spiked ferrules and all of the problems that went with them. The waterproof ferrules fixed many of the problems that went with the non-waterproof ferrules, like rods that swelled when wet, stuck together and would not come apart.

J.B.Crook & Son Makers
New York, circa 1880s
3/2, 8'6" Bait casting Rod

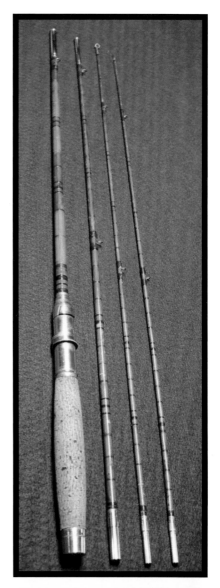

J.B. Crook was in the tackle trade for approximately fifty years, covering the time frame from 1837 to 1887. This rounded Calcutta cane rod is extremely well made. The seams and nodes are basically nonexistent in this rod. It has NiS hardware and has a sheet cork grip. J.B.Crook & Son would have made this rod at the very late stages of their production. The rod has the early style of English twist splayed foot snake guides out of very heavy NiS. The rod is wrapped in Chinese red tipped with black and has full intermediate wraps. Crook was a competitor with the Conroy firm. In the last few years of his known existence in business he occupied the old Conroy shop at 52 Fulton street in New York. Known J.B. Crook rods are very rare and few are known to exist. Fly tackle by Crook would be a truly great find. Jabez Crooks last known advertising was in 1884.

This rod is from the private collection of Tom Kerr.

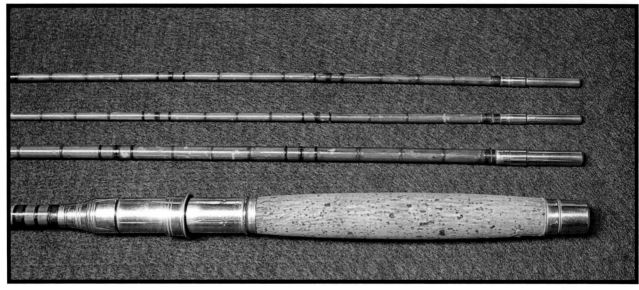

Grip, reel seat and male ferrules and the wrap pattern used by J.B.Crook&Son.

J.B. Crook ferrules and 3 ring tiptop.

"J.B. Crook & Son, Makers, N.Y." mark.

Photo above is an enlargement of the J.B. Crook & Son reel seat.

At the left is a close up of the straight drawn rolled welt female ferrule and 3-ring tiptop used by Crook.

N.K. Waring S.N. 282
8 strip casting & trolling
Circa 1880s-1890s

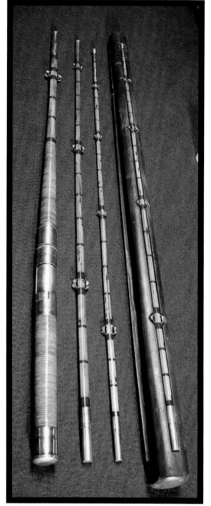

*N*orman K. Waring rods are very rare and only four are known to exist at this time. This eight-strip casting and trolling rod is serial numbered on the blank at the ferrule stations. His use of ink markings on the shaft is one of the earliest known uses of that style of marking a rod. The other makers who were known to do that at the time are C.F. Orvis, John G. Landman and T.H. Chubb. All of these pre-date the ink signature on the shaft that Eustis Edwards is credited with inventing in the early 1900s. This rod is wrapped in silk and has doubled bell guides that are stamped "E. vom Hofe, N.Y.". This is another example of collusion amongst rodmakers in the late 1800s. The reel seat is doubled, as are all of the guides. All of the hardware is nickel silver and the shafts are Calcutta cane.

Mr. Waring in his time was a nationally known builder of bridges and trout ponds.

*T*his rod is from the private collection of Tom Kerr.

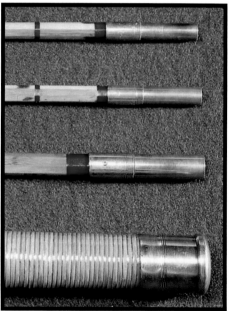

Reel seat, doubled EVH bell guides and the butt cap and male ferrules used by N.K. Waring.

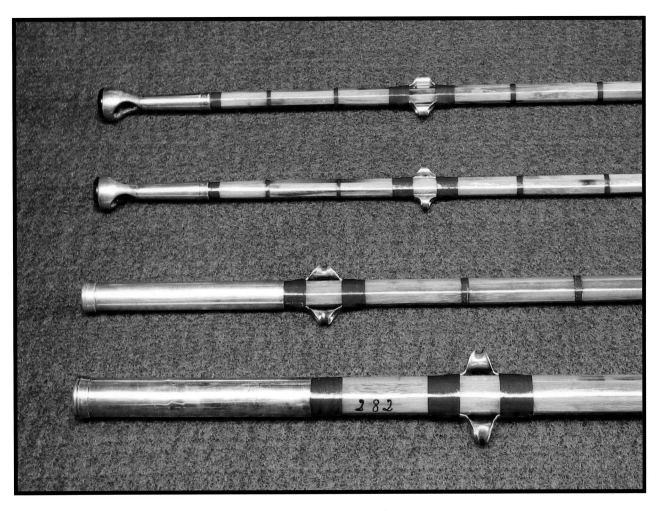

"Waring ferrules, serial number and agate tiptops.

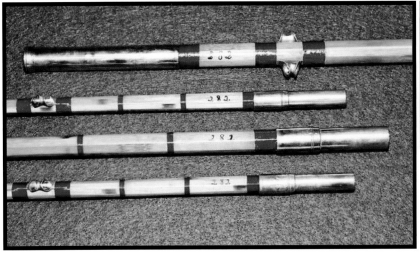

Serial numbers on the shafts from the late 1800s.

Pictured above is the "N.K.Waring Newark Valley N.Y." makers mark.

This rod has been restored and a very good job has been done. The maker should be happy with his work at one hundred and ten years plus and at this point it is ready for the next one hundred and ten years plus.

T.H. Chubb, Post Mills, VT. Lancewood Fly Rod 10' 2/2 with independent grip circa 1880-1891

*T*his rod is an example of a signed and guaranteed Chubb rod. The Chubb star logo is stamped into the reel seat identifying it as a Chubb made rod. The rod has the classical 1880 Chubb patented drawn reel seat out of NiS. The grip is rattan with the traditional wraps of red silk up through the rattan. The guides are hanging rings wrapped with Chinese red silk, and it has full intermediate wraps of Chinese red silk. The tiptops are a soldered wire ring with a straight tail wrapped to a tapered section of the tip. The ferrules are Chubb NiS ferrules. Note the Chubb ad and how this rod was not deliverable by mail even then. The ad pictured is from the 1891 ninth edition of the Chubb catalog. This one is from the reprint done by Tom Kerr, which has allowed the knowledge to be shared by a greater number of people. The original Chubb catalogs when you can find them sell for almost obscene amounts of money depending on condition. This rod has its original form fit case but is missing its ferrule plugs. This rod is from the Authors private collection.

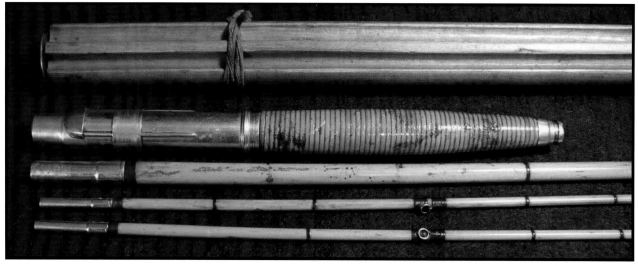

Chubb independent grip and reel seat and the form fit case. Note that the star logo is just above the raised rails on the reel seat.

Chubb male ferrules.   *Chubb female and male ferrules and the NiS wire tiptop.*

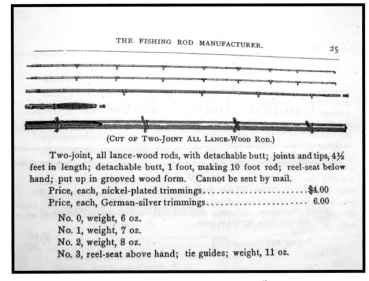

Advertisement for this rod in the 1891 9ᵗʰ edition of the Chubb Catalog above left and a close up of the Chubb star logo stamped into the reel seat above right.

To the left is an excerpt from the 1891 Chubb catalogs about their Lancewood rods and above are the guides and tiptop.

T.B. Mayell, New York Casting & Trolling Rod 8'6" 3/2 Calcutta Cane

*H*ere is an example of a rod that has not been covered in any of the works that are recognized as the primary reference works for the old rod collector. The only mention of Ten Broeck Mayell is from the Albany city directories for the years of 1889-1891. Tom Kerr found this thru Ancestry.com on the Internet and is the owner of this rod. The grip is made of celluloid-like material similar to the grips made by H. Prichard. The metal components are plated brass. The guides are hand soldered out of brass. The rod is wrapped in red silk and has full intermediate wraps. The butt cap is stamped with "T.B.Mayell, Maker, New York". The rod is 6-strip construction and from the quality of the work Mr. Mayell was an aspiring rodmaker at that time and was not real proficient with his work.

*T*his rod is from the private collection of Tom Kerr.

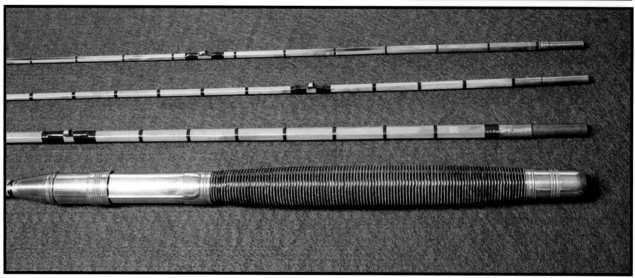

Pictured above is the Mayell rubber or celluloid grip and the plated reel seat and butt cap and male ferrules.

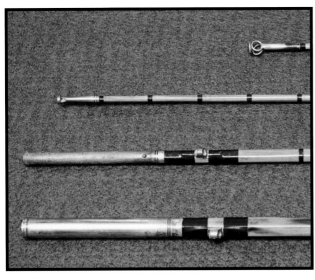

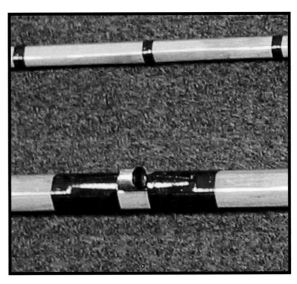

Female ferrules, funnel tiptop and 3-ring top.   *Close up of the handmade brass guide.*

T.B.Mayell Butt cap.   *Close up of the "T.B. Mayell, Maker, New York butt cap stamping.*

Close up of the reel seat used by Mayell.

J.B. Daniels, Auburn Me.
Tonkin cane Fly Rod
9' 3/2 circa 1880-1900

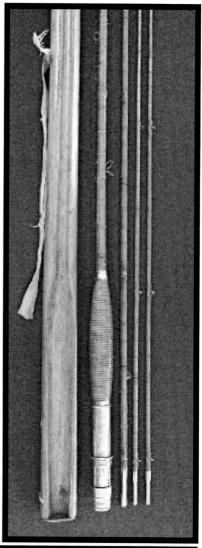

This is an example of one of the rods produced by John Barbour Daniels while he was living in Auburn, Maine. J.B. Daniels was a rod maker who made his own shafts but purchased his hardware from T.H. Chubb and then from Montague after they purchased the Chubb firm in 1891. The notable features of this rod are the Chubb reinforced female ferrules with the hex shoulders, the Chubb reel seat and the signed Daniels form fit case with the leather end caps. The rod is wrapped in three colors of silk, maroon, tan and orange. The guides are very early NiS snake guides with the English twist. The grip is rattan with the single spiral of red silk up thru it. This rod is in need of a full restoration and was photographed before a full restoration was started.

This rod is from the private collection of Bruce Handley.

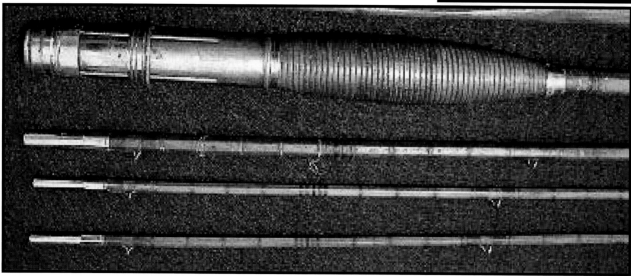

Rattan grip and Chubb hardware used by J.B.Daniels on the Auburn rod pictured above. Also pictured are the NiS snake guides and the Daniels wrap pattern.

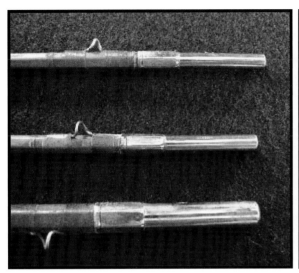
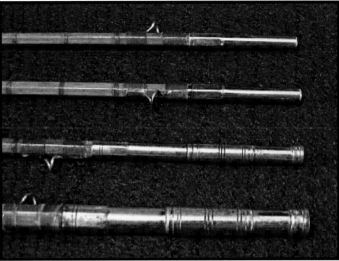

Chubb hex shouldered male ferrules above left and the reinforced female ferrules.

J.B. Daniels ink stamping on the form fit case well faded but still readable.

Close up of the Chubb reel seat used by J.B. Daniels.

G.W. Boyd, Harrisburg Pa.
Calcutta cane Fly Rod
9'6" 3/2 circa 1880s
Charlie Fox's first fly Rod

This rod was Charlie Fox's first fly rod and his dad gave it to him. This rod and the photos of it are courtesy of Russ and Erica Gooding, owners of Golden Witch Technologies, Inc.

Many thanks to Erica for the photographs.

Charlie fox despised the original hanging ring guides and so he stripped the rod and sporterized it with snake guides. This is one instance of a rod that has been sporterized and should be left alone because of who did the rework on the rod. Charlie Fox is known for such notable books on angling as "Armchair Adventures for the Angler", "Rising Trout", "This Wonderful World of Trout"," The Book of Lures" and his first book "Advanced Bait Casting" published in 1950. G.W. Boyd of Harrisburg, Pa. is one of the small time makers who has been overlooked in the entire major literature on rod makers from that time frame. We can assume the rod originally had full intermediate wraps to go along with the hanging ring guides that were replaced. The grip is rattan and the reel seat is a mortised cedar butt. The ferrules are seamed and soldered indicating that they are most likely original. He built rods from 1883.

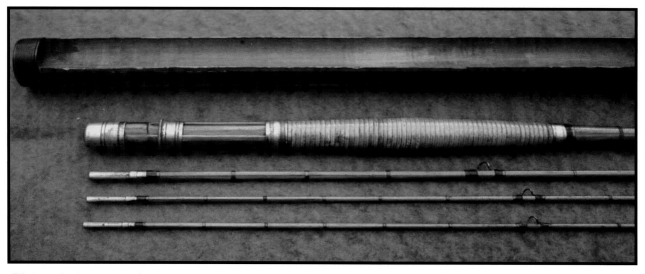

Pictured above are the cedar mortised butt section with the rattan grip and the mortised reel seat with the NiS cap and ring hardware. Note the original form fit case with the unusual end cap.

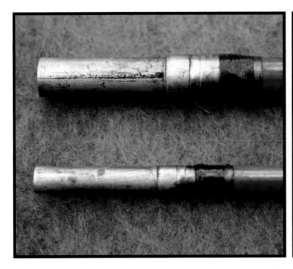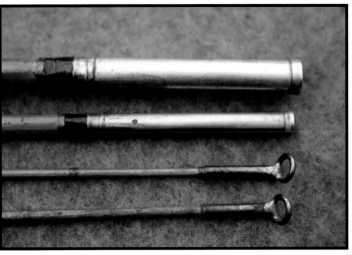

Male ferrules from the G.W. Boyd rod. Female ferrules and the tiptops from the Fox / Boyd rod.

Pictured above are close ups of the reel seat hardware, butt cap and slide band above left and the fixed front hood and grip check above right. Note the slide band's similarity to the mass produced Chubb hardware. And below is a complete view of the reel foot mortise in the mortised butt.

Will Cruttenden, Fly Rod Cazenovia, N.Y. 1880s 10' 3/1 Lancewood

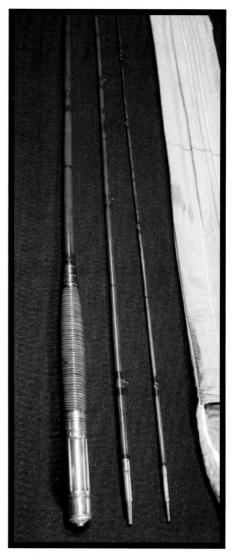

*W*ill Cruttenden is one of the more obscure makers from the late 1800s. The patented reel seat and ferrules were purchased from John McHarg of Rome N.Y. This rod originally had hanging ring guides and would have been wrapped in silk. The grip is rattan and has the spiral of red silk wound up thru it. The components are all NiS plated. The ferrules are classic examples of a large doweled ferrule not spiked.

*T*he reel seat is a typical example of John McHarg's work, as are the ferrules. When a rod of this age has been upgraded or "sporterized" by changing guides or other hardware, it makes it very tough to learn from the rod what could have been learned if it had been left in original condition. Within the written literature of today, there are very few mentions of Will Cruttenden making this an extremely rare rod.

*T*his rod is from the private collection of Tom Kerr.

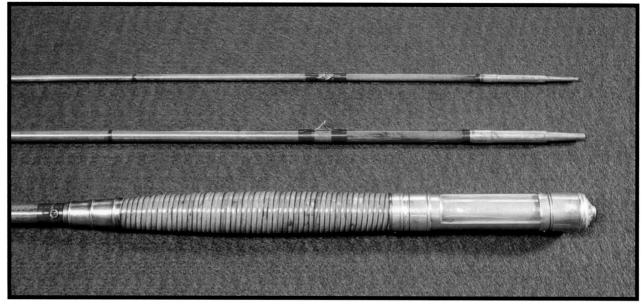

Pictured above are the rattan grip and the McHarg reel seat on the Cruttenden fly rod.

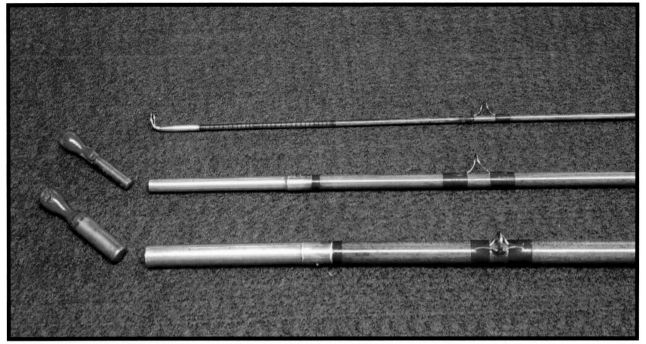

The female ferrules and ferrule plugs used by Will Cruttenden.

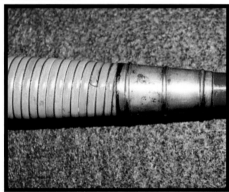

McHarg, Mar.18.73 patent and Cruttenden stampings pictured above left. Rattan grip showing the silk spiral and the front grip check above right. Note the rounded shape of the butt cap and the screw securing it. They are both Identification features of a McHarg reel seat.

Pictured to the left is a close up of the McHarg patent date of Mar.18.73. And the W.H.Cruttenden stamp on the reel seat.

T.H. Chubb, Lancewood Fly Rod, 3/1 7ft. circa 1880-1891

This is an example of a fairly uncommon short length lancewood rod. Note the refinished mid section showing the original light color of the lancewood. The varnish on the butt and tip are very well aged and original and thus the much darker color. When the refinish job was done, the person who did it had no clue of rod building. They had to reset the female ferrule on the butt section and it was reset backwards making the rod un-useable at that point in time. I would estimate that to have taken place in the late teens or early twenties of the 1900s at the latest because of the aging of the varnish on the mid section. The rod has very early NiS Chubb components and the slide band is seamed and soldered. The guides are NiS bell guides and the ferrules are non-waterproof, straight, non-welted, and seamless. The reel seat is the Chubb patented reel seat of 1880. It is wrapped in black silk and has full intermediate wraps. This rod is from the private collection of Jerry Schaeffer.

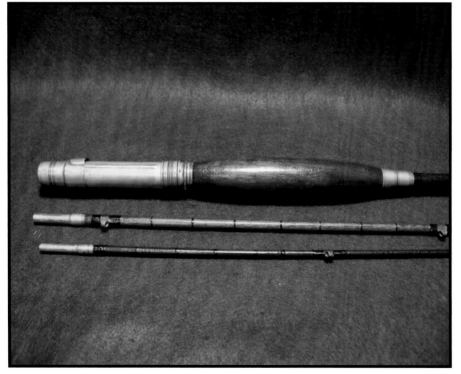

Wooden grip and Chubb reel seat, straight drawn ferrules NiS bell guides on this un-marked Chubb rod

Close up of the non-waterproof male ferrules above left and a close up of the female ferrules and the bell guides.

Close up of the early Chubb butt cap above left and a close up of the seam in the slide band above right, which is an indication of age.

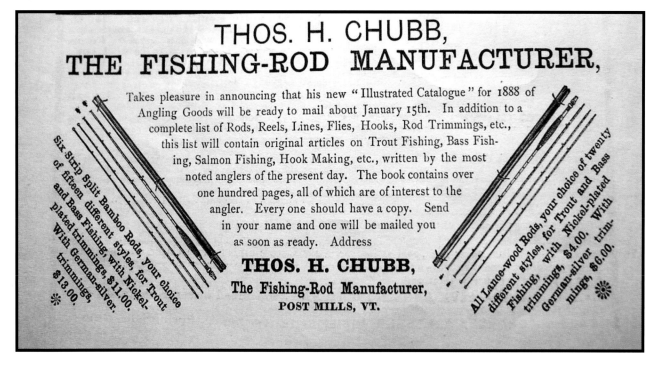

THOS. H. CHUBB,
THE FISHING-ROD MANUFACTURER,

Takes pleasure in announcing that his new "Illustrated Catalogue" for 1888 of Angling Goods will be ready to mail about January 15th. In addition to a complete list of Rods, Reels, Lines, Flies, Hooks, Rod Trimmings, etc., this list will contain original articles on Trout Fishing, Bass Fishing, Salmon Fishing, Hook Making, etc., written by the most noted anglers of the present day. The book contains over one hundred pages, all of which are of interest to the angler. Every one should have a copy. Send in your name and one will be mailed you as soon as ready. Address

THOS. H. CHUBB,
The Fishing-Rod Manufacturer,
POST MILLS, VT.

Six Strip Split Bamboo Rods, your choice of fifteen different styles, for Trout and Bass Fishing with Nickel-plated trimmings, $11.00. With German-silver trimmings, $13.00.

All Lance-wood Rods, your choice of twenty different styles, for Trout and Bass Fishing, with Nickel-plated trimmings, $4.00. With German-silver trimmings, $6.00.

Pictured above is the ad from Harpers weekly from Dec. 1887 advertising his new 1888 catalog.

T.H.Chubb Trolling Rod
Calcutta Cane
7'4" 2/1 circa 1880 – 1891

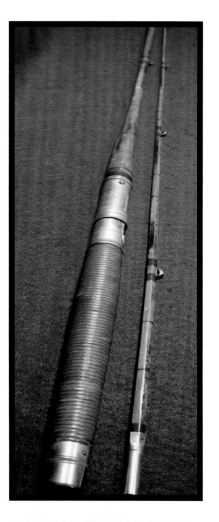

*T*his early unmarked Chubb trolling or bait casting rod has the 1880 patent reel seat for rods with dual guides. The patent number is 235,513 and it was awarded to T.H. Chubb on Dec. 14th 1880 (Notice the screw in the picture below, it is original). This rod has the most intricately knurled hardware of any Chubb I have ever seen. A historical feature of this rod is the markings on the shafts. It is the earliest rod in my collection marked that way. It predates Edwards's shaft markings by a couple of decades plus. The rod has anti friction raised tie guides and a three-ring tiptop. The reel seat has a seamed slide band indicating an early date of manufacture {1880} as opposed to a later date {1891}. The rod is wrapped in Chinese red silk and has full intermediate wraps of the same silk. All of the hardware is NiS.

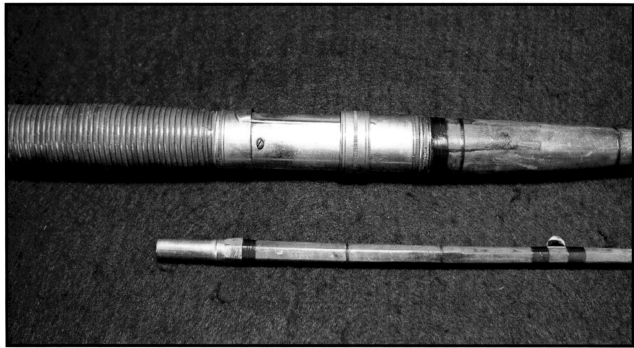

Pictured above are the rattan grip and the 1880 Chubb patent adjustable reel seat.

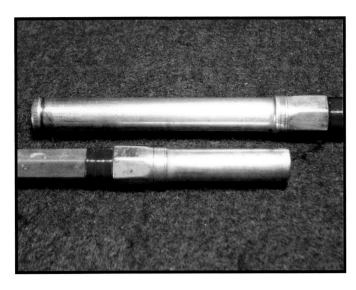 

Male and female hex shouldered ferrules.   Close up of the slide band with the visible seam.

Close up of the welt n the female ferrule to the left and a close up of the # 8 shaft markings to the right.

Close up of the anti-friction raised tie guide above left and a close up of the three-ring tiptop above right.

T.H. Chubb, Post Mills VT.
Ash & Lancewood
Black Bass Bait Rod
9' or 10'6" 3/2 Circa 1880s

*T*his unmarked rod is a Chubb built rod or rod kit at least. Due to the fact that the rod is not stamped with the Chubb star logo leads us to the possibility it may have been built by the original owner. The rod does have the Chubb braided grip or "wound patent whipping" as, described in the 1880s Chubb catalogs. This grip is very rarely seen. The best description for it would be a Chinese finger cuff or a braided leader but large enough to slip over the shaft of a rod. The reel seat and butt cap are NiS plated brass with the well-worn plating, as are the ferrules, which are a straight non-welted style. The rod is in original condition with no broken pieces and even has a near mint short tip contained in the hollow butt. The ad for this rod was featured in "Great Fishing Tackle Catalogs of the Golden Age" by Samuel Melner and Hermann Kessler, which were published in 1972 by Crown publishing of New York. The rod has Prichard patented guides made of NiS. It has a three-ring tiptop on the full-length tip and a Chubb patent funnel tiptop on the short emergency tip.

*T*his rod is from the Author's private collection.

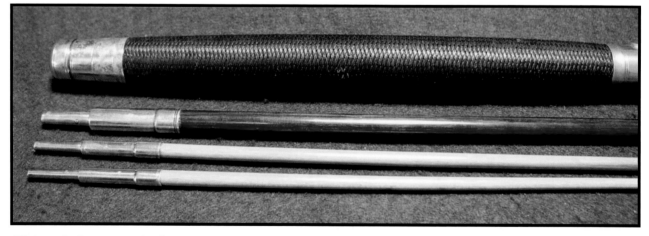

Pictured above are the "patent wound whipping' used as a grip on the Chubb Black bass bait rod circa 1880s. By the last Chubb catalog produced in 1891 before their last fire, which put them out of business, this rods grip was listed as rattan and not the wound whipping.

Male and female ferrules and tiptops pictured above, note the difference in color of the hardware on the tip that has been stored inside the butt of this rod for over 100 years. That tip has been very well protected.

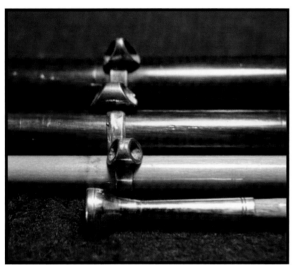
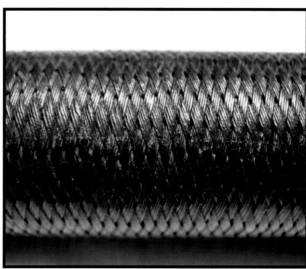

Prichard patent guides and the Chubb funnel tiptop above left and a close up of the Chubb Wound whipping grip that is rarely seen today.

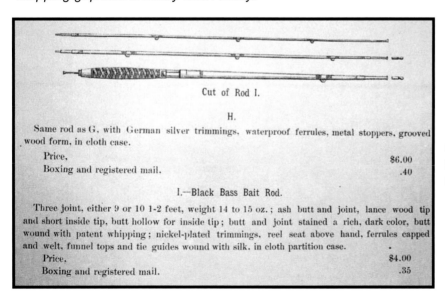

Cut of Rod I.

H.

Same rod as G, with German silver trimmings, waterproof ferrules, metal stoppers, grooved wood form, in cloth case.

Price, $6.00
Boxing and registered mail. .40

I.—Black Bass Bait Rod.

Three joint, either 9 or 10 1-2 feet, weight 14 to 15 oz.; ash butt and joint, lance wood tip and short inside tip, butt hollow for inside tip; butt and joint stained a rich, dark color, butt wound with patent whipping; nickel-plated trimmings, reel seat above hand, ferrules capped and welt, funnel tops and tie guides wound with silk, in cloth partition case.

Price, $4.00
Boxing and registered mail. .35

Pictured to the left is the advertisement for that rod from the mid 1880s Chubb catalog in the Authors library.

T.H. Chubb, Post Mills, Vt. Calcutta Cane Fly Rod 10'6" 3/2 circa 1880-1891

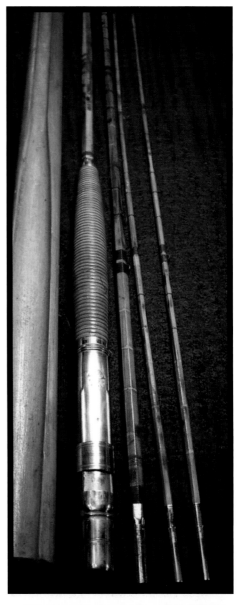

Signed rods by T.H. Chubb are not very common but they do appear from time to time. This rod is one of those odd rods with the Chubb star logo stamped into the reel seat. This also signified that the rod was one of the first rods to carry an unconditional guarantee against breakage due to materials and workmanship for one full year from date of purchase. The rod has the 1880 Chubb patent reel seat with the flat rattan grip that Chubb rods were noted for. It is wrapped in Chinese red silk and has full intermediate wraps. The hardware is all NiS plated with the ferrules being the hex shouldered Chubb ferrule. The guides are hanging rings. The rod is in its original form fit case and is unfortunately missing its original canvas bag. This rod is awaiting a full restoration.

This rod is from the private collection of John Oppenlander.

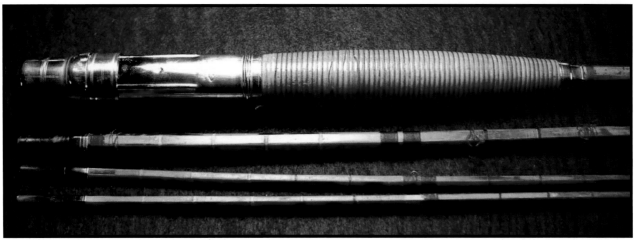

The T.H. Chubb patented reel seat, rattan grip, male ferrules and hanging ring guides pictured above.

T.H. Chubb male and female hex shouldered ferrules above.

Hanging ring guides and the front grip check. Chubb star logo stamping on the reel seat signifying a warranted Chubb rod pictured above right.

Pictured to the left is a close up of the T.H. Chubb single ring tops showing their seamed and soldered construction style.
And to the right is an engraving of Thomas H. Chubb from an 1888 advertisement from Harpers weekly.

John Forrest, Fly Rod Kelso Scotland, 12' 4/1 circa 1880-1920

*T*his is an example of an earlier John Forrest rod. I am dating this rod to this period due to the turned wood butt cap and the hanging ring guides. It has the "Forrest, Maker, Kelso" stamping on the butt cap and has all brass components. The ferrules are doweled ferrules with the wood exposed. The rod is wrapped in black silk and has its original cloth bag and tapered mahogany ferrule plugs. Note the English tradition of the tie off loops for the ferrules. This showed their complete distrust of a properly fitted friction ferrule.

The workmanship on this rod in all respects is of the highest quality. This rod is finished with a shellac finish that is stunning.

This rod is from the private collection of Tom Kerr.

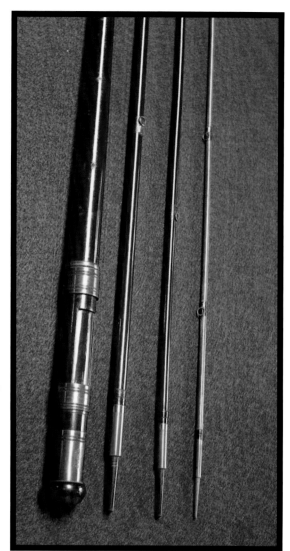

Reel seat with the turned wood butt cap and the exposed wood doweled ferrules.

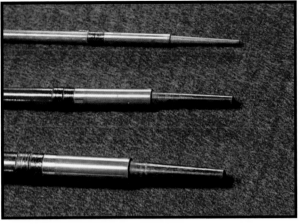

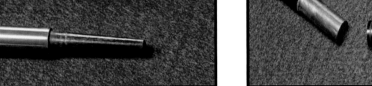

Male brass ferrules with exposed dowel.   *Female ferrules with their mahogany ferrule plugs.*

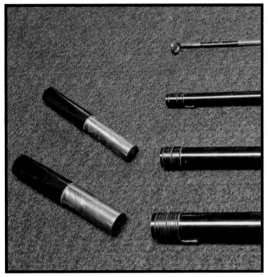

Makers butt cap mark. Female ferrules, tie off loops and ferrule plugs.

Close up of the Forrest of Kelso reel seat and butt cap.

Abbey & Imbrie 3/2 Calcutta Cane "Best Eight Strip" circa 1881-1900

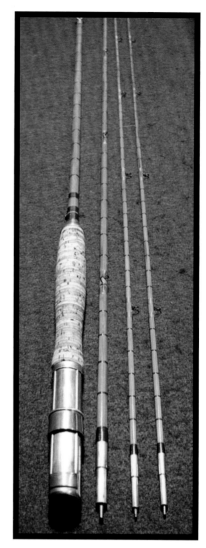

As a collector every once in awhile you come across a rod that just does not fit. Well here is one of them. It is a signed Abbey&Imbrie " *Best Eight Strip*". The rod has the Harry Pritchard Jan. 10th 1888 patented slide band. All of the components in the reel seat are rolled and soldered NiS. The ferrules are copper-bottomed spiked NiS. And the grip is 1/8th inch cork rings. The rod has been "sporterized" with American twist snake guides {circa 1930}. The patented reel seat slide band indicates it is a Pritchard rod but the grip of 1/8th inch rings and the seamed main body of the reel seat are T&E like and the copper-bottomed spiked ferrules point to a John Landman origin. It does show some ghosting of its original doubled intermediate wraps at the ferrule stations, also indicating a John G. Landman origin. The eight strip rods are not very common and at this point in time we know that 8-strippers were made by N.K. Waring, H.P. Buckingham, Fred D. Devine, T.H. Chubb, the Pritchard brothers and the Hardy firm in England. A.H."Doc"Fowler also produced 8 strip rods. Edward vom Hofe also was a maker of marked 8 strip rods.

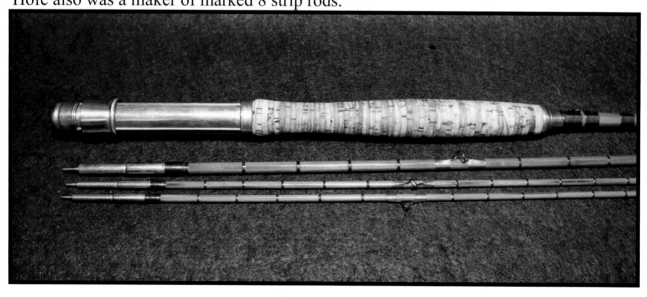

Seamed and soldered reel seat, grip of 1/8th" cork rings and the Landman copper-bottomed spiked ferrules above.

Reel seat and male ferrules.

Male and female ferrules.

Reel seat stamping.

Close up of the copper bottom in the ferrules.

Slide band stamping "Pat.Jan.10.188?

T&E style Grip check.

During the late 1800s we see a fair amount of collusion between rod makers, which makes the identification of rods that have been tampered with a tough thing to do. I would love to be able to say that this is a Pritchard eight strip but I am not sure. The rod is most likely John G. Landman built due to the doubled intermediate wraps and the ferrules. But what is it doing with a Henry Prichard patented beveled slide band? More proof of the A&I /J.G.Landman connection. The shafts are the true mystery because John G. Landman did not make his blanks. He purchased or traded components for them.

John Krider, Valise rod Philadelphia, circa 1880s
1/5/6 = 8 different rods

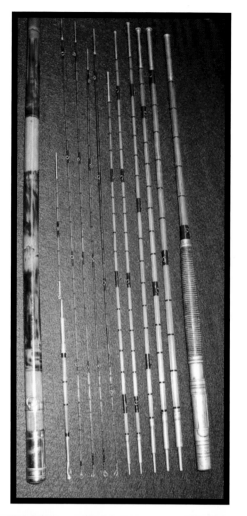

John Krider of Philadelphia rods are a very rare find. The valise rod pictured here is likely a one of a kind in this original condition. The butt and 1st mid are 9 strip construction with the rest being 6-strip. With the pieces supplied you can make a 4-piece 6'4" bait casting rod. The other configurations (7) make up into fly rods from a 5-piece 9'6" to a 6-piece 11'6". The rod is fitted with rolled and seamed hardware that are all handmade. The rod has hanging ring guides. The tiptops are funnel type on the two heavier tips and the rest are a looped NiS wire tiptop. The grip is rattan with the traditional spiral of red silk. The rod is wrapped in Chinese red silk and has Chinese red intermediate wraps. It has its original form fit case and Calcutta cane tip tube.

This rod is from the private collection of Tom Kerr.

Krider Reel seat.

Butt cap stamping.

John Krider's rods were not a cheap item even when they were new, a bamboo spliced 4 joint with extra joint and tips sold for $60.00 in 1878. That would be a 1Butt / 2 Mid / 3 tip rod. Would that make this rod cost $120.00 at a per piece price not counting the form fit case and tip tube?

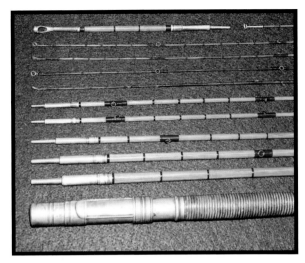

Reel seat, Male ferrules and tiptops.

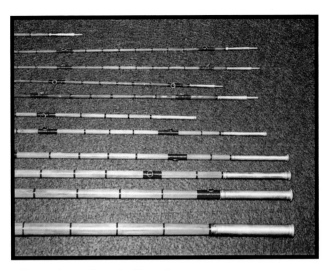

Female and male Ferrules.

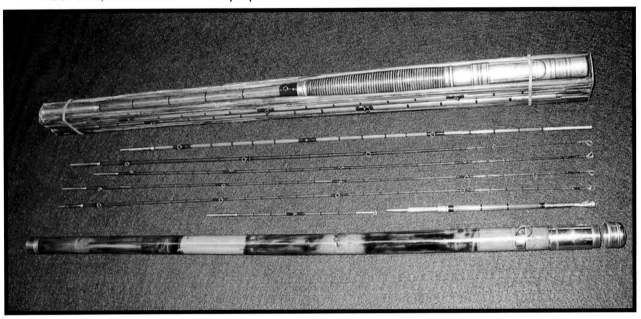

Rod in its form fit with the tip tube out of the form fit and the tips out.

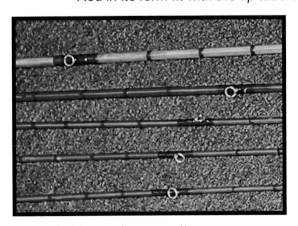

Guides and wrap pattern.

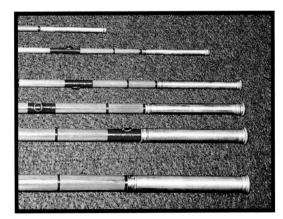

Close-up of Female ferrules.

Edward vom Hofe, N.Y. Calcutta Cane Fly Rod 10'6" 1/2/3 circa 1880s

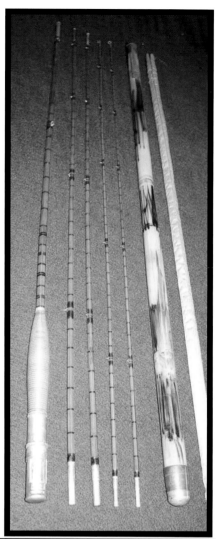

This rod is an early example of an Edward Vom Hofe marked fly rod. The rod originally had three tips with it but one is lost to time. The rod does have its original canvas bag and Calcutta cane tip tube and cloth bag for the tips. The rod is wrapped with Chinese red silk trimmed with green silk and it has full intermediates of Chinese red. The grip is rattan and the reel seat and ferrules are NiS. The rod has NiS snake guides when it should have hanging rings. I am dating this rod to this time frame due to the configuration of the rod. Also, the marking of the rod is a clue to its age. E.V.H. did use antiquated fittings on his rods as late as the 1930s. These fittings included rolled and seamed hardware and rattan grips. So in essence this rod could be dated anywhere from the mid 1880s to the mid 1930s. But I personally feel it is an early model of pre 1900 or earlier. This rod is from the private collection of Tom Kerr.

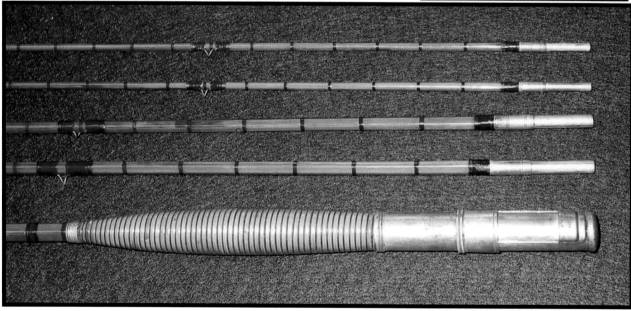

Edward vom Hofe rattan grip and seamed and soldered reel seat and male ferrules.

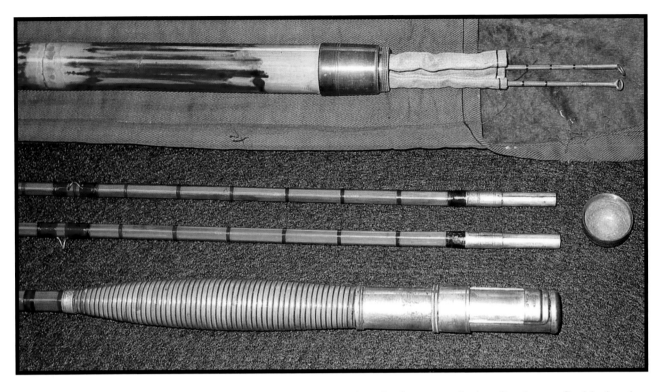

All that is lacking from this picture to make it complete is the one missing tip. A rare find indeed.

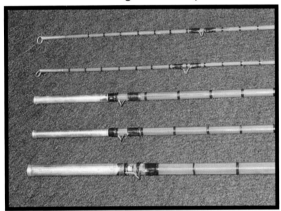

E.V.H. female ferrules and tiptops.

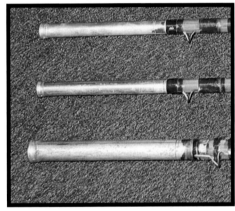

Close up of the seamed and soldered female ferrules.

"Edward vom Hofe Butt cap marking.

Edward vom Hofe reel seat.

Charles F. Orvis fly rod
10' 3/2 Calcutta cane
Circa 1882-1900 S.N.259

Charles F. Orvis started making wood rods in the early 1850's. Twenty-two years later he began production of split bamboo rods. Two years prior to his introduction of split bamboo he introduced the first modern fly reel in 1874, which is still the basis for 90% of the fly reels produced today. This rod is basically complete except for the butt section having been shortened by about 12" and 1 tip is a replacement from a later rod. It is serial numbered 462. The rod is made of Calcutta cane and has the Hiram Eggleston patent reel seat. Patent #258,902 was awarded on June 6th 1882. The grip is 6 strips of 3/8" wide sheet cork. The rod is wrapped in Chinese red silk and has hanging ring guides. The ferrules are the very early rolled and seamed and soldered NiS. It still has its original wood tube and cloth bag.

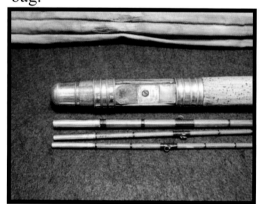

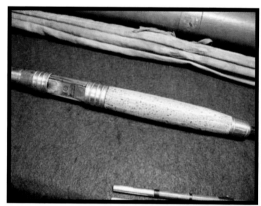

Eggleston reel seat at left.

6 Strip sheet cork grip at right.

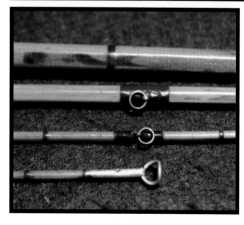

Hanging ring guides and tip top at left.
Guides and grip check at right.

Reel seat
stamping at left.

Front hood of reel
seat at right.

Spring plate in reel
seat at left.

Rear reel seat hood
showing the serial #
259 and the slot
allowing adjustment of
the reel seat.

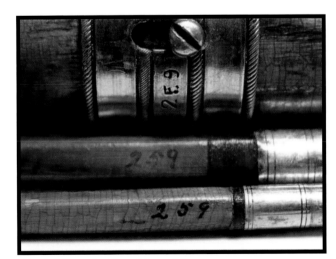

Serial # on butt, mid and tip.

Serial # on the front hood of the reel seat.

Close up details of the original cap and wood tube. Cap at left and splice in the middle of the tube at right.

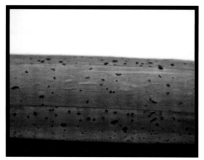

Close up of 3/8" sheet cork strips.   *Makers mark on butt cap.*   *Orvis female ferrule welt.*

Male ferrule that is split on its soldered seam.   *Butt cap and rear hood.*

    The Charles F. Orvis Co. is still in business and can claim to be one of the pioneers in American rod making. They have contributed much to our sport in the last 140 plus years, and they are still one of the foremost outfitters in the fly-fishing industry.

Orvis ad from the Anglers guide 1908 pictured to the right.

Michigan Grayling.

Pictured above is an engraving of the "Michigan Grayling" from the 1908 Anglers guide by Charles Bradford.

W. Mitchell&Son N.Y. Snakewood Salmon Rod 16' 1/2/3 circa 1883-1889

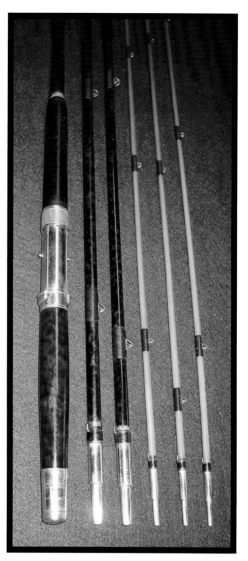

William Mitchell & Son was the stamping used by Mitchell and his son during their final years in business. The snakewood rods made by Mitchell are some of the most beautiful fishing rods ever made. The combination of the heavily grained snakewood and the golden yellow of the lancewood tips are stunning to see in person. This rod is wrapped in Chinese red silk. The reel seat is doubled and the rod has hand made 2-ring standing guides. The metal work is all seamed and soldered. The upper grip is the typical Mitchell cord wrapped, black lacquered grip and the lower grip is ash stained to look like snakewood. In the tradition of his home country of England he applied tie off loops to the ferrules due to his mistrust of the friction fitted ferrules. This rod originally had a fourth tip but it has disappeared along the way. This rod does have its original canvas bag with a compartment for the fourth tip. This rod is from the private collection of Tom Kerr.

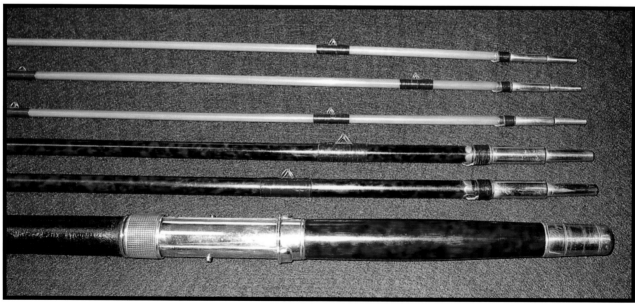

Mitchell doubled reel seat, male wrapped over fluted ferrules.

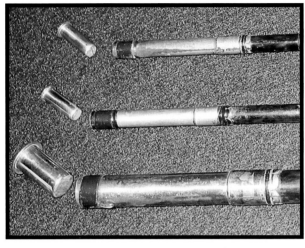

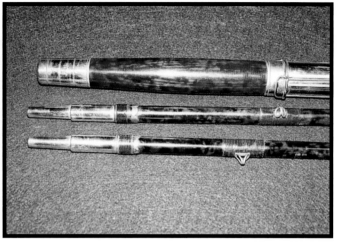

Female ferrules and ferrule plugs.   *Lower grip and male ferrules.*

Close up of Mitchell reel seat. Note the Mitchell knurled slide band.

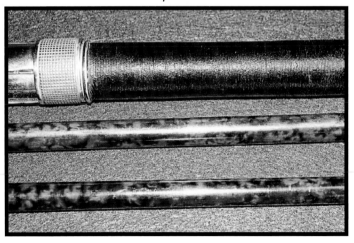

Close up of the snakewood shafts and the Mitchell corded grip at left. Note the intricacy of the grain in the snakewood it is one of the most stunning woods in existence in my opinion.

William Mitchell & Son Snakewood & Lancewood Fly Rod 1/2/3 New York City circa 1883-1889

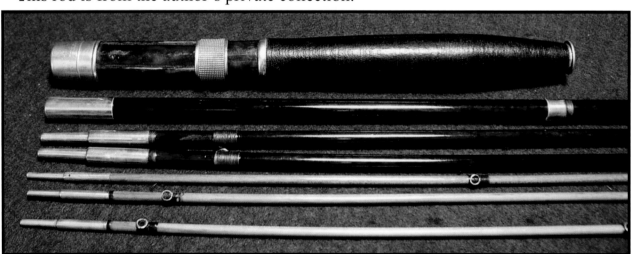

William Mitchell was an Englishman living in New York City in the mid to late 1800's. He was one of the pioneers in the making of split bamboo rods but the odd thing about his work is the fact that more of his snakewood and lancewood rods show up today than do his bamboo rods. The snakewood rods are in my opinion the most beautiful of all the fishing rods ever made. The graining in the wood itself is spectacular.

This is one of his later production rods, marked "William Mitchell & Son, New York". It is one of his rods with the removable handle, for which he was awarded his Jan. 9th 1883 patent #270,460.

Key main features of the rod include its rolled and soldered and unwelted ferrules. The hanging ring guides were right at the end of the time period when they were used. The rod is almost complete. It is missing the extension tube and cap which would have carried the grip and screwed onto the end of the Calcutta tube pictured.

This rod is from the author's private collection.

Pictured above are the removable grip and reel seat that were the first patented removable handle. Also note the richness of the grain and color of the snakewood sections.

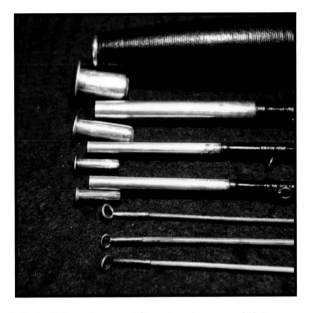

Male Mitchell ferrules.   *Female Mitchell ferrules and ferrule plugs and tiptops.*

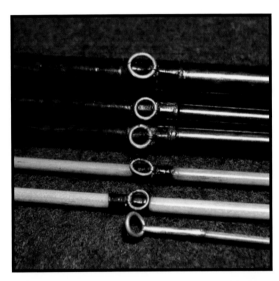

Close up of the hanging ring guides to the left.

Close up of the Mitchell slide band showing the solder seam at the right.

The above three photos show the butt cap stampings "W.MITCHELL&SON, N.YORK, Ptd JAN.9,1883"which were the last markings used by Mitchell. His wooden rods are true pieces of art in the quality of the workmanship and finish of the rods.

E. Bartlett, Amherst Mass. Salmon Rod, Calcutta Cane 17'6" 1/2/3 circa 1885

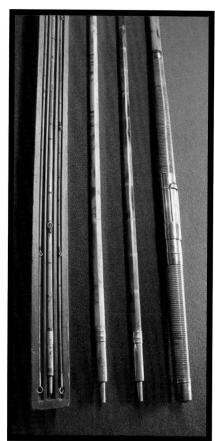

This is one of the largest split cane rods you will ever see. The individual sections are seventy inches in length. The rod is put up in the old style of one-butt two mid sections and three tips. It is in its original form fit case. The rod's reel seat and ferrules are made out of NiS plated brass. It is wrapped in Chinese red silk and has full intermediate wraps. The guides are hanging rings and the tiptops are a single flat ring. The grip is made of rattan with the red silk spiral up thru the rattan. The ferrules are a heavy covered doweled type of ferrule. The Bartlett brothers started their rodmaking efforts in 1872 under Calvin Gray. They continued on under the tutelage of Joseph G. Ward after the death of Calvin in 1873 in the prime of life. Eventually becoming the Montague City rod Co. in 1889. This rod is from the private collection of Tom Kerr.

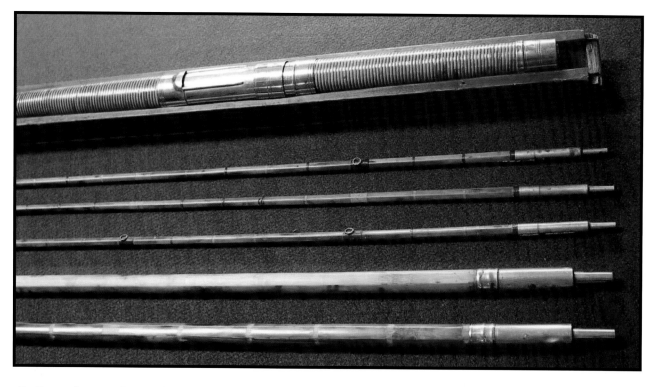

Rattan grips, reel seat, heavy doweled ferrules and hanging ring guides and the mid sections stripped and ready to rewrap pictured above.

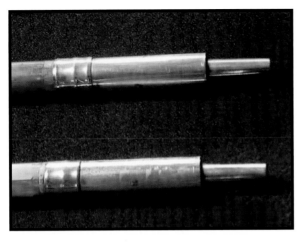

Close up of the male and female ferrules and the female ferrule plug pictured above.

Close up of the Bartlett reel seat

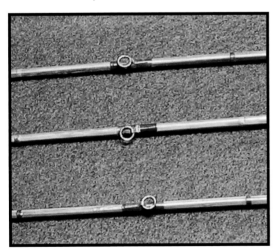

Hanging ring guides.

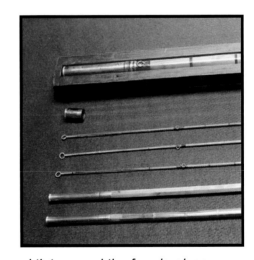

Female ferrules and tiptops and the ferrule plugs.

Fred D. Divine
Utica, N.Y.
Bethabara Casting Rod
9' 3/2 Circa 1885-1888

*T*his is a rod that you can be sure was made by Fred D. Divine himself. The stamping is the confirming fact. Fred used it only for a 3-year period. The rod is wrapped in Chinese red silk and has 2 ring standing guides and 3-ring tiptops. The reel seat is the 1885 Divine patent reel seat, Patent #331,380. All of the hardware is made of NiS. The grip is rattan with a single wrap of red silk spiraled up thru it. The rod is in its original greenheart form fit case and it does still have its original canvas bag. Rods made from Bethabara are very uncommon and are almost as stunning visually as rods made from snakewood.

*T*his rod is from the private collection of Tom Kerr.

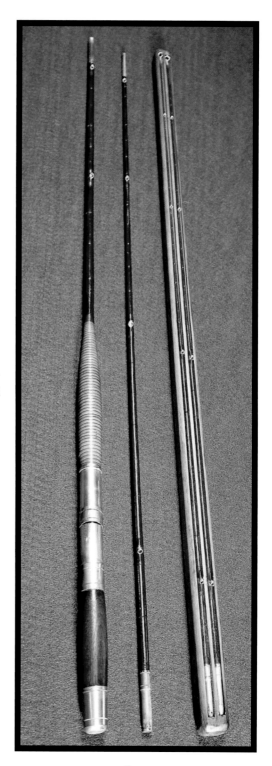

Pictured above left is a close up of the"F.D.Divine,Maker, Utica,N.Y. Pat Dec 1st 1885"reel seat markings and above right is the full length view.

*R*ods by Fred Divine are very rare and are a part of our angling heritage making them almost too rare and valuable to fish at this point in time.

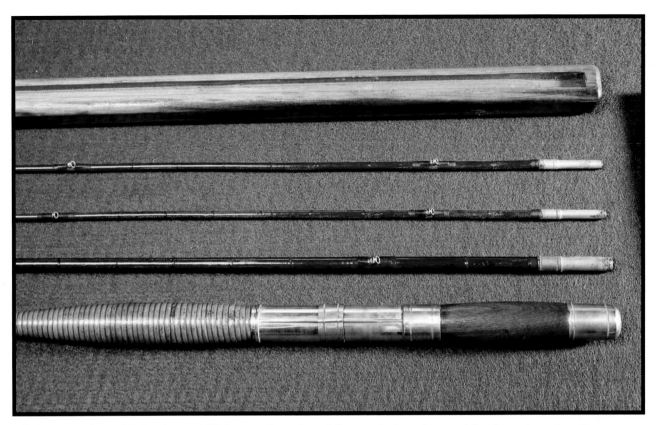

Above are the rattan grip and Divine reel seat and the male ferrules and the two-ring standing guides.

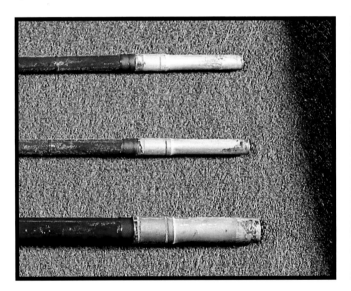 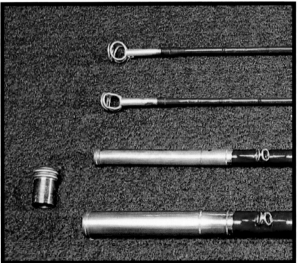

Pictured above are the male ferrules used by Fred Divine on the left and the female ferrules and the three-ringtiptops and the original ferrule plug on the right. Note how stretched the one ring on the lower tiptop is. Makes you wonder what they had ahold of, a rock fish or a real fish or one of those darn tree fish. Whatever it was it had to be big and or solid to stretch a tiptop that way.

A. Fowler, Ithaca, N.Y. 3/2 9' Calcutta Cane Fly Rod circa 1885-1890

*A*lonzo "Doc" Fowler was a dentist from Batavia who made a small number of split bamboo rods both six and eight strip. He is also known for his cast gutta-percha reel the "Gem". This rod has the later capped non-spiked hex based Chubb ferrules dating it to 1885 or later. The reel seat is very similar to the reel seats of B.F. Nichols. The main differences are the butt cap and the slide band. The main body of the seat is very much like the Nichols reel seat, as shown in the picture comparing the two reel seats. The rod is wrapped in Chinese red silk and has full intermediate wraps. The rod has hanging ring guides and Chubb single ring tops. The grip is rattan with the spiral of red silk up thru it. The Fowler rods are very rarely seen. A find that would make any collector go nuts would be a matched Gem reel and a Doc. Fowler rod stuffed away in an attic or barn, the things dreams are made of. Doug Kulick of Kane Klassics restored this rod.

*T*his rod is from the private collection of Tom Kerr.

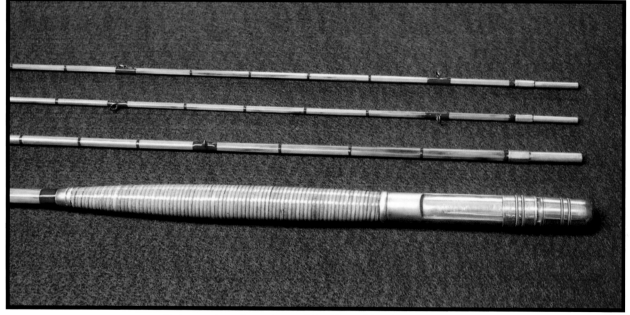

Grip and reel seat used by Doc. Fowler.

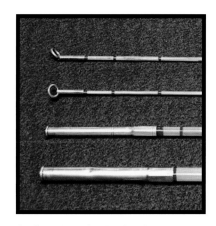

Male hex shouldered Chubb Ferrules.

Female ferrules & single ring top.

Pictured to the left is a Fowler Reel seat above and a B.F. Nichols seat below.

The similarity is the recessed/mortised reel seat done in the metal.

One other man who was known to use that style was John B. McHarg of Rome, N.Y. Is this an example of collusion amongst

Rodmakers? I think so. Fowler used both Chubb and Nichols components on this rod. A great example of a small time rod maker using whatever he could get his hands on to produce what was the best possible rod in his opinion.

Pictured to the left is the "A.H.Fowler, Ithaca.N.Y." reel seat stamping.

Dame Stoddard & Co. "High Grade" B.F. Nichols 9'9" 3/2 Circa 1883-1900

*T*his fly rod is an example of a Calcutta cane trade rod made by B.F. Nichols of Boston for the Dame Stoddard & Co. sporting goods retailer, also of Boston. The reel seat is the typical Nichols reel seat, as are the ferrules. The form fit case is an original Nichols case. The rod is wrapped in red silk with full intermediate wraps and has a rattan grip with the single spiral of red silk up thru the rattan. The hardware is all NiS. The guides are hanging ring guides and are also made of NiS. The rod is marked on the butt "HIGH GRADE" Dame Stoddard & Co., Makers, BOSTON" in four lines with the Dame Stoddard & Co. being in an arched line over the word Maker. The winding check on this rod is slightly different than the other winding checks used by B.F.Nichols, possibly as a small difference between the trade rods and the B.F. Nichols marked rods. This rod is from the private collection of Bob Carolan who also photographed the rod.

*M*any thanks to Bob for the donation of the photographs of the rod!

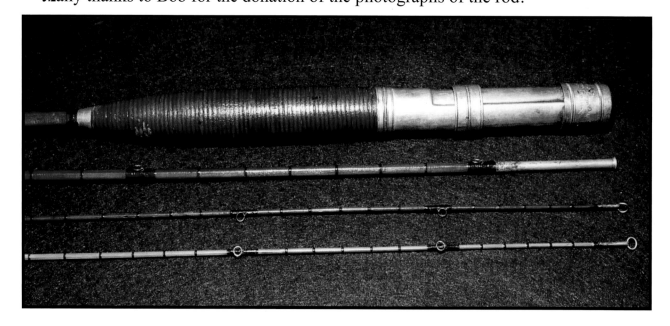

Pictured above are the Nichols reel seat and rattan grip and hanging ring guides, and the male ferrules on the Dame Stoddard & Co. "High Grade" trade rod.

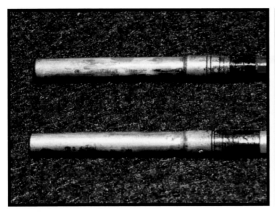

Pictured above left are the Nichols male ferrules. And the Nichols female ferrules showing the soldered seam, and the hanging ring guides are pictured above right.

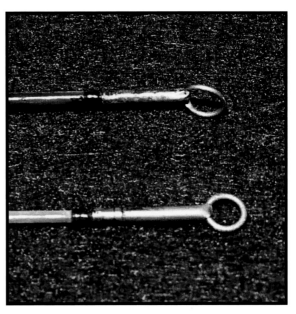

Hanging ring guides.   *Tiptops.*

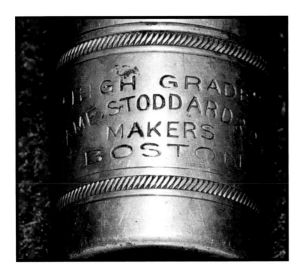

"HIGH GRADE" Dame, Stoddard & Co. Makers, Boston, butt cap stamping above left and the bottom of the Nichols form fit case above right.

William Read & Sons T.H. Chubb Trade rod 10' 3/2 Calcutta Cane circa 1885-1891

The William Read & Sons firm traced their lineage back to the partnership of Lane & Read in 1848. This rod has the 107 Washington Str. Address dating the rod to 1885 or later. This rod is a trade rod made for them by the T.H.Chubb Rod Co. of Post mills Vermont.

The rod is in its original Form fit case and canvas bag. The rod is mortised with cedar and has NiS plated components. One of the most interesting features of this rod is the Chubb sculptured reel rails. That is a feature that is rarely seen today. The rod is wrapped with Chinese red silk trimmed with a black tip and has Chinese red and black alternating intermediates. This rod is from the Author's private collection.

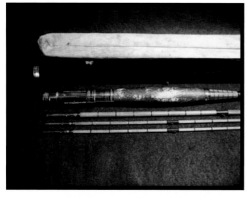

Grip and reel seat at left.

Close up of the Chubb sculptured reel rails at right.

Mortised butt and the hanging ring guides and tip top and reel seat stamping below.

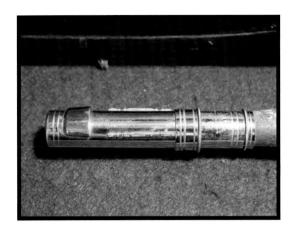

Chubb reel seat.

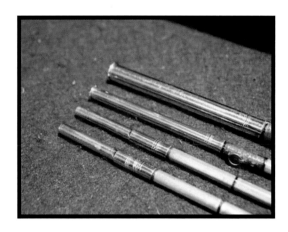

Chubb straight drawn rolled welt ferrules.

Hanging ring guides and wraps.

Cedar mortise and front grip check.

Soldered rear hood.

Signature wraps and mortise and sheet cork grip.

This is a classic example of a higher quality Chubb trade rod sold before the influence of George I. Varney at Montague in the early 1900s. Note the soldered hood and rails that are very prevalent among Rodmakers at that time.

Horton Mfg. Co. Bristol, Ct. Steel Telescoping Patented Line Through the Rod 10'4-piece telescoping plus grip circa 1887-1920

*H*ere is an example of the rod that was patented by Everett Horton on March 8th 1887. The rod is designed to be guide-less. The line runs up through the hollow tubular steel shaft obviating the need for guides. The tiptop is made of brass and is well worn showing that this rod was fished quite a bit. This is substantiated by the set in the rod in the full-length picture to the right. Note the similarity of the reel seat to a Chubb production seat. The grip is a turned wood grip that is hollow to accept the telescoping portions of the rod. The steel rods have always been touted as unbreakable and the answer to Bamboo and wood. Even still to this day you can buy a low quality steel-telescoping rod.

*T*he Bristol rod pictured here is from the collection of Dr. Richard Collar D.D.S.

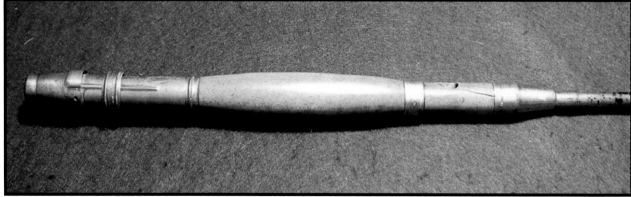

Pictured above is the grip and reel seat, notice the hole at the top of the grip in the wood allowing the threading of the rod.

Line guide at the front of the grip pictured above and to the left is the ad for Bristol steel rods from the back cover of the 1908 "Anglers Guide" by Charles Bradford. Below are the reel seat markings on the Bristol steel-telescoping rod by the Horton Mfg. Co. of Bristol Ct.

Pictured to the left is a close up of the brass tiptop. Note the line grooves in the end of the tiptop. Pictured above are the "Pat'D. MAR.8.87" markings on the front grip check.

H. Prichard/Abbey&Imbrie Greenheart Bait & Trolling 8'9" 3/2 circa 1888-1898

*T*his very dark greenheart rod from the great old tackle house of Abbey&Imbrie is an example of a rod that is normally attributed to the Prichard brothers (Harry and Tom). It may be, but it is more likely the work of John Landman. The rod has the Prichard Dec. 13th 1881 patent rubber grip and also the Jan. 10th 1888 patent slide band. One reason why I am fairly positive that this rod is the work of Landman is the fact that the ferrules are spiked copper bottomed Landman ferrules and also the fact that 50% of each of those patent rights were assigned to Abbey&Imbrie giving them the right to produce those patented items under their own name. Very few rods if any can be directly attributed to Henry Prichard. You see two levels of rod quality in the rods with Prichard patent components; one is a very high quality rod with rolled and seamed NiS hardware and very close attention to detail. The lower grade carries NiS plated brass components and could possibly be the work of either Bartlett / early Montague City Rod Works or by Chubb as a trade rod.

This rod has the rolled and seamed components and high quality NiS bell guides and is wrapped in black silk. The one remaining tiptop is a NiS stirrup tiptop.

*T*his rod is from the Author's rest home for the old warriors collection.

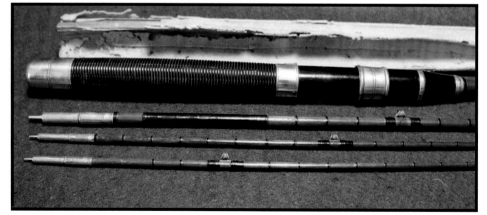 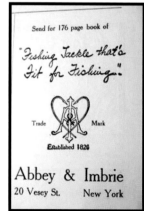

Prichard patent rubber grip and Landman copper bottomed-spiked ferrules and the extremely moth eaten form fit case above left and a late 1890s ad from Abbey & Imbrie above right.

Landman copper-bottomed spiked NiS male ferrules above left and the females and the bell guides and the stirrup tiptop above right, note the seams on the female ferrules.

  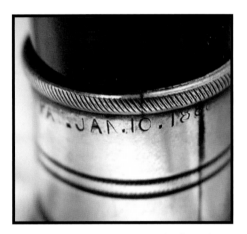

Above row of photos show from left to right a close up of the copper bottomed spiked male ferrule, the bell guides and stirrup tiptop and the Jan. 10. 1888 patent markings.

Pictured above is the Prichard Dec 13th 1881patent date on the rubber grip above left and the Abbey&Imbrie New York markings on the butt cap.

This rod is a visual delight because of the contrast from the dark greenheart to the black grip and reel seat to the bright NiS hardware.

Abbey&Imbrie 6 strip 8'6" 1/2/3 Calcutta Cane circa 1888-1898

*T*his rod is another example of a rod with both Pritchard patent components and John G. Landman built components. There are very few known examples like this rod that have a single spiked ferrule on the mid sections. The tips have a standard waterproof design with the waterproofing cap being made out of copper, indicating the Landman made ferrules. The rod has its original form fit case. All of the NiS components are seamed and soldered also indicating a possible Landman origin. The grip and reel seat are a single piece of wood with the reel seat mortised out of it and having a NiS cap and ring with the Henry Pritchard Jan 10th 1888 patent stamping. The guides are hanging ring guides with the rod being wrapped in Chinese red silk. It has full intermediate wraps and was put up in the old configuration of 1 butt, 2 mids and 3 tips.

*T*his rod is from the private collection of Richard Collar D.D.S.

Finished wooden grip and reel seat with the Henry Pritchard Jan 10th 1888 patent pictured below.

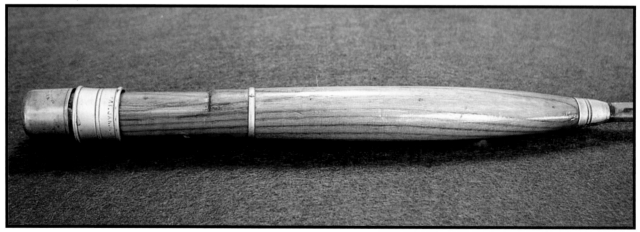

Abbey & Imbrie stamping on the butt cap at left with a close up on the right of the Pritchard patent stamping on the slide band.

Copper bottomed spiked and non-spiked male ferrules.

Female ferrules and hanging ring guides.

Some of the signs of extreme age of a rod are grooved line guides and alligator-ed finish. Even with this rod exhibiting those features, it would be fishable today. But, as a complete and rare example of an early trade rod by either Landman or Pritchard, it is too rare to fish or even cast.

Close up of grooved guide and alligator-ed finish.

Abbey & Imbrie 8-Strip 8'6" 1/2/3 Calcutta Cane circa 1888-1898

*T*he connection between John Landman and Abbey & Imbrie must have been a strong one. The number of A&I marked rods by Landman that have surfaced in the last ten years is actually a surprise. I have held 4 rods in the year of 2003 and they are all marked as A&I rods but John G. Landman made them. Out of that group three were 8-strip rods. This rod is a great example of that connection. Note the doubled intermediates at the ferrule stations and the Landman Bakelite reel seat. This rod is a later model than the 6-strip pictured on page #88. This rod does not have spiked male ferrules on the mid sections, but it still has the copper bottomed waterproofing caps so unique to Landman. The rod has a grip of 1/8th inch cork rings. This rod has early English twist snake guides that are wrapped in Chinese red silk with full intermediate wraps of the Chinese red silk. The stripping guide and tiptops are all agate inserts in NiS frames.

*T*his rod is from the private collection of Richard Collar, D.D.S.

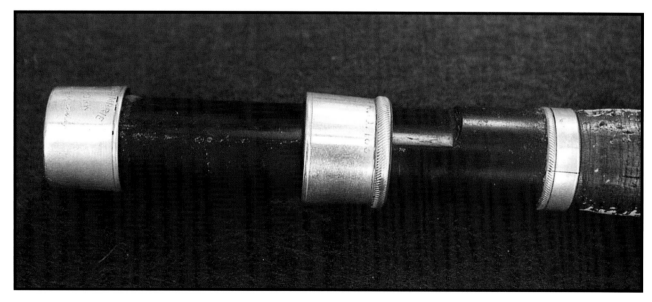

Close up of the Landman Bakelite reel seat with the Pritchard patent slide band.

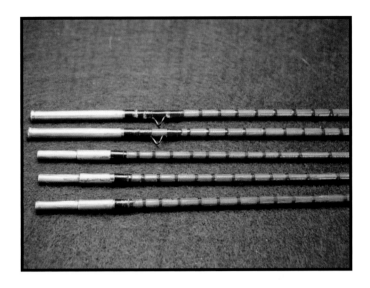

Male and female ferrules and the doubled intermediate wraps at left. "Abbey & Imbrie, New York, Best Eight strip" stamping on the butt cap at right.

Close up of the agate stripping guide and agate tiptops pictured above left and close up of the tiptops at right

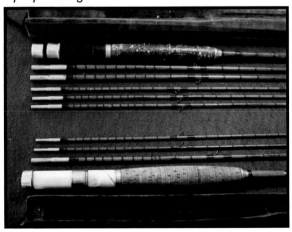

Pictured here at the left is a side by side comparison of two marked Abbey & Imbrie best eight strip rods. Both of the rods have Landman made components and each has the doubled intermediate wraps that Landman was known for.

B.F. Nichols, Boston
H.C. Litchfield & Co
12' 3/2 Calcutta Cane
circa 1888-1898

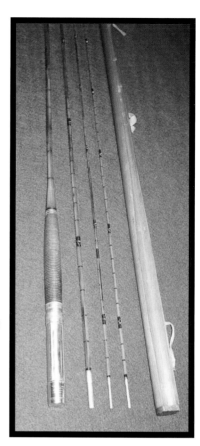

*T*his rod has the "B.F. Nichols" H.C.Litchfield & Co. Makers, Boston, Mass. stamping on the butt cap. This is the 3rd and last known marking used by Benjamin F. Nichols and it is also one of the more rare markings. It was used only after late 1888. This rod has its original form fit case. The rod is wrapped in Chinese red silk and has full intermediate wraps of Chinese red. The grip is rattan and the reel seat and ferrules are NiS and of Nichol's own manufacture. The rod has hanging ring guides and single ring tops. The Nichols reel seat is similar to one other early makers patented seat and that was John McHarg of Rome N.Y. Both seats styles have a recess for the reel foot mortised right into the barrel of the reel seat.

*T*his rod is from the private collection of Tom Kerr.

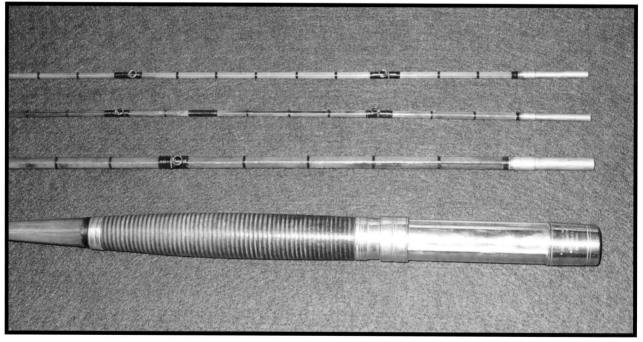

B.F. Nichols rattan grip, swelled butt and hardware pictured above. Note the style of the wood form fit case, which is typical to Nichols rods.

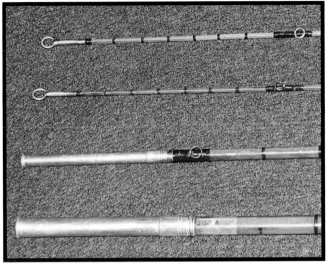

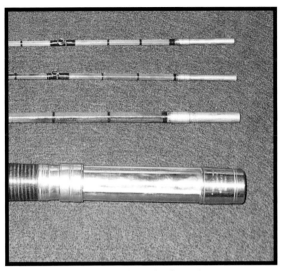

Nichols female ferrules and single ring tops.　　　　*Reel seat and male ferrules.*

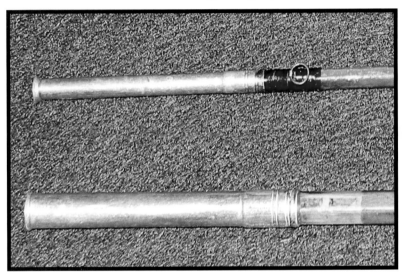

Close ups of female ferrule and hanging ring guide and the male ferrules.

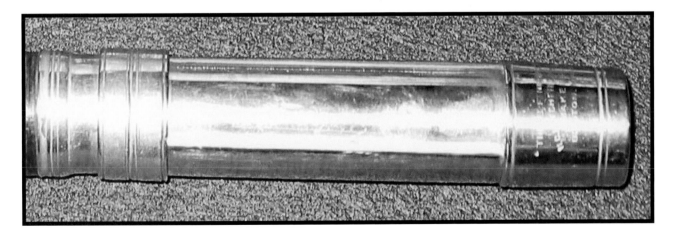

The Benjamin F. Nichols reel seat showing the stamping on the butt cap.

The "B.F. Nichols"
H.C. Litchfield & Co.
Boston circa 1888-1898
Fly Rod 1/2/4

*B*enjamin F. Nichols had a long career as a rodmaker starting in 1880 He operated the "Boston Split Bamboo Rod Co. for a period of approximately 1 year. After that year the name was changed to the "B.F. Nichols & Co.". Some of Mr. Nichols work consisted of a 6-strip butt and 4 strip mids and tips showing the early influence of Murphy, Phillipe or Green. This rod has the top quality NiS reel seat with the foot mortised into the seat as opposed to the normal raised rails. That is another feature that is very reminiscence of the reel seats mortised into the Bamboo that Charles F. Murphy did. The rod retains its original ferrules and form fit case. It is of 6-strip construction and is put up in the old style of 1 butt 2 mids and 4 tips. The rod is stamped with the very rare 3rd marking reading

"The B.F. Nichols" H.C. Litchfield & Co., Makers, Boston, Mass. stamped in 4 lines on the butt cap. The rod has its original rattan grip and form fit case. The rod should have hanging ring guides and full intermediate wraps, not snake guides. This rod is from the Author's private collection.

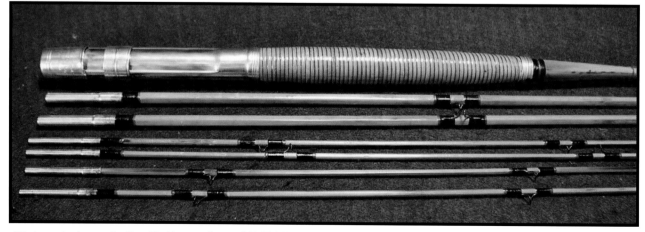

Pictured above is the Rattan grip and B.F.Nichols reel seat and male ferrules and the non-original snake guides.

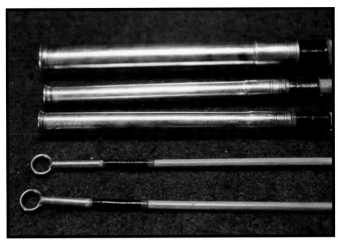

B.F. Nichols male ferrules.

Female ferrules and flat single ring tiptops.

Close up of the welt on the female ferrules used by B.F. Nichols above left and a close up of the rattan grip above right.

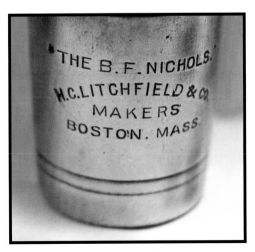

Pictured to the left is the butt cap stamping reading "The B.F.Nichols" H.C.Litchfield & Co. Makers, Boston, Mass. To the right is a comparison of the tiptops. The two at the top are what the rod should have and the two at the bottom have not been replaced yet.

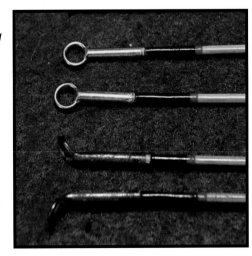

George B. Appleton & Co.
Boston, circa 1888-1893
9'6" 3/1 Calcutta Cane

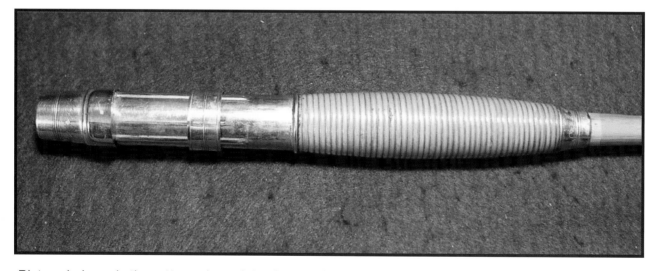

*T*his is a fairly rare example of a rod that is marked " *Geo. B. Appleton&Co.*" This rod was a trade rod made for Appleton by the Kosmic crew. It is the equivalent of a low grade KOSMIC that was the ISAAC WALTON. This rod is an old warrior. The mid section is a couple of inches short and its one remaining tip is very short. This rod was sporterized with snake guides in probably the early 1930s or the late 1920s. When that person stripped the rod to change the guides from the original hanging rings, he made a serious mistake in his rebuilding process, he removed the outer layer of power fibers of the cane by probably sanding the rod. The sanding also removed the burn marks of the Calcutta cane and over 90% of the ghost of the original wraps. He also rounded the corners of the hexagonal shape of the shaft thus decreasing its strength and durability.

*T*he rod has a Chubb reel seat and the one original female ferrule is most likely not a Chubb. The other ferrules have all been replaced. The rod is ready for a light chemical strip of the varnish and then it will be ready to start on the restoration.

Pictured above is the rattan grip and the Chubb reel seat and grip check that are all of the remaining original hardware from the "Geo. B. Appleton&Co." Rod. Note the swelled butt which is not really a sign of a Chubb origin.

Female ferrule above left and a close up of the welt on the female ferrule above right, note the witness mark for alignment of the rod. Some modern rod making companies call the witness marks an alignment dot. I prefer the more historically correct witness marks.

In the above row of pictures are the butt cap markings, which extend almost all of the way around the butt cap.

Pictured to the left is a close up of the grip check and the rattan grip. To the right is one of the remaining ghosts of one of the original intermediate wraps. It is hard to see due to the sanding of the blank when it was sporterized. The ghost is the slight band of discolored cane in the center of the picture.

T.H. Chubb, Post Mills Vt. Lancewood Fly Rod, 9' 3/2 Circa Late 1880s

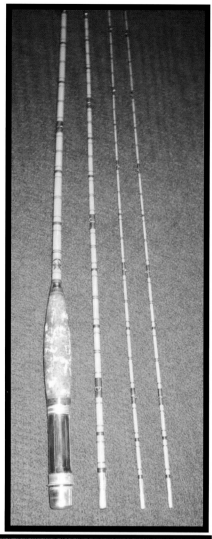

*T*his rod is a later example of a Chubb built lancewood fly rod because of its wood insert cap and ring reel seat. The rod is wrapped in red and green silk and has full intermediates with signature wraps in the intermediates. The ferrules are the Chubb straight rolled welt NiS, with a single knurled band on the females and a single incised band in the male ferrules. The rod has hanging ring guides and a NiS soldered wire tiptops.

*T*his is one of the more intricately wrapped Chubb's that I have seen. The rod has a sheet cork grip. If this rod was not made by Chubb prior to late 1891 then it is a Chubb/Montague which could date the rod as late as 1910 or so due to the hanging ring guides. In the late teens the use of hanging ring guides was fairly well over giving us a fairly well set date when it was not made.

*T*his rod is from the private collection of Tom Kerr.

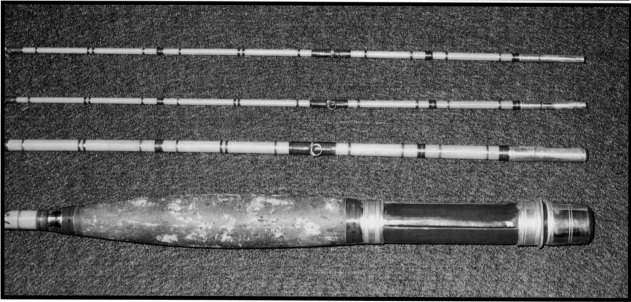

Close up of the T.H.Chubb wood insert reel seat hardware and grip pictured above.

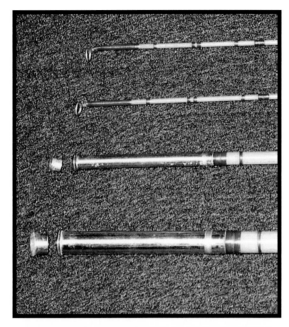

Close up of the Female ferrules and ferrule plugs and NiS wire tiptops at left. Wrap pattern and hanging ring guides above.

Close up of hanging ring guide.

Close up of the male ferrules.

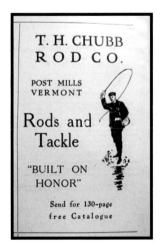

The signed Chubb rods are not a frequently seen item, whereas unsigned Chubb's are very common. Chubb warranted the signed rods for 1 year against defects in material and workmanship. This is one of the earliest known examples of a rodmaker guaranteeing his work in writing. The unsigned rods could have been made by almost anybody due to the fact that every rod that Chubb sold, you could buy as a kit with the components and build it yourself. In the 1891 Chubb catalog there are almost 30 pages of rods listed followed by 3 pages of components for the listed rods. You had your choice of components from either brass, nickel plated brass or Nickel silver. The ad to the left is from 1908.

George Morgan, Fly rod Syracuse N.Y. circa 1889-1909 9'6" 3/1 serial # 022

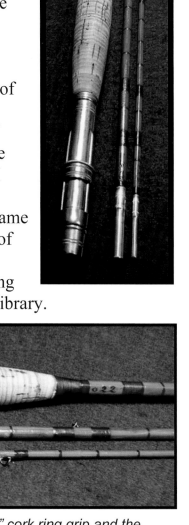

*T*his rod is an example of the small time maker that appeared after T.H. Chubb and the other mass producers made quality components available to the public at reasonable prices.

*T*he reel seat is the Chubb patented reel seat and the female ferrules with their rounded welt are very Chubb–like. The grip out of 1" cork rings suggests a date of 1900 or later. Rods by George Morgan of Syracuse, N.Y. are extremely rare. I personally know of three that are stamped "G. Morgan, Syracuse N.Y.". Two are fly rods, serial numbers 022 and 016, from the Author's collection. Serial number 016 is being restored at this time. another is a Baitcaster in a 3/2 configuration floating around southern Colorado somewhere. The hardware is all NiS and is of high quality. The snakes are THS that were blued. The rod is wrapped in red silk with olive trim wraps and it has a group of three olive wraps tipped with red as the signature wrap with the first of those wraps being a thread winding check on the grip. I have dated this rod to a time spread that is fairly wide with the likelihood of the rod being made at the later end of that time frame {1900-1909}. These dates are the known period of G.Morgan of Syracuse building rods per his claim in the 1909 "The Anglers Guide" published by Forest and Stream. See the ad on the facing page, which is an excerpt from that issue out of the Author's Library.

Chubb reel seat used on the "G.Morgan, Syracuse N.Y." rod. Note the 1" cork ring grip and the serial numbers of India ink on the shaft above the thread winding check.

Male ferrules.

Female ferrules with the oval welt with the knurling.

Pictured above is the hardware used by George Morgan.

And to the left is his advertisement from the 1909 issue of "The Anglers Guide". Note his nasty little remark aimed at those makers using a powered beveler at that time. "My rods are made after the old system".

Pictured at the left is the beveled tip with the soldered loop tiptop and to the right are the markings used by George Morgan Of Syracuse N.Y.

Pictured to the left are Hiram Leonard's personal creel and fly box and Nottingham reel from the Harmon Leonard collection.

REUBEN WOOD.

And the lower picture is of Reuben Wood from Fred Mather's "Men I Have Fished With" published in 1897. This man was an expert fly caster and maybe even more of a gentleman than that. He was known to throw casting competitions on purpose he would let a lesser angler win on a quite frequent basis. He usually did it out of respect for one particular angler. The history of the sport of casting has a considerable amount of material about Reuben Wood, as does Fred Mather's book. There are a couple of terms that he made up that just make people howl. One of them is " Wrinkle-Hawk " which he used for wind knots and tangles. Another term is "Flugemocker" which he used for any long stemmed pipe. And if Reuben caught a big fish it was "an Old Codwalloper". He would have been a true pleasure to fish with.

T.H. Chubb circa 1889-1891 Post Mills, Vermont Greenheart Fly rod 9' 3/2

*T*his is one of the rare signed T.H. Chubb rods from pre-1900. It has his 1889 circa reel seat and has the Chubb trademark acetate label on the shaft above the grip. The reel seat is an up-locking mortised wood seat. The rod is wrapped in red silk with yellow trim and intermediate wraps and has hanging ring guides. It is in its original form fit case and is missing one tip. The remaining tip is very short. The rod has a sheet cork cigar grip and the ferrules are straight rolled welt NiS. The varnish on this rod is very dark amber covering the greenheart. The knurling on the reel seat is very finely done. Like most lancewood fly rods this one is very slow and soft in action. This rod also could be a later Chubb/Montague, circa 1891-1925. This rod is from the private collection of Mr. John Oppenlander.

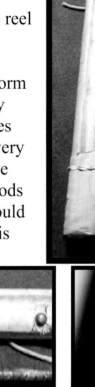

Chubb wood reel seat and sheet cork grip.

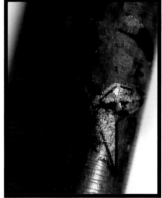

Acetate sticker.

Chubb wood up-locking reel seat.

Chubb star logo.

Chubb female Ferrules.

H.L. Leonard Fly Rod "Adirondack Tourist" 10' circa 1890s Calcutta Cane, 1/2/2/2

*H*ere is an example of the Leonard "Adirondack Tourist" rod as described in the Wm. Mills & Son catalog of 1894. This rod is missing one tip from the description in the catalog, which listed it as a three tip, two mids, two-butt sections and the removable grip. This rod is wrapped in Chinese red silk and has black trim wraps. The intermediate wraps are Chinese red and black. The rod has the Leonard patent ferrules. One of the two rods in the set has been "sporterized" at some point in its life with snake guides. The rod should have the hanging rings on all pieces. The grip is out of 5/16th inch cork rings. It is in its original wood tube with the extension tube to carry the grip.

*T*his rod is from the private Collection of Tom Kerr.

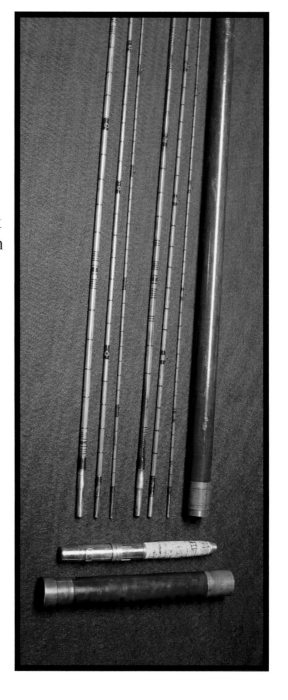

Pictured above is the full-length view of the rod and all of its parts.

Pictured to the left are the removable grip and the male ferrules and the original greenheart tube for the rod.

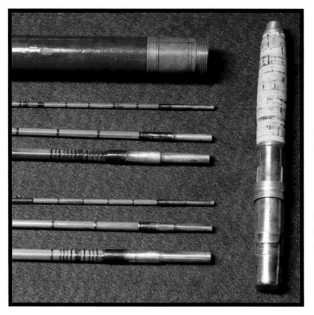

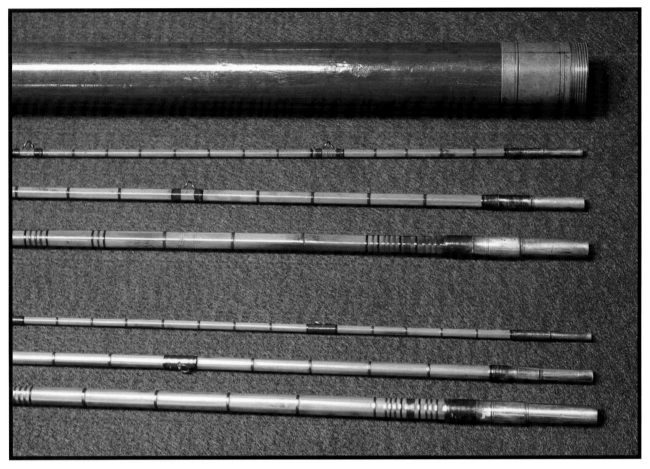

Male ferrules and the original greenheart rod tube.

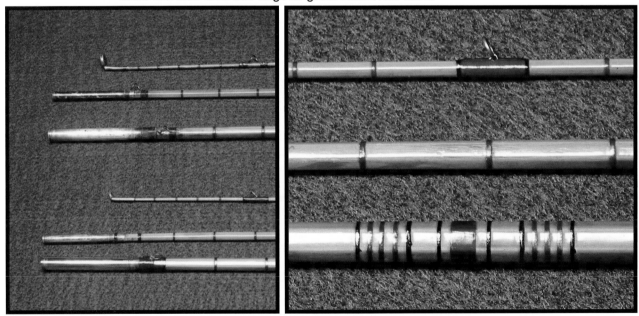

Female ferrules and the tiptops.   *Close up of the signature wrap in the intermediate wraps.*

The invention of the waterproof and serrated or slit ferrule allowed for rods that were better built and would perform better and would last longer. Great selling points for the Leonard rods at that point in time.

Henry Pritchard, N.Y.
Bait rod Circa 1890s
Lancewood 3/2 92"

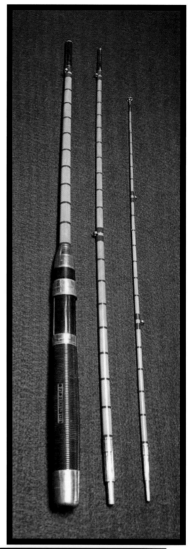

This lancewood bait rod has the Dec. 13th 1881 patented celluloid grip that became known as "Harry's rubber handle" and also has the Jan. 10th 1888 patented slide band with the beveled wedge inside of it. To say that Henry Pritchard made this rod is a stretch. To say that it has Pritchard patent components is a fair statement and that it was most likely built under the supervision of Harry Pritchard could also be accurate. Abbey & Imbrie were the main sellers of rods with Pritchard patent components. Note the greenheart Pritchard bait rod in the pages before this rod. That rod has very high quality handmade NiS components and its ferrules are spiked copper bottomed denoting a John Landman origin. This rod has plated components and is a mystery as to who made it due to the fact that Abbey&Imbrie dealt with multiple different makers. The rod has a three-ring top and has NiS three ring coil guides. It is wrapped in Chinese red silk and has full intermediates. This rod has been restored.

This rod is from the private collection of Tom Kerr.

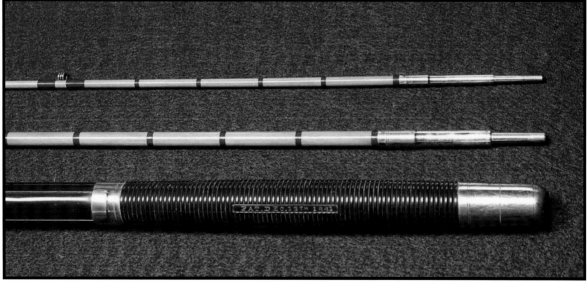

Harry Pritchard Dec13th 1881 patent reel seat and spiked male ferrules

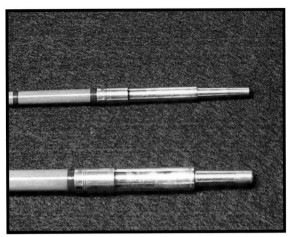

Three ring tiptop, guides and female ferrules.

Closed up of the spiked male ferrules.

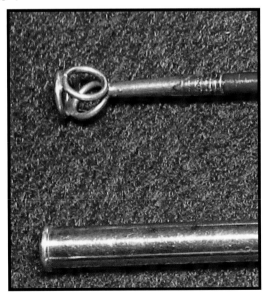

Patent markings on the celluloid grip and slide band.

At left is a close-up of the butt cap showing its plating loss. And at right is a close-up of the three-ring top and the female ferrule welt.

John Forrest, Kelso Scotland *2/2 9'* Greenheart Salmon rod Circa 1890-1930

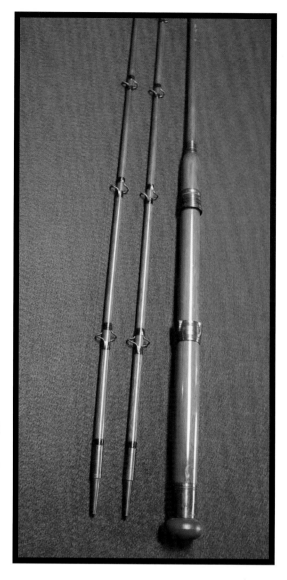

*T*his is a classic example of a John Forrest two-piece rod from around the time frame of 1890-1930, denoted by the rubber butt cap. The rod is wrapped in black silk and has doubled heavy wire English twist snake guides. The reel seat is also doubled. The hardware is made out of brass. The rod has doweled ferrules with the tie off loops. The butt cap is stamped " Forrest, Maker, Kelso". This rod retains its original canvas bag and is in extremely good condition. The finish work on this rod like the other Forrest rods pictured herein is immaculate.

*J*ohn Forrest of Kelso was a major supplier of high quality rods and flies and other terminal tackle to the American trade as early as the middle 1800s.

*T*his rod is from the private collection of Tom Kerr.

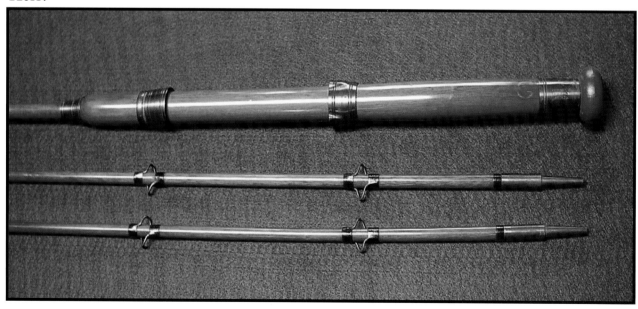

Forrest of Kelso grip, butt cap and doubled guides and the male doweled ferrules.

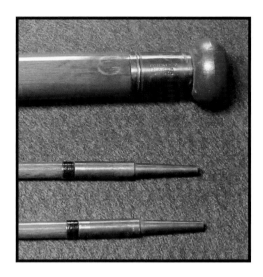

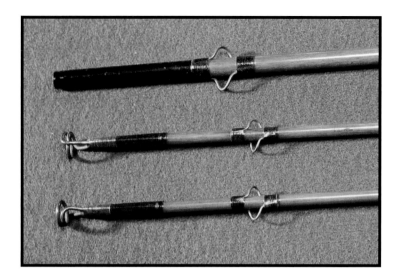

Male ferrules and butt cap with rubber button, and female ferrule and wire stirrup tiptops.

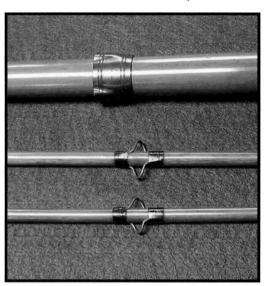

Doubled reel seat rear hood and snake guides at Left.

Front slide band and doubled snakes at right.

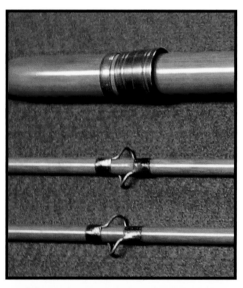

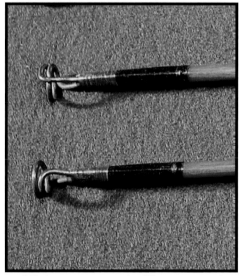

"Forrest, Maker, Kelso" butt cap stamping above left, spiral looped tiptops wrapped with copper wire above right.

John Forrest, Kelso Scotland Grilse Rod 16' 1/2/3 1890-1930

*R*ods made by John Forrest of Kelso Scotland can be very tough rods to date due to the consistency of build style used over many years. John Forrest and Forrest & sons can trace a business lineage from 1836-1837 up to 1967. One of the notable identifying features of this rod is the rubber butt cap, which was used on the later era rods by Forrest, as were the smaller NiS wire English guides. The butt section and mid sections are greenheart stained a dark mahogany with natural lancewood tips. The reel seat hardware and ferrules are brass. The ferrules have the traditional tie off loop and are also doweled. The tiptops are done in the English/European style of looped NiS wire wrapped on with copper wire. The rod is wrapped in black silk and has a "Forrest, Kelso" stamped butt cap

*T*his rod is from the private collection of Tom Kerr.

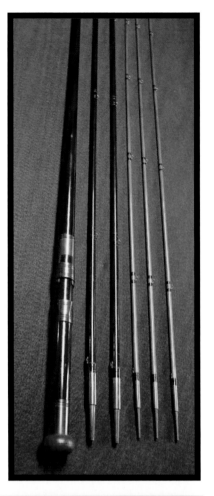

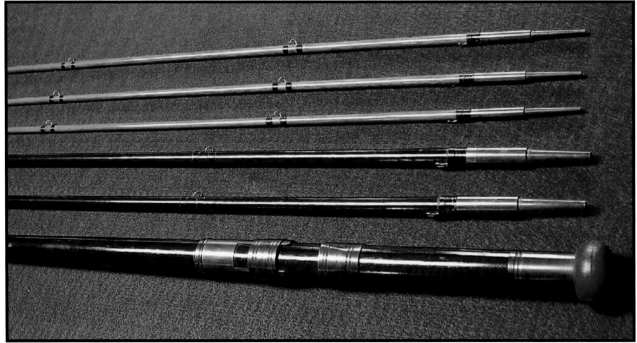

Grip and reel seat and doweled male ferrules with the tie off loops.

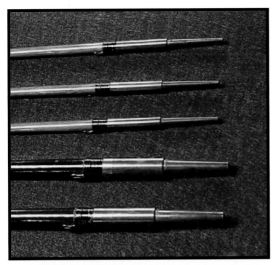

Female ferrules and the mahogany ferrule plugs above.

Male ferrules at the left

John Forrest reel seat above. NiS looped tiptops and NiS English twist snakes below.

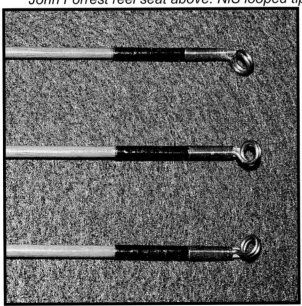

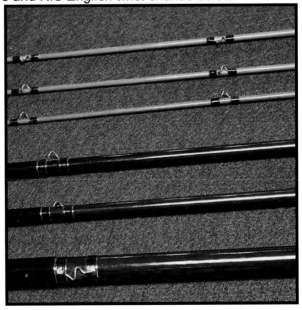

John G. Landman, N.Y.
8 Strip Calcutta Cane
8' 3/2 circa 1890-1900

*T*he features that identify this rod as to who made it and when are the Landman Aug 19th 1890 patent reel seat, the doubled intermediate wraps at the ferrules and the copper bottomed male ferrules. The reel seat has the spiral groove in the ivoroid insert which is what the patent was granted for {as a locking mechanism}. The rod is wrapped in Chinese red tipped with black and has full Chinese red intermediates. The grip is made of 1/8th inch cork rings and has the very typical landman winding check. The rod has English twist bronzed snake guides and is in its original velvet covered form fit case. All of the NiS hardware is rolled and soldered leaving the seams visible. This rod exhibits smith age features at the end of the expansion era due to the hardware-making machine that Landman had acquired from France in the late 1870s. The doubled wraps at the ferrules so often attributed to Landman were actually Landman copying what C.F.Murphy had already done as a signature mark on his rods. See the Murphy on page #12.

*T*his rod is from the private collection of Richard Collar D.D.S.

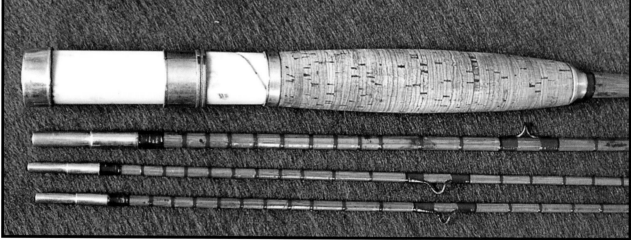

John G. Landman August 19th 1890 patented spiral locking reel seat and 1/8th inch cork ring grip and doubled intermediate wraps at the ferrules.

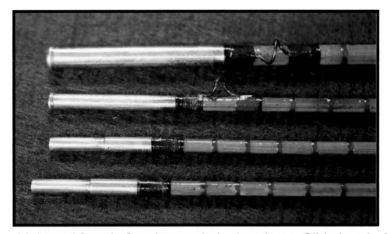

Male and female ferrules made by Landman. Slide band with the Aug. 19th 1890 patent stamping.

Close up of the Landman patent screw lock reel seat with the Ivoroid insert at left.

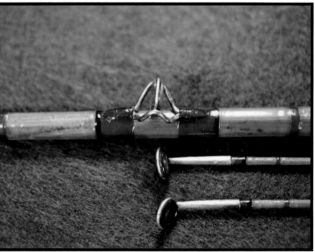

English twist snakes and the agate-stripping guides pictured above left and the agate tiptops and agate stripping guide above right.

John G. Landman should have a place alongside of Chubb and Wheeler and Leonard and the Bartlett brothers as Fathers of mass production of high quality fishing tackle in the late 1800s. He supplied much of the high quality rolled and seamed hardware used by many different makers.

John G. Landman VL&A Chicago, Striped Bass Rod 2/2 with Independent grip Circa 1890-1898

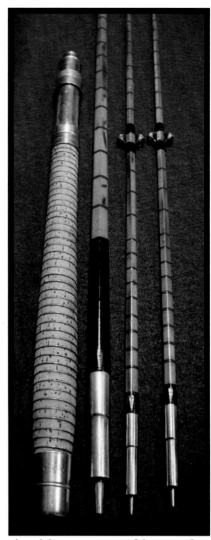

John G. Landman was in business as a tackle maker from about 1880 to 1900. He imported a French machine designed to manufacture guides. This is a very rare example of a John G. Landman light saltwater rod. It exhibits several of Landman characteristic components and also it is signed in a fashion as a John G Landman. He did this by doubling the intermediates at 6" from the ferrule stations on rods of his own make that were not signed as such. Also this rod has the NiS wire wrap over the sheet cork and also one of the finest examples of his August 19th 1890 patent locking reel seat, which was the first of its kind. The rod is constructed of Calcutta cane and has agate stirrup tip tops and doubled bell guides on the tips and doubled agate guides on the butt section. The agate guides on the butt section have a most unusual frame composed of a flat strip foot with the banded agate raised by means of loop of NiS wire. John G. Landman was one of the early originators of the American sweatshop. Another distinctive feature of rods by Landman is copper-bottomed spiked NiS ferrules, which are a sure sign of a Landman made rod or rod with Landman made components.

This rod is from the Author's private collection.

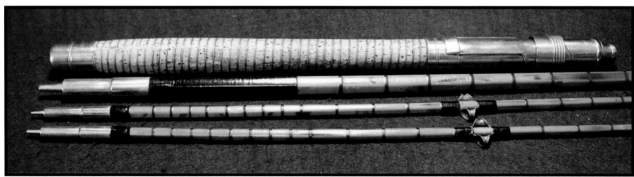

Pictured above are the NiS wire covered sheet cork grip and the Landman Aug. 19th 1890 patent reel seat. The reel seat consisted of over 10 hand soldering operations to make. Also note the doubled intermediate wraps at the ferrule stations.

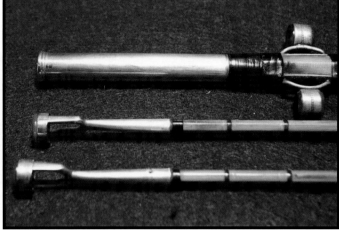

Spiked copper-bottomed male ferrules.   *Female ferrule and agate stirrup tiptops.*

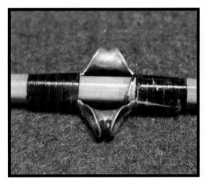

Doubled agate stripping guides and tiptops above left, doubled NiS bell guides in the center and the Aug.19th 1890 patent stamping on the reel seat barrel above right.

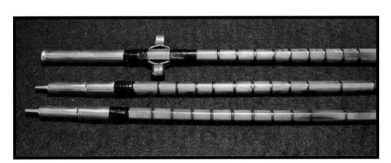

Pictured above are the doubled intermediate wraps and to the right is a close up of the copper bottomed spiked ferrules.

Von Lengerke & Antoine was a tackle and sporting goods outlet in Chicago from 1891 to 1927. In their early years they dealt in high quality tackle, with this rod being an example of the highest quality saltwater tackle available at that time. This rod is double built and was pictured in A.J. Campbell's book "Classic & Antique Fly fishing Tackle" on page #112. A.J.Campbell also featured it in the fall 1993 issue of "Fishing Collectables Magazine" in an article about John G.Landman.

John G. Landman, Fly Rod. Brooklyn N.Y. 1890-1898 9'3/2 Calcutta cane # 806

*H*ere is a truly rare signed example of a John G. Landman built six-strip rod. This rod has the "J.G.Landman, Maker, Brooklyn N.Y." stamping on the butt cap. The other notable features of a Landman built rod displayed by this rod are the August 19th 1890 spiral locking slide band, the doubled intermediates at the ferrule stations and the copper-bottomed ferrules. This rod is a spitting image of the high grade KOSMIC rod of the same time frame. From the 1/8th inch cork ring grip and the Ivoroid reel seat to the Chinese red wraps tipped with black and the full intermediate wraps of Chinese red. The signature wrap and ferrules on this rod and a KOSMIC of the same time frame are dissimilar. John G. Landman did not make his own shafts for the rods he produced. He most likely traded components for them, which were his specialty. This rod is in its original form fit case and has what is most likely its original leather capped canvas bag. John G. Landman built Abbey&Imbrie marked rods are much easier to find than Landman Maker marked rods. Both are not very common but you do see them on an infrequent basis. This rod is from the private collection of Tom Kerr.

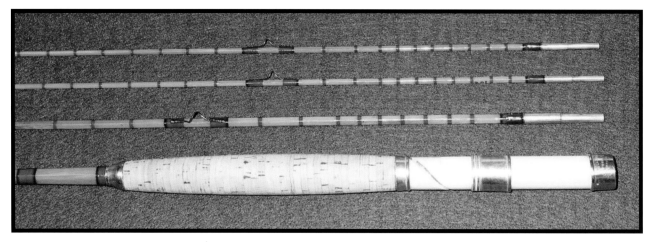

1/8th inch cork ring grip Landman patent reel seat. Note the Landman doubled intermediates, which were originally done by C.F.Murphy.

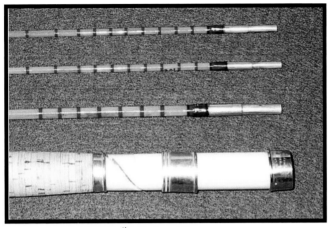

Landman Aug. 19th 1890 patent reel seat.

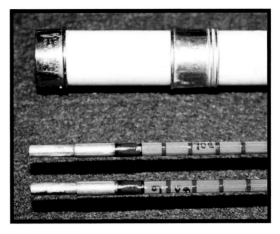

Serial numbers and makers mark.

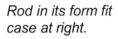

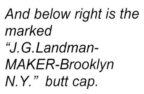

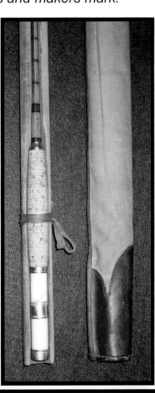

Close up of female ferrules and NiS tiptop at left.

Rod in its form fit case at right.

And below right is the marked "J.G.Landman-MAKER-Brooklyn N.Y." butt cap.

*J*ohn G. Landman in my opinion has a place alongside George I. Varney as one of the most under appreciated and under recognized Master Rodmakers of the late 1800s. His impact on the formative years of the classic fly rod cannot be truly known at this time, but it had to be a large one. A substantial amount of high quality work of his that has surfaced in the last ten to twenty years. From double built striped bass rods to short eight strip fly rods. The rods have run the gamut in length, size and function, but all have been of very high quality.

Wm. Mills & Son, Fly Rod "The Standard" 10' 3/2 Calcutta, circa 1890s

This rod is one true anomaly. It is stamped "The Standard" on the butt cap, which was a mark used by Wm. Mills & Son for the rods that they produced as a slightly cheaper alternative to the rods made by Hiram L. Leonard. This rod has some very unusual features all rolled up together starting with the 1880 Chubb patented reel seat. The male ferrules are non-waterproof and are so similar to a non-waterproof Leonard ferrule that it cannot be a coincidence. The female ferrules are straight with a hand welt and are also seamed, indicating a handmade origin. The rod is wrapped in red silk and has green trim wraps and red and green intermediate wraps. The ferrules are all NiS with the reel seat being one of the high grade all NiS seats sold by Chubb and Chubb/Montague at that time. The rod has NiS hanging ring guides with NiS straps. The tip tube cap is made to be exactly like the waist on the ferrules down to even matching the incised bands with the tip tube being made out of Calcutta cane.

This rod is from the author's collection.

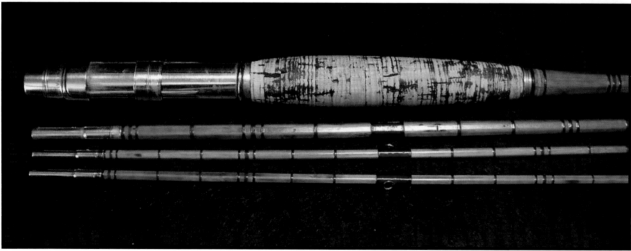

Note the Chubb patent reel seat with the Leonard copy male ferrules below it. Also pictured are the hanging ring guides and the 3/8th inch cork ring grip and the Leonard or Varney style of swelled butt.

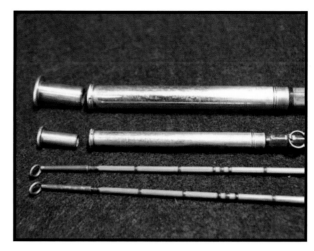

Male ferrules used on "The Standard" rod by Mills above left and the female ferrules and ferrule plugs and the tiptops pictured above right.

Hanging ring guides, close up of the collar on the male ferrule and the seamed and soldered hand welted female ferrule with the ferrule plug partially inserted pictured above.

Pictured above from left to right are guides found in the tiptube, and a close up of the exposed cane at the bottom of the non-waterproof male ferrule. "The Standard" butt cap stamping

As a collector some times you get lucky and find at least some of the missing guides from a rod hidden away in the tiptube as was the case with this rod. Only a few are missing.

Unsigned Chubb 3/1,4/1 Lancewood Combination 11' Fly, 8'6" Bass, 1890s

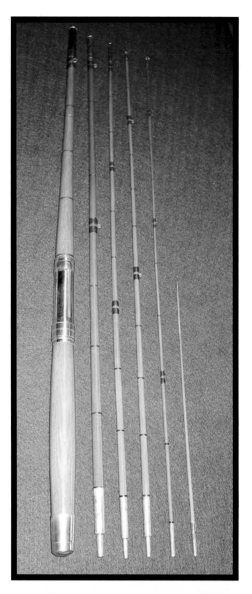

*T*his is a museum quality example of an unsigned Chubb/Montague combination rod from the mid 1890s. The butt and first mid section are made of white ash with the rest of the rod made of lancewood. The rod has a hollow butt where the short 15" emergency fly tip is hidden. The hardware is all NiS. The male ferrules are a large spiked on the mids and the tips are a straight non-spiked with the females being a rolled welt ferrule. The rod has 3 ring coil guides for the Henshall bass version at 8' 6" and the tip for that version is a Chubb funnel style tiptop. The tips for the fly rod have hanging ring guides and Chubb single ring tops. The mid section for the fly rod has hanging ring guides the other mid section has three ring spiral guides. The rod is wrapped in red silk. This rod is from the private collection of Tom Kerr.

Ash butt with the 1880 Chubb patent seat and the male spiked ferrules on the mids and the straight non-spiked male ferrules on the tips pictured below.

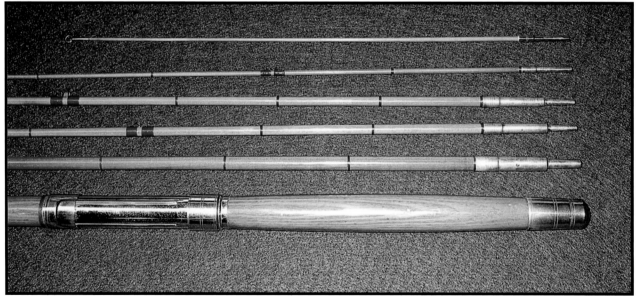

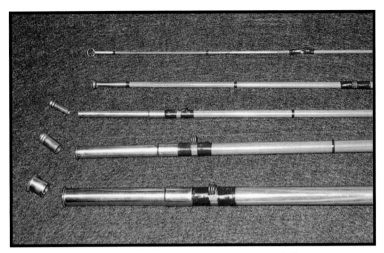

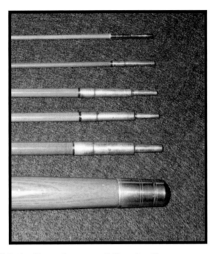

Female ferrules and ferrule plugs and tiptops. *Male ferrules and the butt cap.*

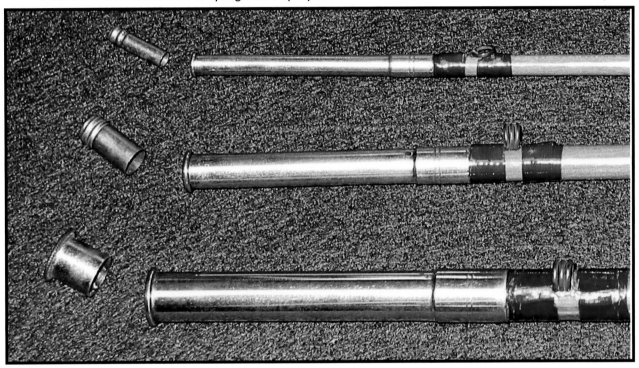

Close up of the female ferrules and the ferrule plugs and the three ring spiral wire guides and the hanging ring guides above and the Chubb 1880 reel seat below.

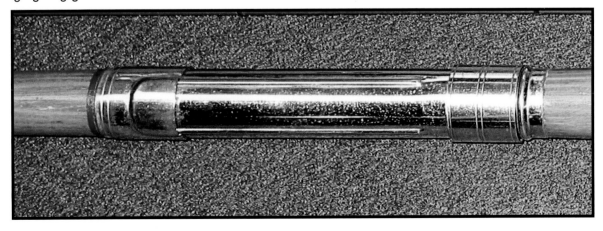

Charles E. Wheeler, 9' 6" 3/2 Calcutta Cane Fly Rod Farmington Me. Circa 1890's

Charles E. Wheeler was one of a group of men who really revolutionized the mass production of split cane rods. The others were Hiram L.Leonard, Thomas H. Chubb and Charles F. Orvis. These men were the very first to use powered bevellers and swaging machines for the mass production of fishing rod components. Charles E. Wheeler is known for his finely mortised rods and his unique Chinese hat end caps for his form fit cases. This rod is an example of his mortised work. The cedar strips used in the inlay are very long and finely tapered. The rod has a sheet cork grip. The rod has NiS plated components and bronzed English twist snake guides wrapped in Chinese red silk and it has Chinese red and gold alternating intermediate wraps. The rod is in its original form fit case with the NiS Chinese hat end caps. The butt and tips are original with the mid being a period mid section of Calcutta used to restore the rod by G.R.W. of Paonia. C.E.Wheeler is one of the more under-recognized makers of the late 1800's.

This rod is from the private collection of Tom Kerr.

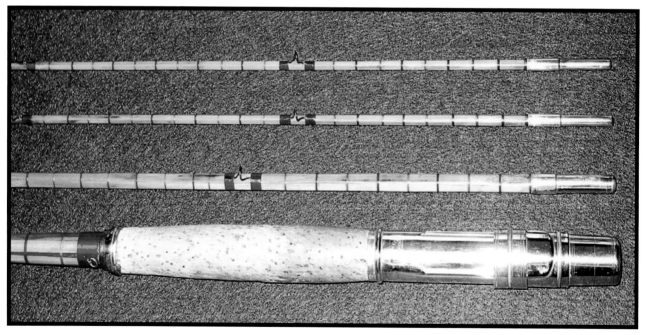

C.E.Wheeler cedar mortise, sheet cork grip, reel seat and male ferrules.

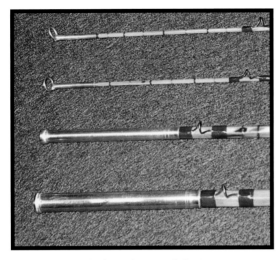

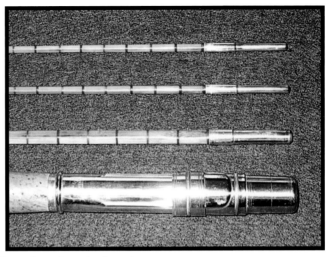

Female ferrules and tiptops.   *Reel seat and male ferrules.*

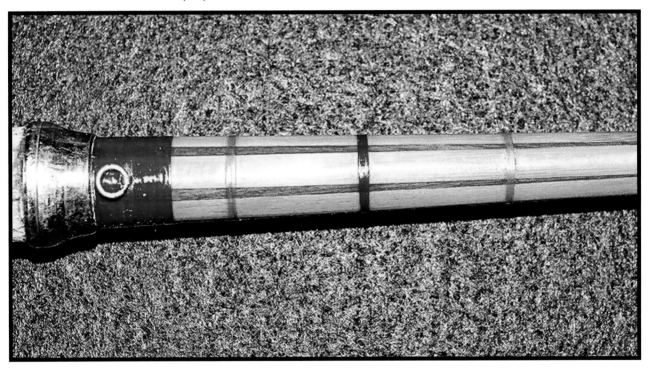

Close up of C.E.Wheeler mortised shaft, hook keeper and winding check above.

Close up of form fit case with Chinese hat end caps at left.

*N*ote the blue velvet covering which can be used to determine age. Wheeler used it from 1890 to 1916 approximately.

Charles E. Wheeler, Me. Calcutta Cane Trolling Rod 9'6" 3/2 circa 1890-1910

*T*his rod is a classic example of a rod that was designed to fish the big 6x to 8x long streamers for landlocked salmon. The technique was to tie on a fly and kick back while your guide rowed you around the lake and you waited for a fish to try to rip the rod out of your hands. The Wheeler rod was used by the first registered Maine guide, known as "Fly Rod Crosby", a lady angler who was recognized as one of the best fly fishers of the time. Not exactly what you expected from a lady of that time period. Bless her for her efforts and the mark she left. This Wheeler rod is wrapped in orange silk with black trim wraps and black and orange intermediate wraps. The tiptops are NiS three-ring tops. The guides are NiS snakes. The ferrules are NiS. The reel seat is a NiS plated with raised reel foot rails giving us a date of 1890 or later. The grips are sheet cork. The rod has its original form fit case with the Chinese hat end caps on it. And also it retains its original canvas bag.

*T*his rod is from the Author's private collection.

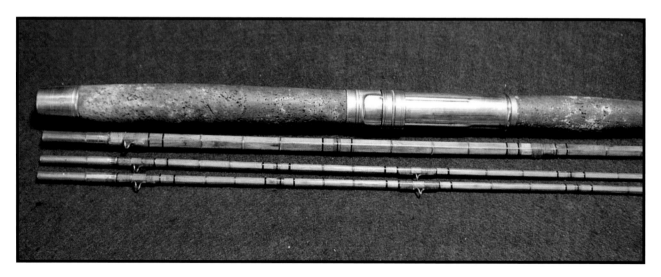

Pictured above are the sheet cork grips, the plated reel seat with the raised rails, the NiS male ferrules and the NiS snake guides. Note the wrap pattern of the intermediate wraps.

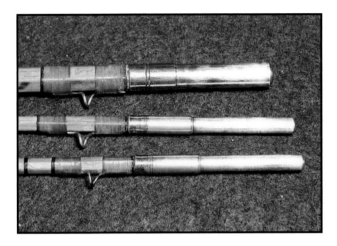

Male and female ferrules on the Wheeler trolling rod pictured above. Note that the male ferrule on the mid section and the female on the butt section are not original Wheeler guides. The female really shows the differences. The top female on the right is the replacement; note the rolled welt as opposed to the oval hand welt on the lower female.

NiS snake guides.

A close up of the three-ring tiptops.

At the left is the "Wheeler, Maker" mark on the butt cap. And to the right is a close up of the very finely mortised butt section showing the cedar mortise a Wheeler specialty. His

mortised rods are truly some of the most beautiful fishing tools ever produced.

'The Kosmic" S.N.1739 circa 1891-1892 9ft 6" Calcutta Cane Fly Rod 3/1

*T*he Kosmic crew who in their early years consisted of the following makers or combinations of made this 10-foot rod. F.E. Thomas, E.Edwards, Loman Hawes and Ed Payne.

*T*his group made some of the most distinctive fly rods ever made. From the ivoroid reel seats obtained from J.G. Landman to the Hawes and Edwards patent ferrules, and especially the taper within the bamboo. The "Kosmic" rod and its little brother the "Isaak Walton" is the high and low grades, produced by Thomas, Edwards, Payne and Hawes. The ferrules have the celluloid insert that was part of the H&E patent ferrules. It was an attempt to get around the Leonard waterproof ferrule patent. This rod has been the victim of a poor restoration. Note the picture showing the ghosting of the original wraps. The least that person could have done was to follow the original wrap pattern religiously.

*M*arked 'The Kosmic" A.G. Spaulding & Bros. Its serial number is 1739 indicating that it should have hanging ring guides on it instead of the snake guides.

*T*his rod is from the author's private collection.

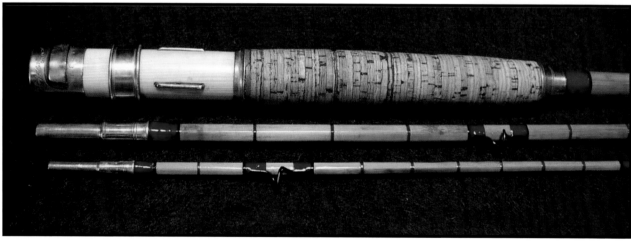

Grip and reel seat used on the KOSMIC. Note the 1/8th inch cork rings and the KOSMIC ferrules and the Landman ivoroid reel seat. The snake guides were an upgrade from the hanging rings as a fishing tool but it is sad to see a rod with out its original hardware.

Reel seat and male ferrules.   *Close up of the female KOSMIC ferrules and the original tiptop.*

"The KOSMIC" stamping.   *The "A.G. Spaulding & Bros" stamping.*

 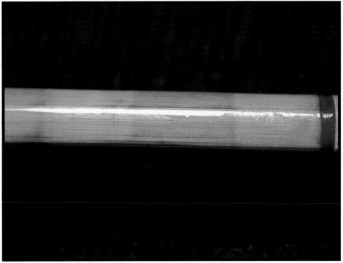

Pictured above to the left is the serial # 1739 and above right is the ghosting from the rods original wraps.

Kosmic 15' 3/2
2-Handed Salmon Rod
circa 1891-1892, N.Y.

*T*his rod is serial # 1746, denoting that it was most likely made in the time frame of 1891 or 1892. It is marked with "The Kosmic A.G. Spaulding & Bros" and the serial number on the butt cap. The rod has a full NiS Varney/style reel seat. It is wrapped in Chinese red silk tipped with black silk and has full intermediates of the Chinese red silk. It is made of Calcutta cane and has hanging ring guides. The tiptop is a round angled soldered NiS wire. The rod also has the Hawes and Edwards patent ferrules with the celluloid insert. Patent dates of May 6th 1890 and May 27th 1890 are stamped on the female ferrules. The upper and lower grips are composed of 1/8th inch cork rings and are 8 1/2 inches and 6 7/8ths inches in length. This rod is in original condition and will have to be rewrapped to maintain the integrity of the rod. The silk is so rotten that if you look at it wrong it falls off. The varnish on the other hand is in almost immaculate condition with the exception of a few salmon scales imbedded in it.

*T*his rod is from the author's private collection.

Pictured to the left is a close up of the reel seat and hanging ring guides and to the right is the butt cap and male ferrules.

At left are the female ferrules and the tiptops and to the right is a close up of the imbedded salmon scale.

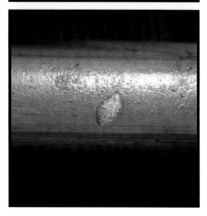

The "Kosmic" stamping.

The "A.G. Spaulding & Bros" stamping.

Close up of celluloid insert in ferrule.

1746 S.N. with a double stamped 4.

Pictured to the left are the Edwards and Hawes May 6th 1890 and the May 27th 1890 patent dates on the female ferrule on the 15' KOSMIC salmon rod.

*T*he Kosmic crew built some of the most impressive of the transition era rods and set the standard for today's rods. My hat is off to Loman Hawes, Eustis Edwards, Fred E. Thomas and Ed Payne for their immeasurable contribution to our angling heritage.

"The Walton" Casting rod By A.G. Spaulding & Bros Calcutta Cane 3/2 9" circa 1891-1895

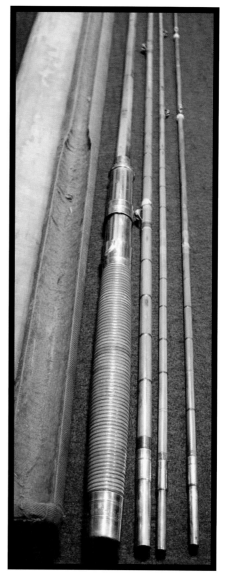

*T*his is an example of the Kosmic crew's lower price casting rod. It has a rattan grip NiS tie guides and NiS ferrules that are welted but not waterproof. The tiptops are 3 ring NiS, and the butt cap is signed "The Walton" By A.G. Spaulding & Bros. This leads me to believe it is a pre 1895 rod. The rod is wrapped in Chinese red silk with full intermediates of Chinese red silk. This rod is complete except for one missing guide on each tip {and in the same darn place on each tip to boot}. Murphy's law at work again I suppose. The reel seat on this rod is very "Chubbesque". At that point in time the tackle trade was seeing a lot of collusion between makers of components and manufacturers of rods and even the small time rod builders are represented by names like Morgan and J.B.Crook. This rod is from the Author's private collection and is in need of a full rewrap. Note the surgical type tape holding the guides on, as a group we will do almost anything to keep fishing.

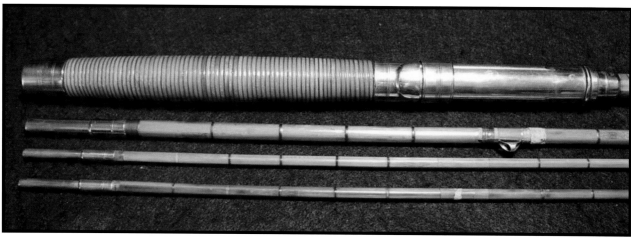

Pictured above are the grip and reel seat and male ferrules and the NiS tie guides on "The Walton" casting rod.

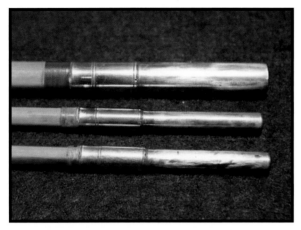

Male ferrules from "The Walton".

Female ferrules and tiptops from "The Walton".

NiS Tie guides.

Close up of the three-ring tiptops.

"A.G. SPALDING & BRO'S." butt cap marking.

"THE WALTON" butt cap marking.

H.A. Merrill, Bangor, Me.
Tonkin Cane Fly Rod
11' 3/2 circa 1890-1920

H.A. Merrill was one of the men who started making rods to fill the void in Maine after Hiram L. Leonard left for New York. His rods are unique in several aspects the first and foremost being his unique four-part male ferrules which consisted of three NiS tubes that were then capped to make waterproof. The rods produced by Merrill were very Leonard like in appearance from the inset reel foot recess to the red wraps with full intermediates and the casting actions of the two types of rod are very similar. This rod has bronzed THS English twist snake guides indicating a later date of manufacture also the fact the rod is made out of Tonkin cane as opposed to Calcutta cane would indicate a date of post 1900 being most likely. The rod has its original form fit case and canvas bag. The grip on this rod is out of composite or burl cork and has taken on a very dark and handsome patina over the last one hundred years or so.

*T*his rod is from the Authors private collection.

H.A. Merrill NiS reel seat {most likely made by Frank Philbrook} and burled cork grip with the THS English twist snake guides and the unique male Merrill ferrules. Note how some idiot has pinned the reel seat with a small brad at the top of the butt cap. Once again reaffirming the lengths we will go to as fisherman to keep fishing our favorite rod.

Merrill 4-part male ferrules. *Merrill female ferrules.*

Nickel silver wire round tiptops. *Bronzed English twist snake guides.*

Recessed reel foot seat and slide band. *"H.A. Merrill,Bangor" signature on the bottom of the butt cap.*

C.F. Orvis, Calcutta Cane Casting Rod S.N. 238 3/1, 8'4" Circa 1875-1900

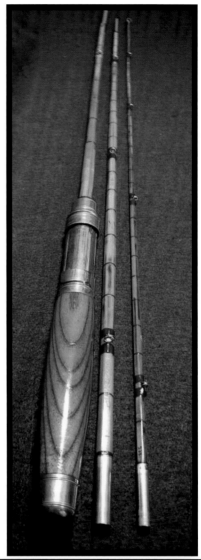

*T*his is an early example of a bait-casting rod in the Henshall style. It is out of Calcutta cane and exhibits some characteristics of a rod made in the late Smith age {Mid 1870s} or the very early transition era {Late 1870s} even though the rod was most likely made at the later part of the 25 year time span and possibly even as late as 1900-1910. Those characteristics include the rolled and seamed handmade NiS Hardware. The ferrules are the very early rolled and seamed and capped waterproof ferrules that Thaddeus Norris preferred along with Charles F. Orvis. They were very modern for their time. The rod has a Sumac grip and standing 2-ring guides. The rod is wrapped in Chinese red silk and has full intermediate wraps. The rod has a three-ring tiptop. I am dating this rod to this time period due to the hardware and style of build. Martin Keane dated this rod to be a very early rod and also fairly rare. This rod is from the Author's private collection.

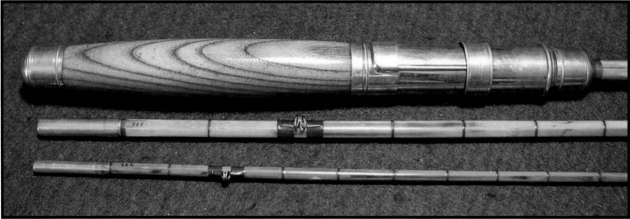

Pictured above are the sumac grip and the standing 2-ring guides done similar to the Richardson 2-ring guide. Also note the straight male ferrules that were common to the very early Orvis rods.

Close up of the soldered and seamed straight male Orvis ferrule above left and above right are the female ferrules and the three ring tiptop.

Soldered two-ring standing guides.

Front grip and winding check.

Pictured to the left is the makers mark on the butt cap and to the right are the serial numbers on the mid and tip shafts. Note the difference with the tip being a later factory replacement.

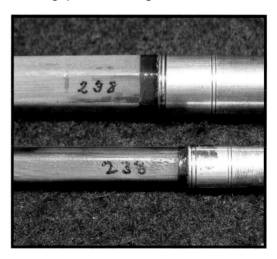

Dingee Scribner & Son St. Johns N.B. Canada Greenheart 1/2/3 spliced Circa 1880-1900

Dingee Scribner was the first man known to produce rods professionally in Canada. He may have even been an influence on the early work of H.L. Leonard along with C.F. Murphy. This rod exhibits many of the features Scribner was known for from the form fit case to the British wood button on the butt cap. His spliced rods based on the Castle Connell rods, which were the predecessor to the modern parabolic action that is usually accredited to Charles Ritz, Paul Young and Jim Payne. The castle Connell style of rod is a very old style going back several hundred years. It relies on the archaic splice to put the rod together. This rod has rattan grips and all of the metal work is NiS with the exception of the brass hanging ring guides and the looped wire tiptops. The rod has its original form fit case.

This rod is from the private collection of Tom Kerr.

Dingee Scribner & Son Makers, St. John N.B. stamping on the form fit case.

The condition of this rod is immaculate considering its age. For the tips to have survived is almost miraculous considering the fragility of greenheart tips.

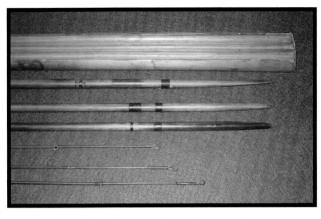

Looped tiptops and spliced joints.   *Splice protectors in the form fit case.*

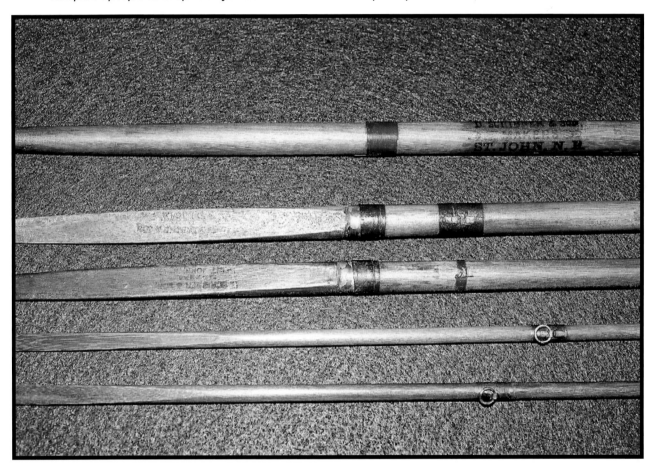

Spliced joints showing the ink stamping used on the splice and on the shaft by Dingee Scribner & Son

Shaft markings of "D.SCRIBNER & SON, MAKERS, ST. JOHN, N.B." in the close up to the right.

Anonymous Maker "Bassett" Fly Rod 9'6" 3/2 circa 1880-1915

*T*his rod is marked "Bassett". The build style and type of components used on this rod indicate it was made by one of the following makers; George H. Burtis, Eugene Bartlett, Montague City rod Co., C.E. Wheeler, F.D. Divine or possibly even T.H. Chubb. This rod's components are all made out of NiS with the exception of the brass hanging ring guides and their keepers, which are also made out of brass. The grip is sheet cork and the butt section is mortised with red cedar. It is wrapped in red silk with black trim wrap and full red intermediates. This rod shows the mortise exposed below the reel seat. This has one purpose that is practical, it extends the butt below the reel seat giving the angler a small fighting butt on the rod. The other purposes is purely decorative. The mortised rods are true works of art in wood and are a challenge to make.

*T*his rod is from the private collection of Tom Kerr.

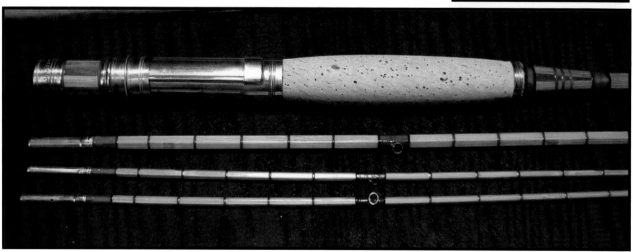

Pictured above is the sheet cork grip, mortised butt section and the guides and male ferrules used on "BASSETT".

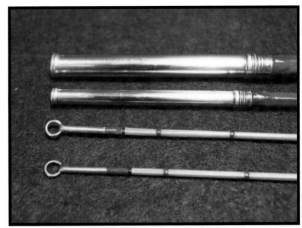

Close up of the male ferrules above left and the female ferrules and tiptops above right.

"BASSETT" Butt cap stamping.

Hanging ring guides and wrap pattern.

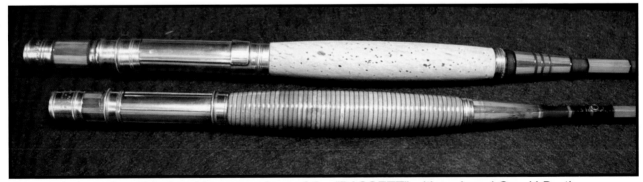

Pictured above is a side-by-side comparison of the "BASSETT" with a signed Geo.H.Burtis mortised rod. And Below is a close up of the mortise at the front of the grip on the "BASSETT".

Thomas & Edwards, Me.
Empire City Marked
9' 3/3 circa 1898-1899

The rods from the short lived F.E. Thomas and E.W.Edwards partnership that were marked, as "Empire City FTM Special grade are truly rare finds. This rod exhibits the fully soldered reel seat with the pocket full length that was most likely a product of the Landman shop as were the ferrules used by the T&E partnership. The rod has its original velvet covered form fit case, which was most likely made by the Montague/Chubb firm. The rod is wrapped in black silk and has full red intermediate wraps. As you can see, this rod sports a short tip and you wonder if a fish caused it or if the pucker brush got it. The rod has the early English twist snakes on it and has an agate-stripping guide and agate tiptops. The ferrules and reel seat are all made of NiS soldered and show their seams. The grip is made of 1/8th inch cork rings.

This rod is from the private collection of Dr. Richard Collar, D.D.S.

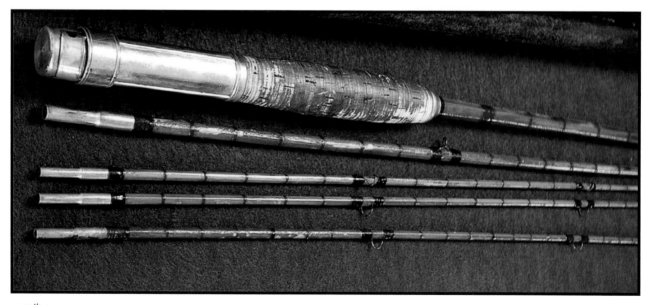

1/8th inch cork ring grip, male ferrules and reel seat that were most likely Landman components used on the "Empire City Special grade".

Reel seat used by T&E.

The "Empire City EFTMC Special grade' stamping.

Male and female ferrule used by T&E. Snake guides and wrap pattern and tiptop and stripping guide missing its agate.

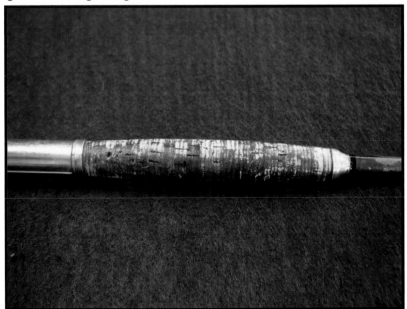

1/8th inch cork ring grip at left.

*N*ote the similarity of the Winding check to the winding checks used on John G. Landman rods. They are identical showing another clue that T&E most likely bought or traded shafts for components from Landman.

Empire City F.T.M. Co. 6'6" 3/2 Bait-casting Rod circa 1898-1899 by T&E

*T*he Empire City logo as used by Fred E. Thomas and Eustis William Edwards is one of the harder trademarks to find in antique rod collecting. The two makers only used it for a period of 2 years. The logo is absolutely identical to a known T&E Fly rod belonging to Richard Collar. If this rod was not made by T&E, the only other possibility would be John G. Landman. This is not likely because of the lack of the copper bottom in the ferrules.

*T*his rod exhibits many of the features that T&E rods were known for, such as rolled and seamed hardware including ferrules and reel seat, ¼ inch cork rings in the grip. The guides are NiS bells with an agate stripper and tiptop. The two remaining original agate guides are some of the finest agates and framework on a guide of that type that I have ever seen. The rod is wrapped in black silk with red intermediates. It is in its original leather tipped velvet covered form fit case. Note the detachable grip. This rod is from the author's private collection.

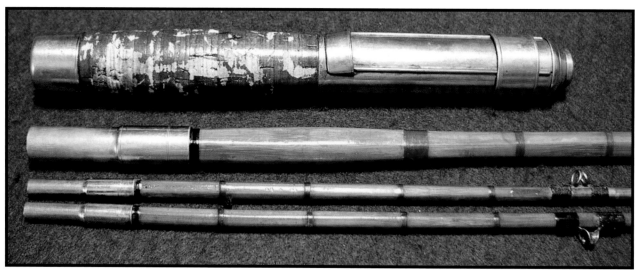

Pictured above is the removable grip and reel seat with the male ferrules. Note the swell of the cane of the butt section and the Richardson standing two-ring guide that is a replacement guide on the first tip, it should be a bell guide.

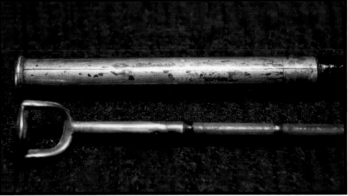

Soldered and seamed male ferrules.

Female ferrule and agate tiptop.

Close up of the agate striping guide and agate tiptop. Agate striping guide and NiS bell guides.

"Empire City EFTCM Hand made makers mark.

Leather end cap from the form fit case.

Von Lengerke & Detmold 8' 3/2 Bait-casting Rod circa 1898-1899 by T&E

*T*his trade rod was made for Von Lengerke & Detmold of New York by T&E. VL&D was a dealer of all ranges of quality of fishing tackle. This rod is a typical example of T&E work. Some of those typical details are the seamed and soldered hardware and the ¼" cork rings in the grip. The ferrules and reel seat are absolutely typical of T&E products. The rod is wrapped in black silk with black silk intermediates. The guides are NiS bell guides with NiS stirrup tip tops. This rod has its original cloth covered form fit case and its light canvas bag. The form fit case has its original cotton ties, which is fairly unusual in the fact that they do not generally survive this long due to use. This rod is in exceptional condition except for a heavy overcoat of varnish on the wraps.

*T*his rod is from the Author's private collection.

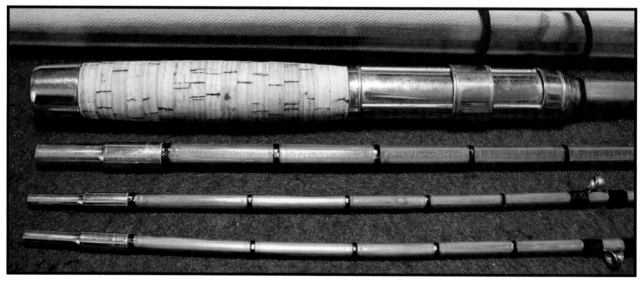

Pictured above are the grip of ¼" cork rings and the soldered and seamed NiS reel seat and male ferrules of the "V L&D casting rod. Note the set in the bottom tip. Also pictured above is part of the form fit case, which is in excellent condition and still retains its original cloth ties at full length.

Male Ferrules.

Female ferrules and the NiS stirrup tiptops.

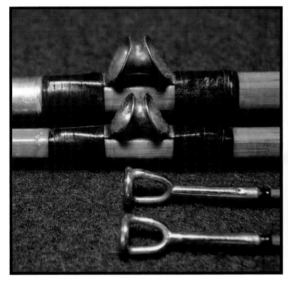

NiS bell guides and stirrup tiptops. casting rod.

Close up of the soldered hood and reel foot rails on the V, L&D

Close up of the pin and soldered seam on the reel seat barrel. "Von Lengerke & Detmold" stamping that is missing the k and e from Lengerke and the d from Detmold.

George H. Burtis, Fly rod Worcester Mass. 9'6" 3/2 Calcutta, circa 1895-1915

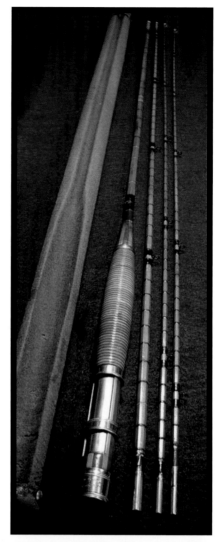

George H. Burtis of Worcester Massachusetts was a rodmaker known to be in business for at least twenty years. This rod is one of the few-signed examples of his work. The rod features a mortised reel footplate of NiS and the butt shaft is mortised with cedar. The hardware is NiS with the exception of the English style snake guides, which are of tool-hardened steel that has been blued. The butt cap is stamped with the "Geo. H. Burtis, Worcester, Mass." Maker's mark. The rod is wrapped in black silk with red intermediate and trim wraps. The rod is stored in its original felt covered, leather end capped form fit case. The ferrules are hand serrated and no color preserver was used on the wraps, allowing them to go translucent. The grip is made of rattan and has the customary wrap of red silk up thru the grip.

This rod is from the author's collection.

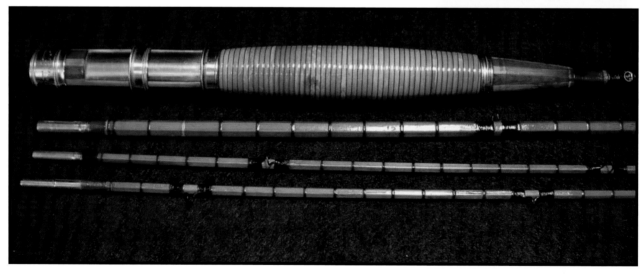

Pictured above is the rattan grip and Burtis mortised shaft and the mortised reel seat footplate of NiS that George H. Burtis of Worcester Massachusetts was famous for. Also pictured are the English twist snake guides on the Burtis rod. Note the added on hook keeper which was not an original feature of the rod.

Close ups of the male and female ferrules used by Burtis pictured above.

Close up of the Burtis reel seat and butt cap pictured above.

"Geo.H.Burtis, Worcester.Mass" makers mark above left, above right is the Geo.H.Burtis ad from the 1908 edition of "The Anglers Guide" by Charles Bradford, from the Author's personal library.

H.J. Frost & Co, Brooklyn, N.Y. Frost Kelso Casting Rod 8'6" 3/1 circa 1896-1920s

*H*erbert J. frost was a traveling salesman who was very good at his job and sold a lot of tackle over a long period of time. He was the primary salesman at U.S. Net and Twine until 1896. The name Frost Kelso is a play on word in a way due to the fact he was pulling on the good will and reputation of John Forrest of Kelso. This casting rod has the ivoroid reel seat produced by John Landman and the shafts appear to be of KOSMIC origin. They are very well made and are finished very nicely. The rod has NiS ferrules and NiS anti friction trumpet guides. The grip is a cigar made of ½" cork rings. The rod is wrapped with deep red silk, and it has yellow trim wraps. It also has full intermediate wraps with signature wraps in the intermediate wrap pattern. The rod has an agate first guide and an agate four-wire basket tiptop. The ivoroid insert in the reel seat is of lower quality than one would see on a KOSMIC thus relegating it to a trade rod.

*T*his rod is from the Author's private collection.

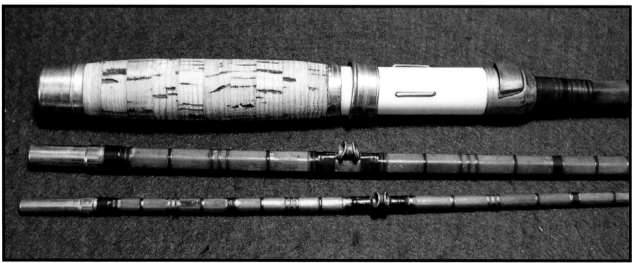

Pictured above are the grip and the ivoroid reel seat and the NiS anti-friction trumpet guides and the male ferrules from the "FROST KELSO" casting rod. Also note the signature wrap pattern at the front of the grip and at midpoint between the guides.

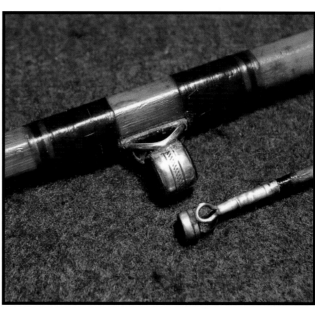

Male ferrules.   *Female ferrules and the 4-wire basket agate tiptop.*

Agate 1ˢᵗ guide and the anti-friction trumpet guides above left and a close up of the agate 1ˢᵗ guide and the 4-wire basket agate tiptop above right.

Pictured to the left is a close up of the "FROST'S KELSO" reel seat marking on the backside of the fixed hood section of the reel seat.

"The Isaak Walton" Fly Rod Calcutta Cane 9' Circa 1895-1905

*T*his is the lower grade produced by the collaborative efforts of F.E.Thomas and Ed Payne and Eustis Edwards. This rod is made of Calcutta Cane and has snake guides. It was made right at the time of change from Calcutta to Tonkin cane. It is the classic configuration of the modern fly rod. I am dating this rod to this time period because it is not marked with A.G. Spaulding & Bros or any of the other outlets for the U.S. Net and twine group/(The Kosmic crew). And was probably made after Loman Hawes had left the original Kosmic crew in 1892-1895. This rod is complete down to its original tip tube with cloth bag for tips. Its ferrule plugs and original canvas bag are also there. It is very rare to find rods this complete from 100 years or more ago. This rod is from the Private Collection of Mr. Richard Wallace and it was photographed after a full restoration by Gnomish Rod Works Of Paonia Colorado.

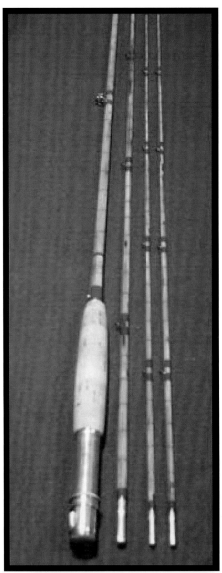

Bottom group of photos show clockwise from the reel seat close up at the right, then the signature wrap, agate stripping guide, tip tube and tiptops and last the female ferrules and the plugs.

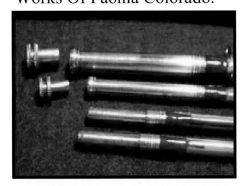

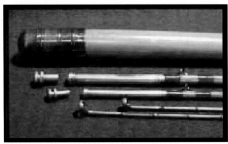

Ed Payne
2 handed Salmon Rod
Calcutta Cane 14' 1/2/3
circa 1899-1910

*T*his is an example of a rod by one of the best makers ever, Edward F. Payne. This salmon rod is put up in the old style of one butt and 2 mids and 3 tips, and is in immaculate original condition. This rod shows some collusion between the E.F. Payne Rod Company and the H.L. Leonard Co. It is put up in a replacement canvas bag with an H.L. Leonard hanging tag and has the Leonard interrupted thread NiS reel seat and yet it is stamped on the soldered hood with the E.F. Payne Rod Co. stamping. The rod has an agate stripper and agate tip tops and is wrapped in black silk with full intermediates. The tips are stored in the original tip tube. This is a classic example of one of the bigger fly rods made in the last 110 years or so. This rod is probably one of the last of that style built in the 1/2/3 configuration. It is 14' long and weighs 20 ¾ ounces.

*T*his rod is from the private collection of Dr. Harmon Leonard.

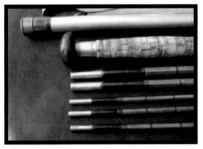

Butt cap and male ferrules. Leonard or Thomas Interrupted thread reel seat and the winding check above left to right and below left to right be the guides, agate tiptops and the female ferrules.

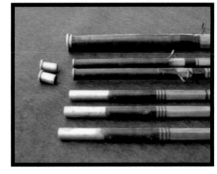

A Classical era tackle collage of gut leaders from S.Allcock's&Co. and even a dozen from Paul H. Young. I have not found a Young rod but I do have some of his leaders. The snelled flies are from Bill Mauldin of Delta, Colorado circa 1960s. The split willow creel is circa 1930's and the aluminum creel is just post World War II. There is a pair of leader tins to the far left against the willow creel.

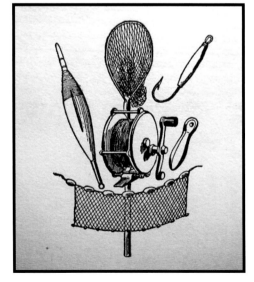

Pictured above is a Paul Young ad from the early 1940's and to the left is an example of an engraving from the 1909 "Anglers Guide" by Charles Bradford.

The classic Era 1900 to 1960

The classic era was dominated at one end by the mass production giants and at the other end by a small handful of men who were dedicated to producing the absolute best product that they possibly could. The classic era saw the innovations of the oversize snake guide with the American twist opposite of the British twist; I.E., left hand as opposed to right hand twist. The modernization of the screw lock reel seat and the addition of the modern tip-top by the Perfection Co. of Denver in 1915 and also the introduction of the super Z ferrule by Lou Fierabend. After World War II we saw the last gasp of the steel rod by the Heddon Co. And the appearance of the fiberglass Wonder Rod first put out by the Shakespeare Co. The. The Bamboo rod maker's were having a rough time and you see the almost complete stop of bamboo rod making. Fiberglass rods could be produced and sold for a fraction of the cost of a bamboo rod after the first production problems were solved. Mass production of fairly cheap fly lines was also achieved during this era due to the invention of the nylon line during World War II. We were finally able to say goodbye to soaking our caterpillar gut leaders to prevent the brittleness that accompanied the use of the clear silk leaders when they were dry {Thanks once again to the nylon fiber}. During the classic era there was a large amount of very high quality tackle made, this incomplete list of those makers include Henry Andrus, Everett Garrison, F.E.Thomas, Hiram Hawes, The Leonard Rod Co. Ed Payne, Orvis, Lyle Dickerson, George Halstead, Pinky Gillum and Paul H Young. The production rod makers included Horrocks & Ibbotsons, Montague, South Bend, Heddon, Phillipson, Cross, Granger, Edwards. The Classic Era saw high quality tackle become more affordable to the masses.

S. Allcock & Co. Fly Rod Redditch, England
9' 6" 3/2 circa Early 1900s

S.Allcock & Co. in Redditch England can trace their tackle making business lineage back to 1803 when Polycarp Allcock began making hooks. They began to make split cane rods in the 1870s after starting the manufacture of reels in the middle 1800s. This rod is from the early 1900s. The rod has a 1" cork ring grip and reel seat with an aluminum slide band and butt cap that has the ever-present wood button found on a lot of English made rods. The rod has blued NiS ferrules and a bridged fully enclosed snake guides. The rod is wrapped in a dark green / olive silk and in the English tradition has very closely spaced intermediate wraps. The rod has its original Cloth bag and is in need of a restoration. Note that the cork in the grip and reel seat is cross cut as opposed to specie cut indicating a lower quality of cork. Which is shown by The large holes in the cork confirm this statement.

*T*his rod is from the private collection of John Oppenlander.

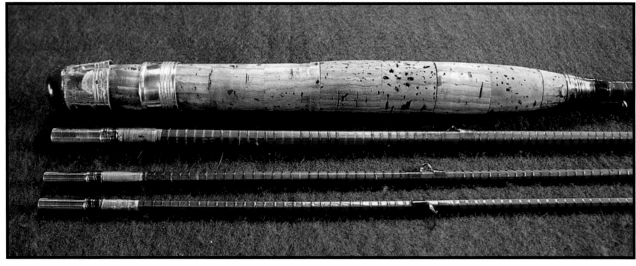

Pictured above are the 1 inch crosscut cork grip and reel seat, along with the guides and male ferrules and wrap pattern.

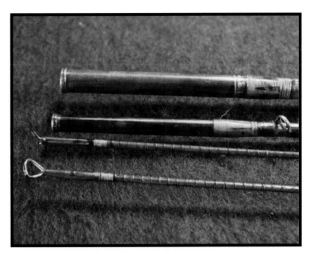

Male ferrules used by S.Allcock & Co.

Female ferrules and tiptops.

Stripping guide and bridged snakes and the tiptops above left and the close up of the butt cap markings above right.

Pictured above right is a close up of the agate-stripping guide and a close up of the bridged snake guide at the left.

Abercrombie & Fitch Yellowstone Special 8'6" 3/2 Fly Rod

*T*his rod is an example that shows the collusion amongst Rodmakers. The Yellowstone Special rods are attributed to the work of F.E.Thomas. The rod has what are unmistakably Montague ferrules with the reel seat being a rail less Montague made seat. The grip work and cane work are very consistent with the work of Thomas. The form fit case is a Chubb/Montague thru and thru. The rod is wrapped in red silk trimmed in yellow with full red intermediate wraps. The reel seat on this rod is exactly the same as the reel seat on the J.F.Schmelzer & Sons. Trout rod pictured on page #160, which is another trade rod that can be attributed to F.E.Thomas or very high quality Montague work showing the Influences of George I Varney after he was hired as their head Rodmaker in the very early 1900s. This rod is from the private collection of John Oppenlander.

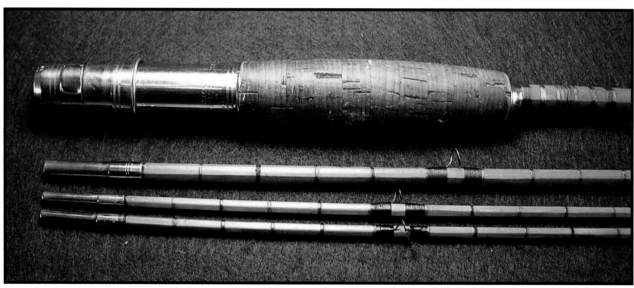

Pictured above are the grip, reel seat and male ferrules and the snake guides on the "Abercrombie & Fitch Yellowstone Special".

Male ferrules. *Female ferrules and the tiptops.*

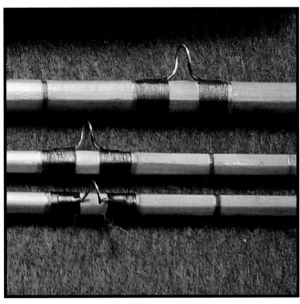

Snake guides and wraps. Close up of the tiptops and rolled welt on the female ferrules.

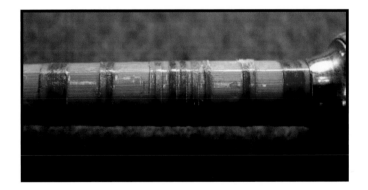

Pictured to the left is the reel seat stamping "YELLOWSTONE SPECIAL, ABERCROMBIE&FITCH NEW YORK", and above is the signature wrap.

Chubb/Montague Fly Rod 2/2 6'6" circa 1900-1925

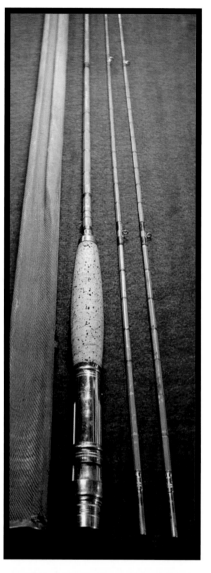

*T*his is an example of one of the last of the rods built under the Chubb/Montague label. It is one of those very rare short rods from that time frame. It has Nickel-plated brass components. The reel seat is a classic Chubb 1880 Patent style seat that is very small and delicate. The ferrules are a drawn rolled welt bottle shaped non-serrated non-waterproof I.E. montague ferrule. The guides are American twist NiS snakes, which are very small in diameter for a very small lightweight silk line. The shafts are Tonkin cane and it is wrapped in Chinese red silk with black trim wraps and full intermediates of the Chinese red silk. It has its original form fit case. The form fit case even still has both of its original end caps but is missing its canvas bag. This model of rod was drawn on page 131 in Michael Sinclair's book "Bamboo Rod Restoration Manual". This rod is from the private collection of John Oppenlander

Pictured below are the Chubb reel seat and sheet cork grip, NiS snake guides and male ferrules.

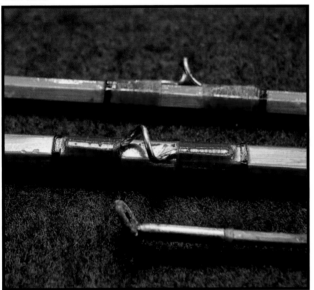

Pictured to the above left are the male ferrules and above right is a close up of the female ferrule.

Nickel silver wire snake guides and wrap pattern above left is a close up of the angled Chubb single ring tiptops.

T. H. CHUBB
R O D   C O.

POST MILLS
VERMONT

Rods and
Tackle

"BUILT ON
HONOR"

Send for 130-page
free Catalogue

Pictured to the left is an ad from the 1908 Anglers Guide and to the right is an ad from the 1909 Anglers guide.

*T*he Chubb rod company was still being run as a separate entity from Montague at least for advertising purposes at this point in time. Chubb was a trade name of Montague at that point in time.

Fish, more than any other game, needs special attention as to rods, lines, hooks, flies, baits, reels, etc. There is a fish-rod for every fish. Chubb's Rods are preferred where quality and variety are desired. Where a fisherman goes Chubb's Rods go, and it results in great luck. Try them.

T. H. CHUBB ROD CO.
POST MILLS   VERMONT
Catalogue free

J.F. Schmelzer & Sons, K.C. Circa 1900-1920 10' 3/2 Calcutta Cane

This rod was advertised in the 1906 J.F. Schmelzer & Sons Arms Co. catalog as being there "highest grade split bamboo fly rod". The ferrules on the rod as well as the reel seat are of Chubb/Montague manufacture. With Chubb/Montague most likely being the maker of this trade rod. The rod is wrapped in three colors of silk, main wraps in red tipped with black followed by yellow and then black then red then black, equaling out to a five wrap trim wrap. The intermediate wraps are red with a centering wrap between the guides of the B.Y.B.R.B. wrap pattern. The hardware is NiS plated. The grip is ½ inch cork rings with a cap and ring rail less seat. The rod is in its original form fit case but has lost its original canvas bag.

This rod is from the private collection of John Oppenlander.

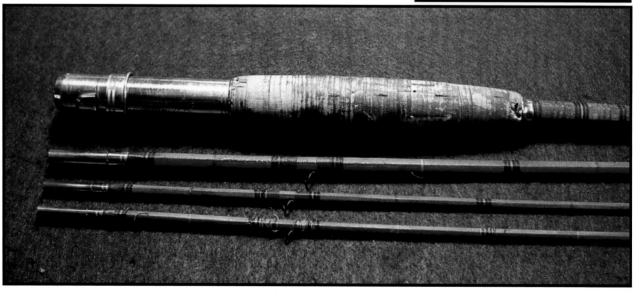

Pictured above are the components used on the Schmelzer "Highest Grade" Fly rod.

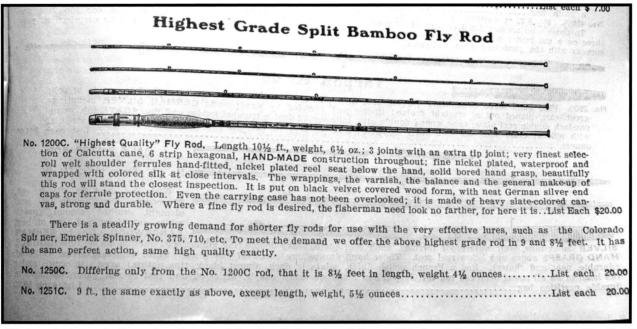

Highest Grade Split Bamboo Fly Rod

...........List each $ 7.00

No. 1200C. "Highest Quality" Fly Rod. Length 10½ ft., weight, 6½ oz.; 3 joints with an extra tip joint; very finest selection of Calcutta cane, 6 strip hexagonal, **HAND-MADE** construction throughout; fine nickel plated, waterproof and roll welt shoulder ferrules hand-fitted, nickel plated reel seat below the hand, solid bored hand grasp, beautifully wrapped with colored silk at close intervals. The wrappings, the varnish, the balance and the general make-up of this rod will stand the closest inspection. It is put on black velvet covered wood form, with neat German silver end caps for ferrule protection. Even the carrying case has not been overlooked; it is made of heavy slate-colored canvas, strong and durable. Where a fine fly rod is desired, the fisherman need look no farther, for here it is..List Each $20.00

There is a steadily growing demand for shorter fly rods for use with the very effective lures, such as the Colorado Spinner, Emerick Spinner, No. 375, 710, etc. To meet the demand we offer the above highest grade rod in 9 and 8½ feet. It has the same perfect action, same high quality exactly.

No. 1250C. Differing only from the No. 1200C rod, that it is 8½ feet in length, weight 4½ ounces.........List each 20.00

No. 1251C. 9 ft., the same exactly as above, except length, weight, 5½ ounces...............................List each 20.00

Pictured above is the advertisement for the Schmelzer&Sons "Highest Grade Split Bamboo Fly Rod" from the 1906 catalog in the author's library.

Chubb/Montague Ferrules.

Signature wrap.

Wrap pattern on snake guides.

"Schmelzers Kansas City" engraving on the reel seat.

Dame Stoddard &Co. "NeverBreak" 3/2 8'6" Trout Fly Rod F.E.Thomas Trade Rod. circa 1898-1905

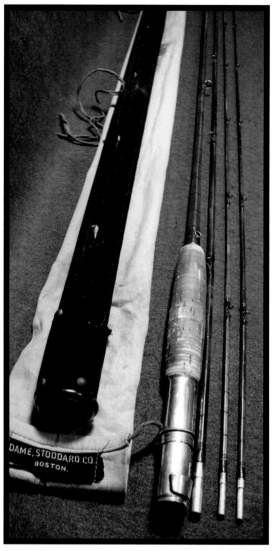

*T*his is one of those odd rods that are actually easy to date because it has a marking that was only used for a few years by the maker for the seller.

*T*he components on the rod are without a doubt a mix. The ferrules and the reel seat could be Chubb/Montague and the shafts appear to be Thomas's work. The cane has a classic Thomas type swell in the butt. The hardware is all NiS. The guides are bronzed snakes. This rod was made between 1898 and 1904 or 1905. It is absolutely complete down to its original form fit case and light canvas sack for the form fit case. This rod does have what are most likely Chubb/Montague made components that F.E.Thomas used on his low-grade trade rods. For example Montague made that style of form-fit case at that time frame. This rod is from the Author's collection.

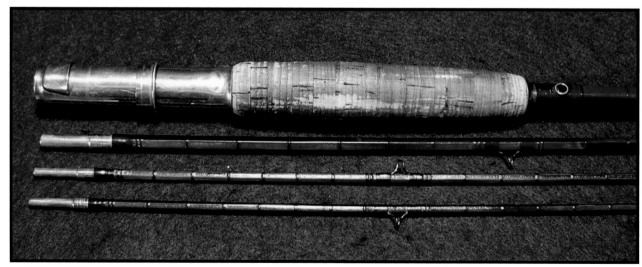

Pictured above are the grip and reel seat from the "Dame Stoddard NeverBreak". Compare this reel seat to the seat on the ISAAK WALTON fly rod on page #150. The two are identical.

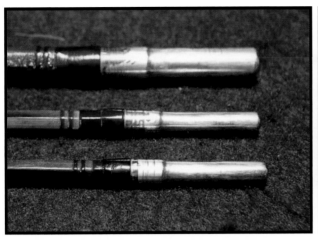

Male ferrules from the "Never Break".

Female ferrules and tiptops.

Guides and tiptop from the "Never break".

Close up of the welts on the female ferrules.

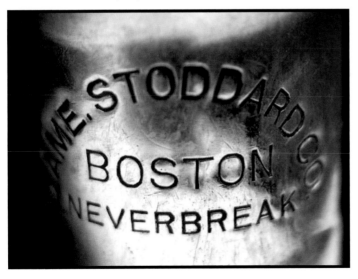

Pictured above is the bag label and to the left is a close up of the reel seat markings.

Dame Stoddard &Co. "NeverBreak" 3/2 12' Salmon Fly Rod F.E.Thomas Trade Rod. circa 1898-1905

*T*he Salmon rod pictured here is the big brother to the trout rod on the previous pages. Some of the noteworthy differences are the reel seat rails and the tip tops are NiS wire done in the English style of being looped and soldered and then tied on to the tip with silk. You can tell the F.E.Thomas Co. made the two by the quality of the work in the cane itself. The attention to detail is surprising for a trade rod. The two rods are very accurate within the taper of the blank. The flat-to-flat measurement variations were under +/- 5 one thousandths of an inch. The rod is wrapped in Chinese red silk and has full intermediates. It is unfortunately missing its original canvas bag. The form fit case is in very good condition.

*T*his rod is from the private collection of Mr. John Oppenlander.

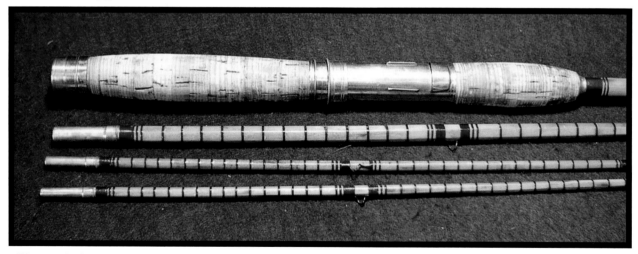

Pictured above are the Varney style raised reel foot rails on the full NiS reel seat and the two-handed cork grip. Note the very closely wound intermediate wraps for reinforcement of this big rod. Multiple makers used the Varney style of reel foot rails.

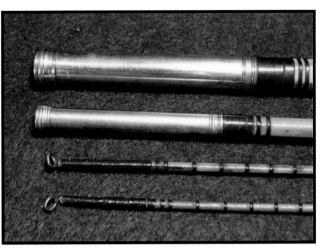

Male ferrules from the "NeverBreak" salmon rod.

Female ferrules and the NiS wire tiptops.

Snake guides and wrap pattern.

Close up of the welt on the female ferrules.

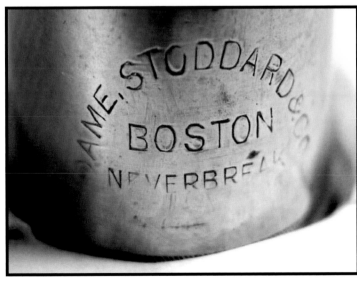

"Dame, Stoddard&Co, BOSTON, NeverBreak" reel seat markings above left and above right is a salmon scale imbedded in the varnish.

George I. Varney, Maker Montague City Mass. Fly Rod 9'6" 3/2 circa 1900-1920

*G*eorge I Varney was another of the master rod makers that left the H.L.Leonard Rod Co. in 1888 or 1889. On March 4th of 1890 he was awarded a patent for a new style of serrated ferrule and a binding ring cap, patent number 422,470. This rod has the Mar 4th 1890 patent ferrules, and the classical Varney reel seat with his signature 5 wrap intermediates the full length of the rod. It also has its original canvas bag and Calcutta cane tip tube with the typical Varney style of NiS cap on it.

*T*his rod is stamped "George I. Varney, Maker, Montague city Mass." indicating the rod was made after he was hired by the Montague City rod works as their master rod maker in the early 1900s. The rod is wrapped in Chinese red with Chinese red and black trim wraps and intermediates. The butt has 102 wraps on it, the mid has 125 wraps and the tips each have 146 wraps equaling a grand total of 519 wraps on the rod. A lot of silk on this rod and unfortunately the varnish is in a full and almost total meltdown on the butt section.

*T*his rod is from the Authors private collection.

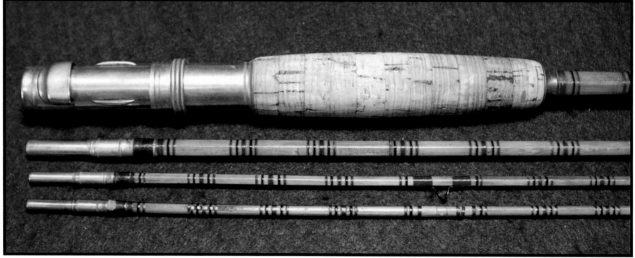

Pictured above are the George I. Varney reel seat and grip and male ferrules from the marked "Geo.I Varney, Maker, Montague City, Mass" rod.

Mar. 4*th* 1890 Varney patent ferrules pictured above.

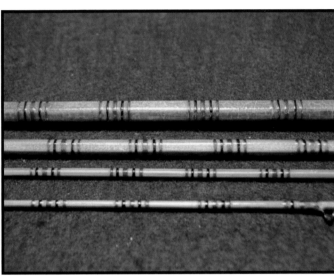

Snake guides and tiptop.   George I. Varney signature five-wrap intermediate pattern.

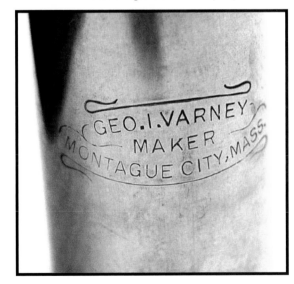
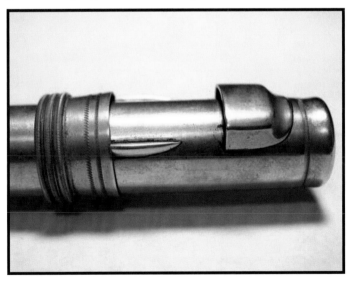

"GEO.I.VARNEY, MAKER, MONTAGUE CITY MASS." Reel seat stamping pictured above left and above right is a close up of the Varney soldered hood and reel foot rails on the NiS barrel.

W.R. Wheeler Hartford, Ct. Lancewood Fly Rod 3/2 circa 1900-1905

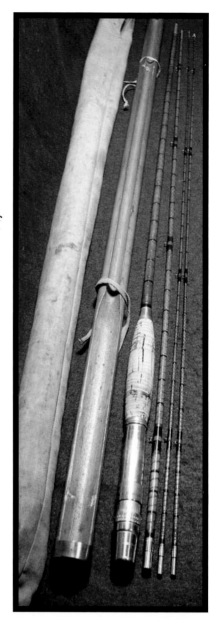

W.R. Wheeler was one of the finest examples of an oddball American Rod maker. Some of the odd things he was known for were his patent for a criss-cross winding of copper wire over the whole rod to an internally operated reel seat. This rod pre-dates his patent for the copper winding. It is only spiral wrapped with thread. The Foster Brothers of England actually invented and patented the practice of spiral wrapping a rod with copper wire. He circumvented the foster Brothers patent by using a flat copper wire instead of a round one.

*T*his rod is wrapped in deep red silk with black and red alternating intermediates over a 2-wrap spiral wrap of gold silk. The reel seat is a Chubb/Montague seat. The ferrules are the earliest version of a severely truncated ferrule that I have ever seen. The male slide portion on the mid is only 9/16th of an inch and the tip male ferrules are only about a 32nd of an inch shorter. They are made out of NiS and have a rolled welt straight female and a shouldered male. The grip is 1" cork rings.

*T*his rod is from the Author's collection.

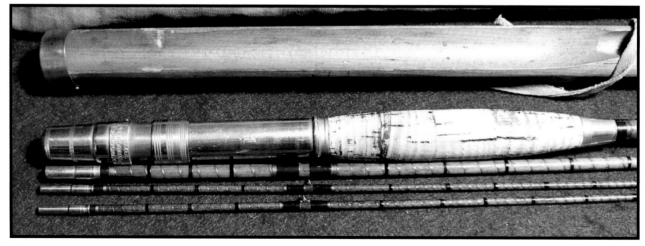

Short grip and long Chubb style reel seat. Note the original form fit case.

W.R. Wheeler's truncated ferrule.

Stripping guide that has been rewrapped.

NiS snakes and a stirrup tip-top.

Guides used by W.R. Wheeler.

W.R. Wheeler wraps.

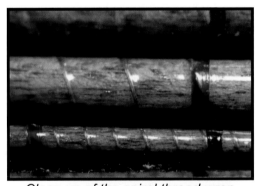

Close up of the spiral thread wrap.

W.R. Wheeler Makers mark at left.

Wheeler truncated male ferrule at right.

Fred D. Divine Co. Utica N.Y. Calcutta Cane Trade Rod for S D&G, New York "Perfection" circa 1900-1920

*T*his is an example of a trade rod by the Divine Co. made between 1900 and 1920. This rod was made for the Schoverling, Daly & Gales Co. This company could actually trace its roots back to John P. Moore, who started his tackle house in 1823. It was one of the oldest continuous tackle dealers in New York City. The rod is made out of Calcutta cane and has NiS hardware. An agate tiptop and trumpet guides. The agate tiptop on this rod is very delicate and the reel seat is very much like a George I. Varney reel seat, with its raised foot rails. Many different manufacturers used that style at that time. The rod is wrapped in red silk and has full intermediate wraps with a signature wrap as an off set tip wrap on the guides and ferrules. The grip is made out of ½" cork rings. This rod is missing its spare tip and its canvas bag or a form fit case and a canvas bag, as was the common practice at that time for a rod like this.

*T*his rod is from the author's private collection.

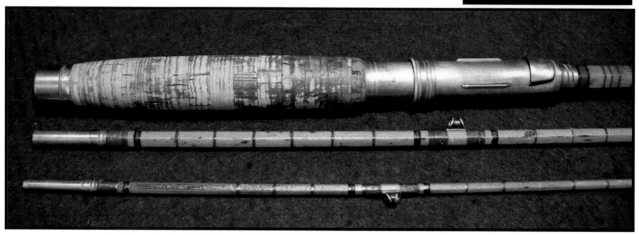

Pictured above is the grip and reel seat from the Schoverling, Daly & Gales Co. "Perfection" casting rod made by Divine.

Male and female ferrules from the S. D&G "Perfection" casting rod pictured above.

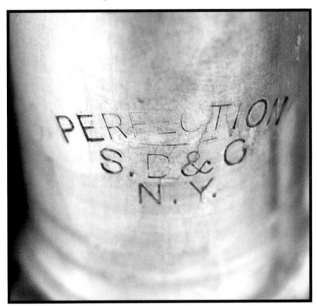

NiS trumpet guides and the offset tip wrap. *The "Perfection S. D&G N.Y. reel seat stamping.*

Pictured above is a close up of the Varney style reel seat used by so many makers during the late 1800s up thru the 1920s and 1930s. Makers who used that style of seat were H.L. Leonard, F.E. Thomas, F.D. Divine and many others.

Herbert Hatton, Hereford England Circa 1900-1925 2/1 8'6" Fly Rod

*H*erbert Hatton of Hereford England was best known for his Devon Wye Spinning Minnow. Some of the typical British style components on this rod are the large rubber butt cap, the English twist snakes and the cork grip and seat with a moveable slide band above a fixed band. The tiny spiked ferrules on this rod are a very tight fit. The rod has the English style intermediate wraps. One of the surprising things about this rod is the very quick action it has. The node spacing in the bamboo is a very tight 3X3. The components are brass that has been blued, and the female ferrule is hand welted. The tiptop and stripping guide are agate. When I saw this rod listed on eBay, the Internet auction service, I knew that I would have to add it to my collection just on the basis of name alone. I do not know if there is any family relation but it would not surprise me one bit if there is. At least once a generation the Hattons produce a trout bum and this go round it is my great pleasure to have the honor of carrying on the tradition of fish crazed fanatic within our family.

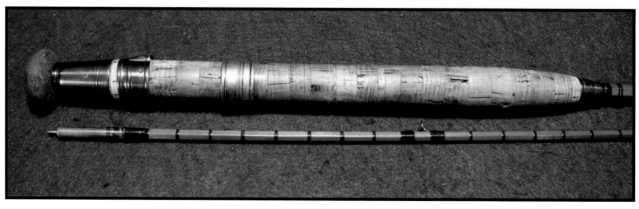

Pictured above are the grip and reel seat of the "Herbert Hatton of Hereford, England rod from the early 1900s.

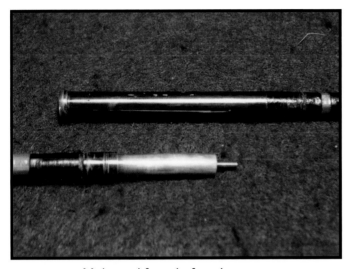

Male and female ferrules.

Close up of the reel seat hardware.

Agate stripping guide and one of the snake guides. grooves worn into the agate from the silk line of that time frame.

Close up of the agate tiptop; note the

Pictured to the left are the butt cap markings "Hatton.Hereford." in a close up.

Vidmar, F.E.Thomas
Trade Rod circa1901-1925
9' 3/2 Calcutta Cane

*T*his is a sort of a mystery rod. I cannot identify it absolutely as an F.E.Thomas trade rod, but if you compare it side by side with my early era Thomas Dirigo the two rods are absolute copies of each other. From the reel seat and grip down to the snake guides and the Calcutta tip tube and canvas bag the two rods are identical to each other. Please see the Dirigo on page #176. The rod has the typical Thomas NiS slide band reel seat. It also has the reverse twist snake guides that Fred was so fond of. It is wrapped in Chinese red silk and has full intermediates. It is in its original canvas bag with Calcutta cane tip tube. The stamping is identical to the ISAAK WALTON stamping on a low grade Kosmic. The shape and size of the lettering are identical. The grip is a cigar full taper and also is quite typical of F.E.Thomas work. The slide band on this rod and the Dirigo are identical. This rod is from the private collection of John Oppenlander.

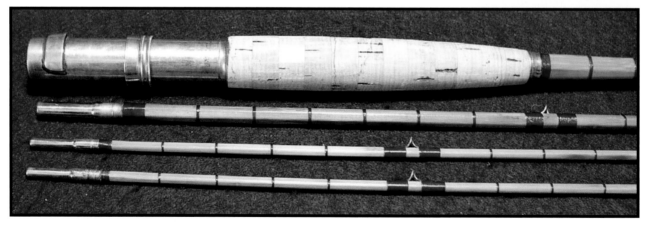

Pictured above are the grip and reel seat and components used on the "VIDMAR" trade rod by F.E.Thomas. This rod has been restored as compared to a rod that has been rebuilt; all wraps were replaced with the proper color of thread and were replaced in the exact same position as they were on the rod originally. Note the rail-less reel seat that was common to the Dirigo grade of rods.

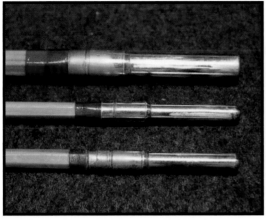
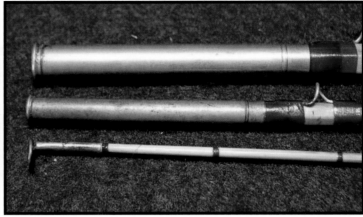

Male ferrules from the VIDMAR trade rod. Female ferrules and tiptop from the VIDMAR trade rod.

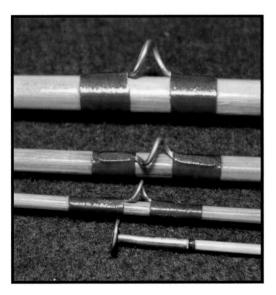

Guides and tiptop.   Soldered hood and slide band from the VIDMAR trade rod.

"VIDMAR' reel seat stamping.   Close up of the slide band

F.E. Thomas "Dirigo"
9' 3/2 Fly Rod Tonkin Cane
circa 1902 – 1920

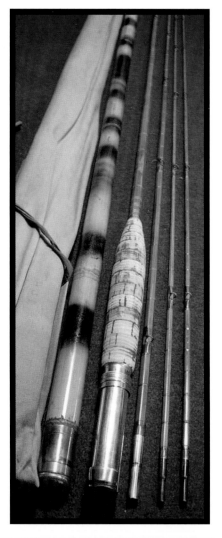

*T*he F.E. Thomas rod company first produced the "Dirigo" fly rod in 1901. It sported a full NiS reel seat and was finished out in a pattern that was very similar to the late Isaak Waltons produced by the Kosmic Rod Co. and T&E and the early Payne rod Co. This rod has its original Calcutta cane tip tube and canvas bag. It also has the signature reverse twist English style snakes that Fred was so fond of. This is one of the early "Bangor. Me." stamped rods identified by the reel seat and the full English twist snakes including the stripper or first guide. The rod is wrapped in gold silk and has full intermediates. The tips on this rod are short by ½" and 2 1/2"s respectively. The male ferrules on the tips are blued and the others are not, but they all are definitely Thomas ferrules. The grip is a ½" cork ring cigar full taper. This rod is a true pleasure to cast even with the slightly short tips.

*T*his rod is from the author's private collection.

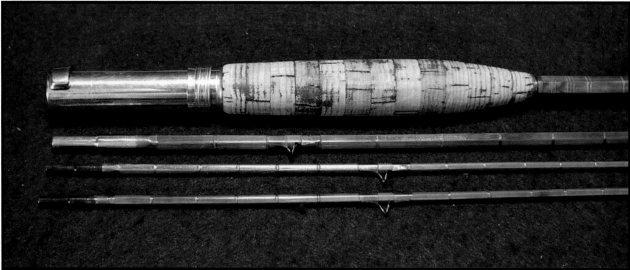

Pictured above is the grip and reel seat and snake guides and wrap pattern of the F.E. Thomas "Dirigo" fly rod circa 1902-1920. Note the factory replacement ferrules on the tips. Makes you wonder if the pucker brush got the original two tips?

Male ferrules on the F.E. Thomas "Dirigo" above left and the females and tiptops above right.

English twist snake guides.

Signature wrap and winding check.

"Dirigo F.E. Thomas Bangor, ME" reel seat stamping above left and a close up of the slide band above right.

Horrocks&Ibbotson,
Ash & Lancewood Boat Rod
Diamond UTK circa 1906-1919
7'6" or 6'6" 3/2

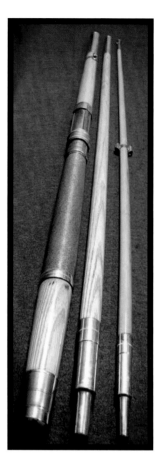

*T*his boat rod is an example of a rod from the first ten to twenty years of production by the H&I Co. after they had purchased the supplies and hardware from two late 1800s rodmakers. They first purchased the supplies of George Kemp of Trenton New Jersey in 1900. A year later they purchased the factory and its inventory of the John B. McHarg Rod Company. This rod has the second marking used by H&I with the first being a sticker on the shaft reading "Clarks, Horrocks & Co". This rod has doubled NiS plated tie guides. The mid section is missing two sets of guides. The tiptops are a funnel and a stirrup with the funnel being on the short emergency tip stored in the butt. The grip is an olive and brown cord wrapped grip with a chrome plated brass reel seat. The ferrules are very large covered doweled ferrules with the ferrules being made out of chrome-plated brass. This rod has a funny story to it. I was sitting at my fly tying bench one morning getting ready to go fish the Gunnison River. My fishing partner Dave shows up and is looking at rods while I finished the flies I needed for the day. I had only recently acquired this rod as a 3/1 configuration off of the on line Internet auction service eBay. Well Dave picks this rods butt up and I am kind of watching him from the corner of my eye as he proceeds to unscrew the butt cap and pull out the mint condition short tip that the seller had not noticed and I too had completely missed. To say the least I about fell out of my chair in surprise and delight at his discovery.

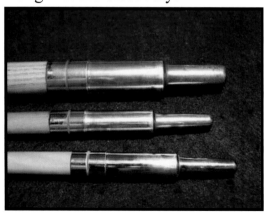

Male ferrules at the left and the female ferrules and the tiptops to the right.

Close up of the butt cap and male ferrules and the lower portion of the corded grip.

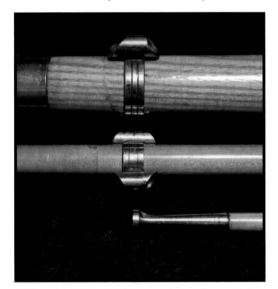

The above two photos show the guides and tiptops. Note that this is a fairly late use of the Prichard style guides. And below left is a close up of the signature stamping on the reel seat.

Pictured above is an engraving of a Mackerel from the 1908 Anglers Guide by Charles Bradford. Put these two together, the rod and the fish and it would have been fun.

Henry Andrus, Hartford, CT. Greenheart/ Split bamboo 8' 5/2 circa 1910-1930

This rod by Henry Andrus of Hartford, Ct. was originally made for R.L. Jones of Hartford, Ct.. This Andrus rod has no date, but the use of the Chubb reel seat with the sculptured reel foot rails suggest a date of 1930 or earlier. The rod is a recreation of a style of build that was mostly used in the first half of the 19th century. Greenheart was used for the butt and mid sections and split-cane for the tips. The oldest complete rod in the American Museum of Fly Fishing in Manchester, Vermont is signed Furman and was made in the 1830s. It is the earliest known example of a rod with split cane as a structural part. The tips are 3-strip and are spliced into the tip section and they comprise ¾ of the length of the tip sections. This rod has 6-strip tips and is actually quite delightful to cast. It has an action that is very similar to the slower models of rods by Leonard. This rod has an agate stripping guide and NiS snakes and round tiptops. The rod is wrapped in red silk with yellow silk offset tip wraps with full intermediates of red silk. The ferrules are a straight rolled welt non-waterproof NiS. The grip is a cigar full taper made out of specie cut ½" cork rings.

This rod is from the Authors private collection.

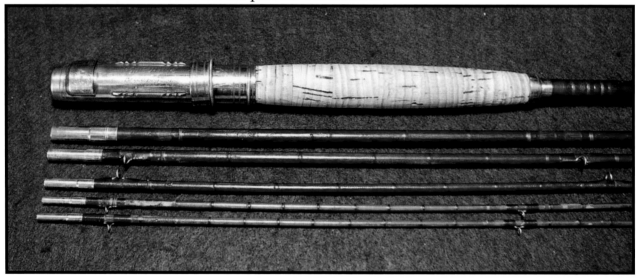

Pictured above are the Chubb reel seat with the sculptured rails, the wrap pattern and the NiS guides and male ferrules.

Male ferrules and NiS snake guides.

Female NiS ferrules with the NiS round tiptops.

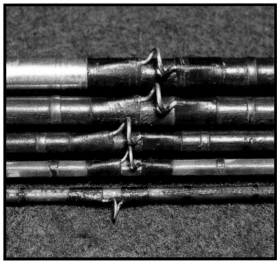

Close up of the guides and wrap pattern. Original owners name and the Chubb sculptured reel foot rails.

Pictured to the left is the "Made by Henry Andrus, Hartford Ct." engraved signature, which is how he marked all of the rods that he produced. This rod is a little unusual in the fact that it is not dated as to the date of manufacture.

F.E.Thomas, Bangor Me.
Thomas "Special"
13' 3/3 circa 1913-1920

*T*his thirteen foot two-handed salmon rod is an example of the early work produced by the Thomas rod company after the split with Eustis Edwards. This rod has the Nov. 9th 1913 patent #1,065,481 reel seat. This reel seat was a near copy of the Leonard interrupted thread reel seat that was designed for use on big game rods. This rod has Blued NiS ferrules and the reel seat is also blued with a large amount of the bluing being worn off at this point in time. The rod is wrapped in black and orange jasper silk and has full intermediate wraps of the same thread. The snake guides are English twist and are also of very heavy gauge wire. The rod has its original form fit case and cloth bag. This rod is from the private collection of Richard Collar D.D.S.

Pictured above is the Thomas reel seat showing the interrupted thread on the barrel and the locking pawl on the soldered and seamed slide band. Note how little of the bluing remains on the reel seat. Authors note; further research has shown that the above reel seat used by Leonard and Thomas is a copy of the Nov. 30 1880 Prichard patented reel seat.

Male and female ferrules pictured above left with a close up of the welt on the female ferrule above right.

Round loop NiS tiptops.

English twist heavy wire snake guides.

"F.E.THOMAS, SPECIAL, BANGOR ME." Reel seat stamping above left and the Thomas bull's-eye on the butt cap pictured above right.

F.D.Divine Rod Co. N.Y. "The Divine Rod" H 4538 8'6" 1/2/2, circa 1917

*T*his rod is a superb example of the rods that helped reinstate the reputation of the Divine rod Co. back to that of a producer of higher quality tackle as opposed to just mass production with little care. Due to the efforts of Frank Wolcott, Frank Becraft and George McDuffie this was achieved by the production of much higher quality rods than during the period between the death of Fred and the introduction of the fairy rod in 1917. This rod has high quality NiS reel seat components and the ferrules are also full NiS. This rod has a factory replacement mid that is so close to the same age of the rest of the rod you would have thought they were made together. This rod is wrapped in Chinese red silk and has black trim wraps and full intermediates out of the Chinese red silk. It has its original canvas bag.

*T*his rod is from the private collection of Richard Collar D.D.S.

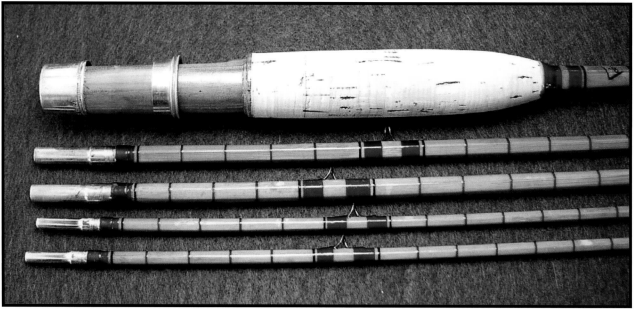

Pictured above is the grip and turned cherry reel seat with the integral grip check turned into the seat. The wrap pattern and the snake guides and the male ferules on "the Divine Rod' from 1917.

Pictured above left are the male ferrules and above right are the female ferrules used on "The Divine Rod" circa 1917.

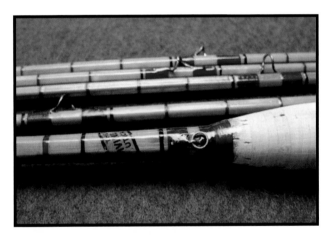

Stripping guide and snake guides and wrap pattern above left. Hook keeper and thread winding check and the acetate label above right.

Serial # H4538 stamped into the butt cap.

"The Divine Rod, Utica N.Y." acetate label.

E.F.Payne Maker
Highland Mills 1920s
8'9" 2/2 Det. Grip

*T*his rod is an example of a very rare two-piece Payne fly rod with a detachable grip in its original form fit case. Martin Keane sold this rod out of his catalog #84 in 2002. The grip has various sizes of cork rings, denoting that it was made during the period when the Rodmakers were struggling to come up with material to work with. The present owner and operator of the E.F.Payne Rod Co. Dave Holloman has authenticated this rod. The hardware is all NiS with an agate-stripping guide and agate tiptops. The rod is wrapped in a deep burgundy silk with a gold tipping. Two-piece rods of this length from that time frame are fairly rare. The rod has what is thought to be its original form fit case.

*T*his rod courtesy of Richard's Rods.

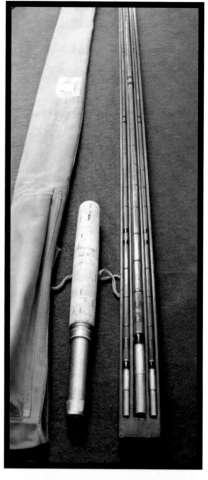

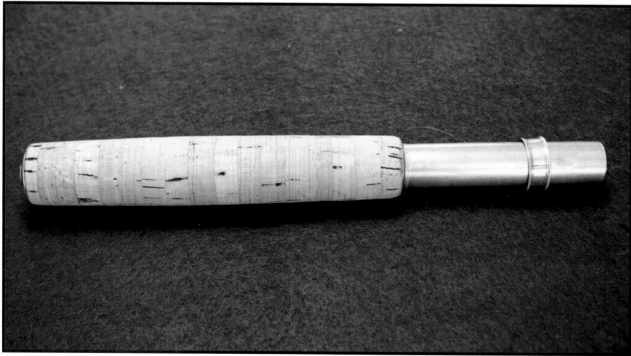

Grip made out of assorted size rings of cork, primarily 3/16th inch and the full NiS reel seat.

Close up of the male Payne ferrules.   *Close up of the female and male ferrules together.*

Agate stripping guide and the snakes and tiptops used by E.F. Payne Rod Co. pictured above.

The "E.F. Payne Maker Highland Mills" Reel seat stamping is pictured to the left.

*T*his rod is a true delight to hold and examine because of the quality of the work in building the shafts and the quality of the hardware.

Montague City Rod Co. "Flipline" Fly Rod 9' 3/2 circa 1920s-1930s

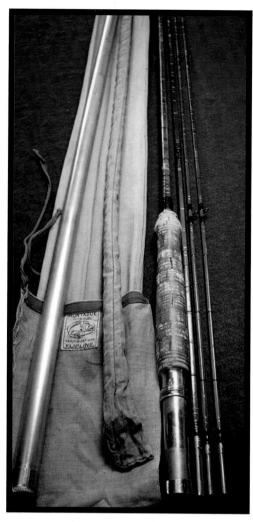

*H*ere is a fairly rare example of a Montague rod that has survived completely intact. The rod, its components and the accoutrements that went with the rod i.e. the labeled canvas bag and the tip tube with its cloth bag for the tips. The rod has a chrome plated cap and ring slide band reel seat. The grip is made out of ½" cork rings that are specie cut. The grip is in the rarely seen "PeckerHead" configuration. The grips popularity probably died from social morals as much as anything. The rod is wrapped in deep burgundy silk and has yellow trim wraps. The intermediate wraps are done from both colors. The rod has SS snake guides and an agatine stripping guide. The tiptops are also agatine. This rod originally would have sold for $15.00 in the late 1920s or early 1930s. Note how clean the rod bags are, which shows how well this rod was stored over the years.

*T*his rod is from the private collection of John Oppenlander.

Pictured above are the components used on the Montague "FlipLine", Note the ill-fated Montague PeckerHead grip. Also note the bag labels, the rear label being the original paper label on the canvas bag.

 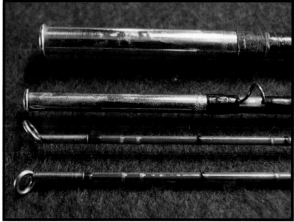

Male Montague ferrules used on the "FlipLine".   Female ferrules used on the Flipline, Note that the females are not the normal shouldered Montague female ferrules.

Snake guides and the agatine stripping guide and the angled Chubb single ring top pictured above left. The intermediate wrap pattern is shown close up above right.

 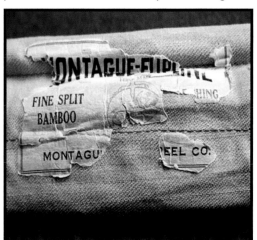 

The acetate label.   The paper label on canvas bag.   The sewn label on the canvas bag.

Tycoon Tackle, Miami Fl.
Medium Salt Water Rod
7' 1/1with Ind. Grip
circa 1920s-1950s

*T*his rod is a fairly uncommon example of what is known as four strip flat laminate construction. The rod consist of four strips three of which are tapered rectangles and the fourth is a rectangle with one side being rounded out for the back side of the shaft leaving the face flat for the guides. The guides are a very small diameter Mildrum style bridged NiS trolling guide. The ash butt section has a Stainless steel reel seat and butt cap that is gimbaled to allow the rod to be used in conjunction with a fighting chair. The rod is wrapped in a heavy olive silk with yellow trim wraps. This rod is stout enough to stop a horse. In short, it is a very fast action and was designed for forcing big fish up from deep water. The decals and general condition of this rod are very good to excellent with the exception that one tip is missing and the remaining tiptop is a later period replacement. Note the heavy spiral wrap at the butt end of the tip section that was used as reinforcement as well as a cosmetic feature.

*T*his rod is from the Authors private collection.

Stainless steel reel seat and male ferrule.

High bridged Mildrum style NiS guide.

Pictured to the left is an extreme close up of the four strip flat laminate blank.

*I*n this picture the backside or spline side of the rod is the rounded face at the top of the picture. The sticker is wrapped around the corner of the rod and extends almost to the joint of the bamboo that is the flat side facing the viewer. Just above the corner of the black edge of the decal is the seam. It is in two dark bands of cane and is very hard to see. The actual shape of this rod is a square with one side rounded outward.

Pictured to the left is "The H.R.H.,Crown, Custom built by" decal.

And to the right is the "Tycoon Tackle Inc.,Miami, U.S.A. Trade Mark, Reg. U.S. Pat. Office." decal on the shaft of the medium to heavy saltwater rod by Tycoon Tackle.

Montague, Fly Rod
The "Pocono"
9' 3/2 circa 1920s

*T*his rod shows the Chubb/Montague influence from the Chubb patent reel seat to the Calcutta cane tip tube. The grip is sheet cork and has the typical stepped winding check used by Montague on the Chubb/Montague trade rods. The snake guides are very small English twist NiS snakes, which were designed to be used with a very small diameter silk line. The tiptops are agate. The ferrules are typical Montague style ferrules. The females are a bottle shaped rolled welt ferrule with the typical Montague waist. The male ferrules are straight. The rod is wrapped in Chinese red silk and has full intermediate wraps of Chinese red silk. The rod has a centering group of three wraps between each snake guide. The rod has its original cloth bag and the tip tube also has its cloth tip bag intact.

*T*his rod is from the private collection of John Oppenlander.

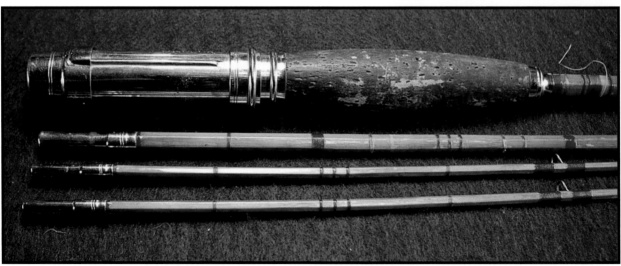

Pictured above are the Chubb patent reel seat and the sheet cork grip with the NiS snake guides and the Montague male ferrules.

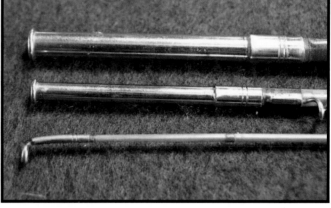

Male ferrules used on the "Pocono".   *Montague female ferrules and one of the tiptops.*

Nickel silver snake guides and the agate tiptop above left and the winding check and the signature wrap above right.

"Pocono" reel seat stamping pictured above.

Winchester Arms Co.
#6035 Fly rod
9' 3/2 circa 1920s

*T*his is an example of the lowest grade of Trade rod made by Eustis Edwards for the Winchester Arms Company. It has NPB components and in the cheapness of quality almost rivaled H&I and Montague for a low quality rod. In the collectable market these rods tend to carry a fairly high price due to the Winchester logo stamped on the reel seat. The higher-grade rods in the Winchester line are very fine fishing instruments. This rod has had a full restoration. It is wrapped in burgundy silk trimmed with black and has full burgundy intermediates. The guides are NiS snakes and the rod is in its original cloth bag. The grip is made out of ½ inch cork rings and is a full taper cigar style. This rod is from the private collection of Richard Collar, D.D.S.

Pictured below are the components and wraps used on the 6035 Edwards Winchester trade rod. Note the similarity of the reel seat to a Chubb reel seat.

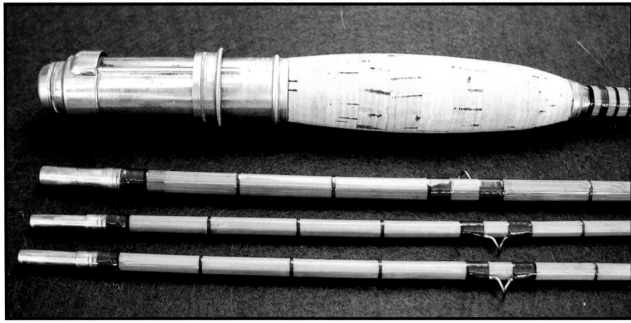

Edwards trade rod ferrules pictured above, males at the left and the females on the right.

Signature wrap on the butt section above left. "Winchester, Trademark, Made in U.S.A. 6035" reel seat stamping above right.

Agatine stripping guide and the snake guide and tiptops used by Edwards on his trade rods above left and a close up of the butt cap above right.

Dr. G.P. Holden Style Rod
9'6" 3/2 Tonkin Cane
circa 1920s

Dr. George Parker Holden is a person who was very prominent in the fishing circles of the early to mid 1900s. He wrote a volume titled "Idyll of the Split Bamboo" which was published in 1920 and gave full directions on how an amateur rodmaker could make his own split bamboo rod. Dr. Holden wrote several other volumes about fishing and the out of doors. He is also famous for having been the gentleman who gave Everett Garrison his first lessons in the art of rodmaking. The rod pictured here is wrapped in the style that Dr. Holden was a proponent of, being done in this way to reinforce the bamboo as opposed to reinforcing it with just intermediate wraps. His reasoning was bamboo breaks in long splinters so therefore a high quality rod will have reinforcing wraps as insurance for the bamboo itself and not so much the seams in the rod. I am sure this is not a rod by Dr. Holden because the spiral wraps are unbroken for the length of the sections. In his book he gives a real muddy set of instructions on how to wrap over the spiral and cut it out underneath the guides leaving a smooth wrap. The person who made this rod got those instructions as well as I did as attested to by the fact he put the guides on right over the spiral wrap. The guides are wrapped in red silk and have a light green trim wrap. The hardware is all of Chubb/Montague origin as shown by the reel seat and ferrules.

This rod is from the private collection of Richard Collar, D.D.S.

Chubb sculptured reel foot and 1/8th inch cork ring grip and the thread winding check so reminiscent of Garrisons work.

Chubb reel seat and a close up of the sculptured rails pictured above.

Stripping guide and snakes and the wire and agate tiptop above left. Close up of the spiral wrap above right.

Close up of the wire and agate tiptops. Close up of the welt on the female ferrule, which shows a certain amount of Varney influence.

*T*his rod is an example of Chubb/Montague components on a rod built in a particular style (Holden wrap style at least). We will never know for sure who made it but it is a beautiful example of a rodmaker at his best whoever he was.

F.D.Divine, "The Fairy"
7'6" 3/2 circa 1920s
Serial # R2988

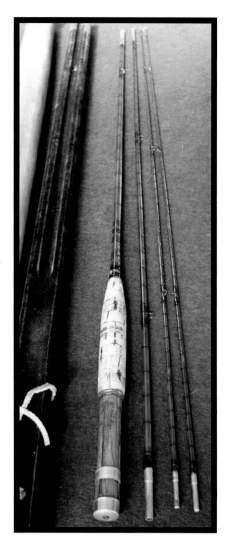

*T*his is a rod that really helped bring the Divine rod Co. back to prominence in the early 1900s, and it was the brainchild of Frank Becraft in 1917. The R in the serial number denotes a 1920s vintage, as does the label on the shaft. The ferrules are all NiS as is the reel seat hardware. The reel seat is the classic Divine cherry wood seat with the grip check turned out of the wood along with the reel seat. The snake guides are English twist denoting an early 1920s vintage also. It is wrapped in three colors of silk, Burgundy, Red and Black. The rod is in original condition and comes in its original velvet covered form fit case. The grip is ½ inch cork rings in the super fine cigar grip used on the "Fairy" model of fly rods. This is one of the earliest of the very small 7'6" or shorter fly rods that have a place in the angler's arsenal.

*T*his rod is from the private collection of Richard Collar, D.D.S.

Divine cherry wood reel seat and male ferrules.

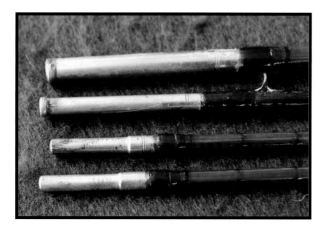

F.D.Divine Rod Co. ferrules.   *Serial number R2988 stamping on the butt cap.*

"The Divine Rod" acetate sticker above left and a close up of the Divine reel seat and male ferrules above right.

The close ups above show the effects of a loose ferrule on the wraps at left and the soldered welts on the female ferrules at right.

This was the rod that created the short rod craze that still lives to this day. They are a true pleasure to cast and an important part of our angling heritage.

Payne Spin Casting Rod
7' 2/1 circa 1920-1940

*H*ere is an extremely rare example of a mint condition never-fished E.F. Payne spin-casting rod. It still has its original paper wrap on the grip and all of the hardware is Jewelry bright. The guides and tiptop are of agate and are all very stunning. The rod has its original ferrule plug. It is missing its original cloth bag and case. The rod is wrapped in the classic Payne brown silk tipped in Gold silk. This rod is another rod that was originally collected by Dr. Harmon Leonard, the grand Nephew of Hiram L. Leonard. I am deeply grateful for his contributions to this work. I cannot say enough about the quality of this rod. The cane work is exceptional and the fittings and cork work are flawless. A true gem from one of the best of the American rod making firms of the early 1900s. And from one of the true old masters E.F.Payne. All of the hardware is NiS with the exception of the rubber butt cap. Dr. Richard Collar who was acting as his broker thru his online tackle service sold this rod in 2003 from Dr.Leonard's collection.

Richards Rods at www.antiquetackle.net.

Paper label on grip.

Hook keeper.

Payne ferrules and ferrule plug

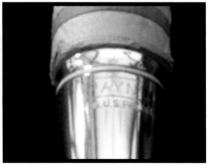

Payne butt cap stamping.

1ˢᵗ agate guide and agate tiptop.

Horrocks&Ibbotson Co. Utica, N.Y. 7'6" 2/2 "Princess" circa 1923-1929

*T*he Princess along with the Tonka King and Queen and Prince are considered by many to be some of the finest of the rod models ever produced by the Horrocks & Ibbotsson's Co. of Utica N.Y. By finest, I mean that they were some of the most fishable tapers produced by H&I. This rod has the circa 1923-1929 trout decal that is rarely seen now. This one is almost 100% complete; it is missing a small piece at the tip of the trout's lower jaw. It is one of the most stunning visually, of all of the decals ever used by any of the production rod makers. It consists of a trout in full color over a setting sun in gold that is reflected in the water below with the rod model name in the bottom. The rod has THS snakes that are very rusty. It is wrapped in orange and black jasper and bordered with an emerald green. The thread is very fine silk. The ferrules have a rolled welt and are chrome plated. The reel seat is a NiS SDL with a Bakelite insert and it has a 6"cigar grip.

*T*his rod is from the private collection of Mr. John Oppenlander.

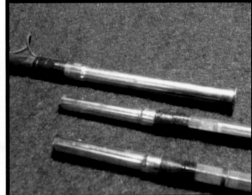

Pictured in the row above are the acetate label close ups and the male and female ferrules.

To the left is the reel seat and to the right are the guides and the winding check.

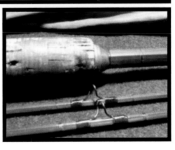

Horrocks & Ibbotson Co. The "Ike Walton" Fly Rod 9' 3/1 circa 1929-1933

*T*his rod is a typical example of the rods that were sold in the price range of $10.00. It has a chrome plated brass cap and ring reel seat. The ferrules are the typical H&I straight rolled welt, low quality ferrule that were infamous for. The grip is ½" inch cork rings in a reversed semi-half wells configuration. The rod is wrapped in garnet colored silk and has full intermediates of the same color thread. The trim wraps are yellow. The rod has THS snake guides and a perfection style tiptop. The stripping guide is similar to a Richardson patent two-ring guide and is obviously a factory item. This rod is about halfway up the quality scale of the rods produced by Horrocks & Ibbotson of Utica N.Y. This rod is missing one tip and a cloth bag and a carrying tube. The H&I company was a major producer of low quality and high numbers, which went hand in hand with each other. Some of their highest quality rods are the equal to most and their low quality rods were worse than most. *T*his rod is from the private collection of John Oppenlander.

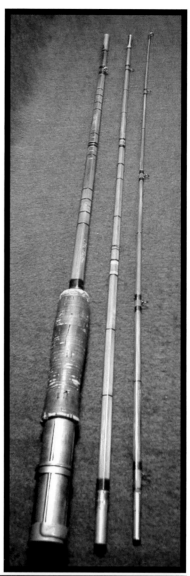

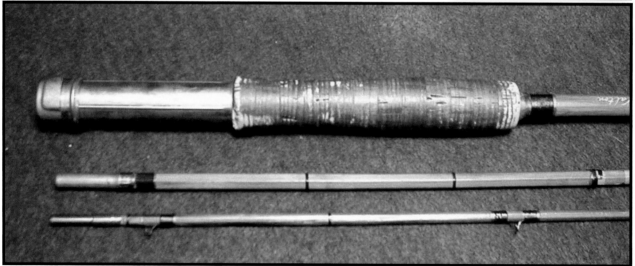

Pictured above is the reel seat and grip, male ferrules and snake guides and wrap pattern of the H&I "Ike Walton" fly rod.

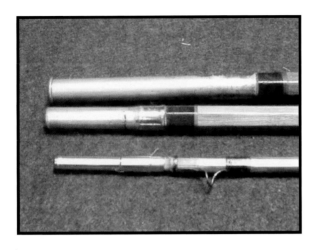

Male and female ferrules used on the Ike Walton by H&I. Tiptop and snake guide and the Richardson style 2-ring stripping guide.

Ink signature on the butt shaft.   Acetate label used by Horrocks&Ibbotsons between 1929 and 1933.

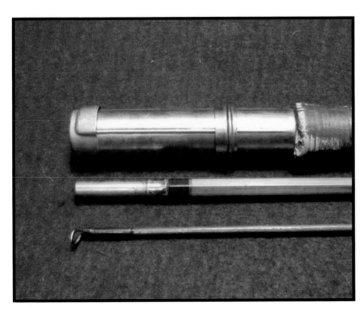

Pictured at the left is the chrome plated brass reel seat and male ferrule and the perfection style tiptop.

Heddon #35 "Peerless" 3/2 9' 1st era Fly Rod circa 1928-1929

*T*his is a classic example of the Heddon peerless or model #35 from 1928 or 1929. The Heddon NiS Hold Tite reel seat and the wrap pattern and the 1/8th inch cork rings in the reel seat are the primary identifying features. The rod has a serial number of 4043 on it. It has the typical spiral signature of that time frame. This rod is complete down to its original aluminum tube and cloth bag. It is wrapped in silk in the following colors, antique gold tipped with black and has full intermediate wraps. The signature wrap on it is also a clue to the age determination of this rod. The Hold tite reel seat was a flop and was only used on the #35 for a couple of years.

Another identifying feature is the Heddon stamping on the bottom of the butt cap. This rod is from the private collection of Mr. John Oppenlander.

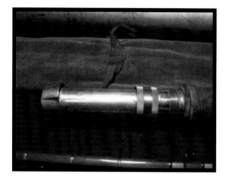
Hold-Tite reel seat.

Heddon Butt stamping.

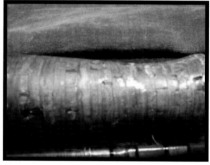
1/8th Inch Cork rings.

Signature wrap & signature.

Serial #4043.

Male and female ferrules.

*I*t is a great delight when you find a rod from seventy plus years ago when it is all complete down to its original tube and or case and is in the shape this rod is in.

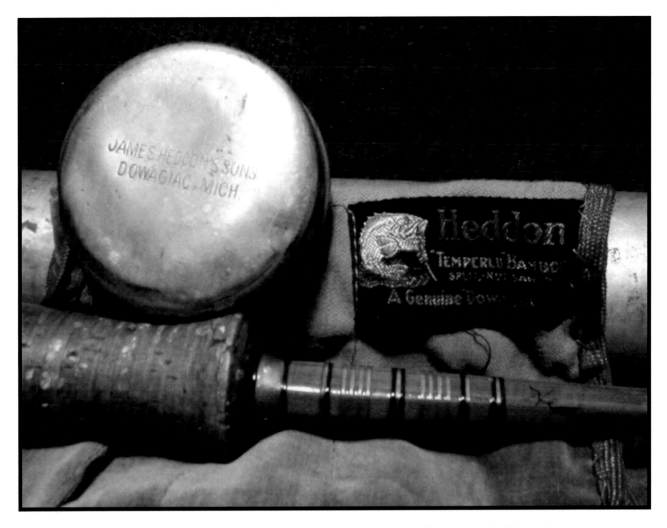

The above picture is a collage of the peripheral pieces you usually do not find in such good condition with the old rods. When you do the rod is usually in very good shape also.

Tube Cap.

Bag tag.

Merritt Hawes
Parker-Hawes, Meridian, Ct.
9' 3/2 circa 1929-1939

*T*his rod was made by Merritt Hawes for the Parker Shot Gun Company after he had taken over his father's company after Hiram's death in 1929. There were only 220 marked models out of a total of only 315 produced by Merritt after his father's death.

*T*he rod has the grip that is most typical of late production rods by M. Hawes. The reel seat is a very light cedar insert with cap and ring hardware. The rod is wrapped in yellow silk and has had one tip replaced. The ferrules are NiS and are serrated and waterproof. They are very similar in style to a Leonard ferrule even down to the shoulders on the males. In the early 1950s Dr. Harmon Leonard had the pleasure of showing this rod to Merritt and discussing some of its history with him. In turn I have been honored in a way that is to me almost indescribable, and that is the help and the relationship I have with Dr. Harmon Leonard who is the owner of this rod. Many thanks Harmon.

*T*his rod is from the Harmon Leonard collection.

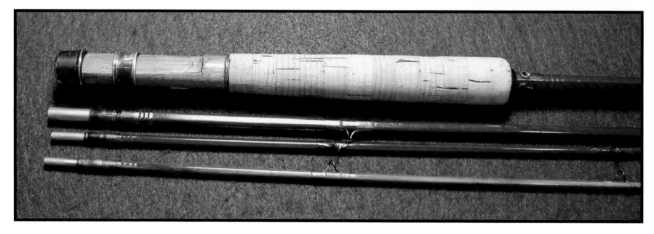

Pictured above are the Hawes grip that is a Phillipe style of grip and the cedar insert cap and ring reel seat.

Male ferrules from the "Parker-Hawes" rod.

Female ferrules and a tiptop.

Pictured above are two close ups of the ferrules, male ferrules above left and the welt on a female above right.

Pictured to the left is the cap and ring cedar insert reel seat with the marked butt cap.

Henry Andrus, Fly Rod
Hartford Ct. 1930
6'9" 3/2

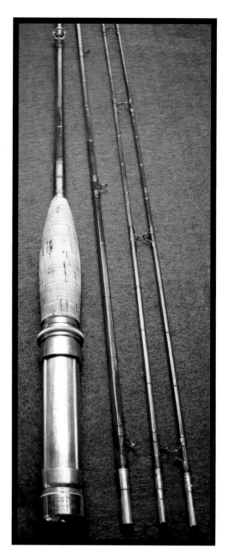

*T*his split cane rod by Henry Andrus helps establish him being a rodmaker up to and including the year 1930. He is one of the less well-known rod makers from early 1900 to 1930.

*T*he rod has a Montague reel seat and ferrules. The snake guides are blued THS with an agate stripping guide and tiptops. The wraps are yellow with a red trim wrap and full yellow intermediates. The grip is made of ½ inch cork rings and is a full taper cigar grip. One of the tips is a replacement that had to have been made by Andrus just a year or two later because of the aging difference of the varnish on the two tips. Mr. Andrus was noted for signing all of his rods with the date and original owners name in engraved script on the reel seat. Some idiot tried to file off the original markings on this rod and almost accomplished the job of removing the original owners name that was B.L. Cooley of Hartford Ct.

*T*his rod is from the private collection of John Oppenlander.

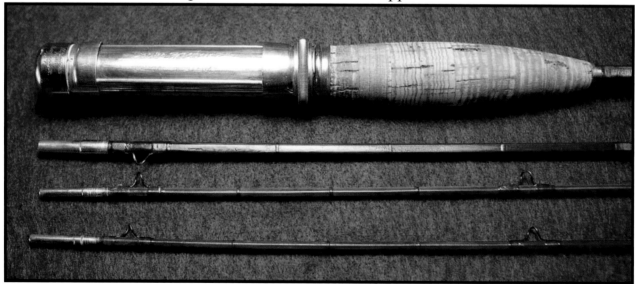

Montague components used by Henry Andrus of Hartford Ct. pictured above.

Male ferrules used by Andrus.

Female ferrules and agate tiptops.

Stripping guide, snakes and tiptop.

Agate stripping guide and tiptops.

H. Andrus Maker Hartford, Ct.1930 Butt cap marking. The Montague slide band reel seat with the screw lock on the slide band.

Fred D. Divine Co. Tonkin Cane Fly Rod "Pathfinder" 8'6" 3/2 circa 1920s –1930s

*T*he Pathfinder is an example of The Divine Company's later production era. The reel seat is not marked but the shaft has a very good example of the Divine acetate sticker. The rod is made of tonkin cane and has a NiS reel seat and ferrules. The guides are bronzed tool hardened steel as is the tiptop. This rod is an old warrior; both tips are a little short and one of them has been spliced back together with a flattened snake guide. I am sure it was someone's "Old Reliable" and could tell some wonderful stories. The grip is ½" cork rings in a cigar full taper configuration. The reel seat is a full NiS plated cap and ring seat. The ferrules are NiS plated and the rod is wrapped in green silk with red trim wraps. The rod has no intermediate wraps indicating a late date of manufacture. The rod has its original cloth bag with the hanging tag still intact.

*T*his rod is from the author's private collection.

Pictured below are the grip and reel seat from the "Pathfinder" by Divine. Note the difference in color of the mid section which has had a poor attempt at restoration or more likely just a case of bad maintenance leading to the mid section being poorly refinished.

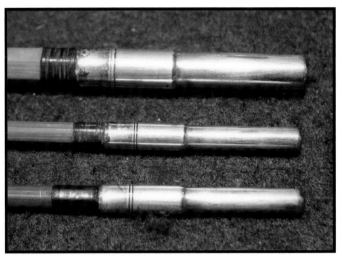

Male later era Divine ferrules.

Female Divine ferrules and tiptops.

Divine guides and tiptop.

Close up of the welt on the female ferrule.

Bottom two pictures are of the Divine Acetate label circa 1920s-1930s.

F.D.Divine, "Rainbow" Fly Rod circa 1928/29 8' 3/2 Serial # R5241

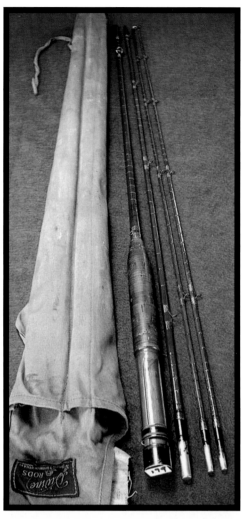

*T*his "Rainbow" model rod from the Divine Rod Company is a typical example produced in the late 1920s, from the turned cherry wood reel seat to the blued ferrules and snake guides. The reel seat hardware is the standard cap and ring used with the turned wood insert by Divine. The rod is wrapped in black and white jasper silk with red trim wraps and full intermediates out of the B&W Jasper silk. The bag is marked with a date of Feb. 19 1929. Most likely the first owner of the rod did this. Note the white tag on the butt cap showing #199, which was the lot number, used by Langs Sporting Collectibles on January 3rd 2004 to auction this rod.

*T*his rod is from the private collection of Richard Collar, D.D.S.

Pictured above are the 1/2 inch cork ring grip and turned cherry wood reel seat with its cap and ring hardware and the male ferrules and snake guides used by Divine on the "Rainbow".

Pictured above are the Male Divine ferrules circa late 1920s at the left and the female ferrules at the right.

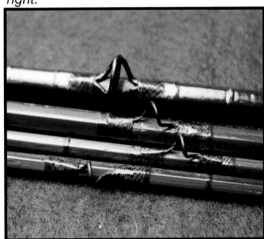

Stripping guide and snake guides above left. The acetate label reading "The Divine Rod, Utica N.Y." and the shaft markings "Rainbow 8' 4 ¼ ounces" above right.

Agate tiptop and the perfection style tiptop pictured above left and the bag label is at the right

The highest quality Divine rods are rods that hold their own with any of the best makers of that time frame or any other time frame. The casting qualities and fishing qualities are the equal of many and better than most production class rods.

Shakespeare Heddon Trade Rod 9' 3/2 circa 1920s-1930s

This rod is a Shakespeare bamboo rod. The Shakespeare Company never made their own rods but bought them as trade rods. The most likely maker of this rod is Heddon or possibly Edwards or South Bend. The rod has the rarely seen Shakespeare banner acetate label on the very nicely swelled shaft that is most like Heddon's work. The rod is wrapped in red silk including the red tip wraps and intermediate wraps. The ferrules are made of plated brass and are a straight rolled welt female. The males are shouldered with two incised bands that are reminiscent of an Edward's trade rod ferrule. The grip is an exaggerated full Wells grip out of ½" specie cut cork rings. The reel seat is a chrome plated brass C&R seat. The rod has its original canvas bag and aluminum tip tube with its original cloth bag for the tips.

This rod is from the private collection of John Oppenlander.

Pictured above is the plated brass C&R reel seat and the exaggerated full wells grip from this Heddon built Shakespeare rod circa late 1920s to the 1930s. Also note the remnants of the spiral banner Shakespeare acetate label on the swelled butt.

Male ferrules.

Female ferrules and tiptops.

Guides and tiptop.

Close up of the winding check.

The above row of photos shows the remains of the "Shakespeare" acetate label.

Weber Of Stevens Point Wisconsin circa 1930-50 Henshall Masterkraft #4500 8'6" 3/2 Fly Rod

*W*eber of Stevens point was a major supplier of fishing tackle for a period of approximately 40 years plus. After 1929 they started selling trade rods made for them by Heddon. Before that, W.E. Edwards made their rods. This rod is an anomaly. There are no records this model having ever been made. It is a #4500 and the hardware and the wrap patterns are all equal to the Heddon model #50.

*T*he ferrules are all NiS that is blued/enameled. Mildrum stripper and THS snake's with perfection tiptops. The rod is wrapped in yellow tipped with scarlet. It has a typical Heddon reel seat and reversed half wells grip. The Heddon Model #50 was one of their longest running and highest quality models of rods. This is a rare trade rod example of a "#50 President".

*T*he rod was purchased on eBay after a very spirited bidding war won by Dennis Nicks who has kindly contributed this rod from his private collection to be photographed for the book.

Pictured above are the grip and reel seat male ferrules and the snake guides used on the Henshall Masterkraft trade rod made by Heddon.

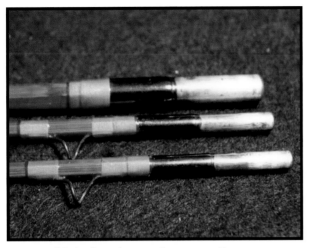

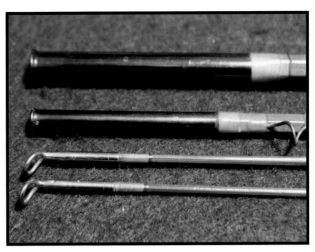

Male ferrules and wrap pattern.

Female ferrules and tiptops.

Close up of the stripping guide, snake guides and tiptops above left and the tube label above right.

The above row of pictures is of the acetate labels found on the Webber "J.A. Henshall MasterKraft #4500".

F.E. Thomas, "Special" Circa 1930-1958 8'6" 3/2

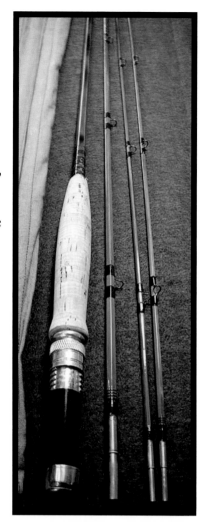

This F.E.Thomas rod is an example of a later era "Special" model as shown by the Hardy style of down-locking reel seat and the lack of intermediate wraps. This rod is wrapped in the deep red-almost burgundy color-that was favored by the Thomas Rod Co. This rod has its original bag and tube, which are in excellent shape. The rod has one tip that is a replacement. You can tell by the wrap colors and also by the lack of the three signature wraps at the ferrule station. The ferrules are the NiS ferrules used by Thomas. The guides are the old style English twist and the tiptops are the pear shaped tanged tiptop used on their higher end rods. The females are waterproof and have a serrated base.

The grip is a reversed half Wells full taper made out of ½" cork rings. Note the hook keeper, which is a feature that is exclusive to Thomas rods.

This rod is from the private collection of John Oppenlander.

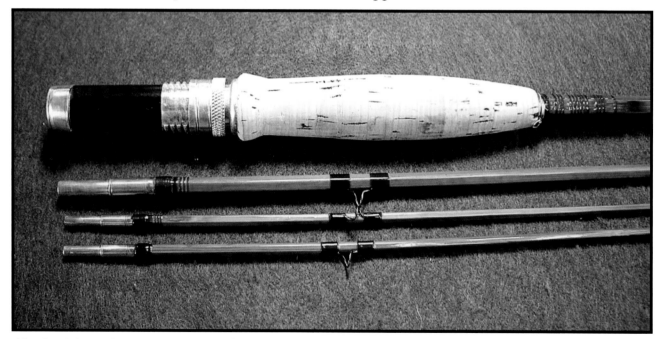

Hardy style reel seat, reversed half wells full taper grip and the English twist snake guides and male ferrules on the F.E. Thomas "special".

Thomas NiS male ferrules.

Thomas NiS female ferrules.

Stripping guide and snakes and tiptop used on the "Special" above left and the signature wrap and the Thomas hook keeper are pictured above right.

Butt cap stamping at the left.

Tube label at the right.

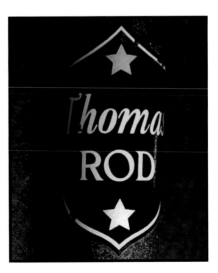

H.L.Leonard, Central Valley. N.Y. Model 50H "Hunt Taper" 8' 3/3 circa 1930s

This rod is the model 50-H or hunt taper which Richard Hunt, an infamous salmon fisherman of the late 1920s and the 1930s, designed. The rod has the classic Leonard NiS cap and ring with the wood insert. The grip is a cigar style out of ½ inch specie cut cork rings. The ferrules are Leonard patent waterproof NiS and were blued at one time. The stripping guide is an agate and the snakes are THS blued. The tiptops are Leonard agate tiptops. The rod is wrapped in deep brown silk. The rod has its original cloth bag and aluminum tube and has a factory original replacement tip giving the rod its three by three configuration. This rod is a very powerful and fast rod for a Leonard, which tend towards a slower softer action as a general rule of thumb. Dr. Harmon Leonard, DVM, donated this rod to this work. He is the grand nephew of Hiram L.Leonard. I owe him a great debt of thanks for allowing me to prowl thru his personal collection.

Pictured above are the NiS cap and ring reel seat with the butternut wood insert and the male ferrules and the Leonard snake guides and wrap pattern of the 1930s

Pictured above on the left are the ferrules and agate tiptop from the model 50-H and a close up of the welt on the female ferrule above right.

Agate stripping guide.

THS blued snake guides from the model 50-H.

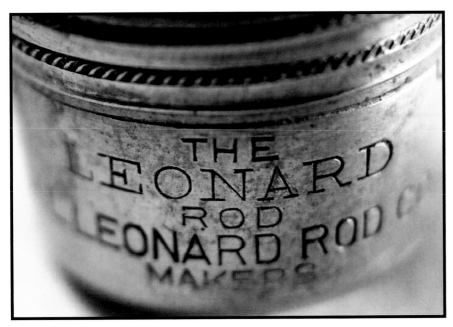

Note the butt cap stamping at the left; this denotes a rod as being made after 1927, which was when the stampings were changed to those pictured at the left.

Edwards Trade Rod
Winchester #6100
9' 3/2 circa early1930s

The old and venerable firm of Winchester sporting goods for a period of time in the early to mid 1900s "1910-1940" sold private label fishing tackle that was produced for them by several makers. This rod is an example of the lowest grade produced by the E.W. Edwards firm for Winchester. The rod has a full taper cigar grip out of ½" cork rings. The reel seat is a NiS cap and ring. The ferrules are typical Edwards trade rod ferrules of a lower quality. The guides are English twist THS blued snake guides. The tiptops are agatine as well as the stripping guide. The rod is wrapped in black silk with gold silk trim wraps. The intermediate wraps are alternating wraps of the black and gold silk. Note the drop in size of the intermediates as you go from the butt section to the mid section and then the tip. The rod has its original Calcutta cane tip tube but is missing the cloth bag for the tips and also the original canvas bag is gone. This rod is from the private collection of Richard Collar, D.D.S.

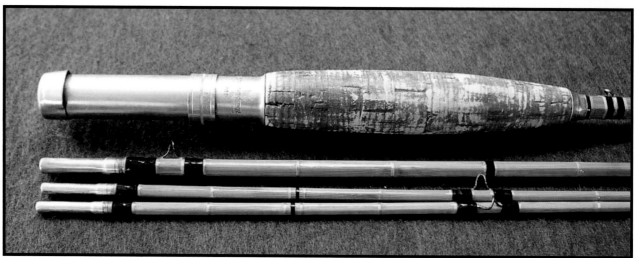

Pictured above is the NiS cap and ring reel seat and the full taper cigar grip along with the male ferrules and the wrap pattern.

Close up of the male ferrules used on Edwards trade rods circa 1920s above left and above right are the male and female ferrules together.

Agate stripping guide and the snake guides and a tiptop from the Winchester #6100 pictured above left and a close up of the reel seat and male ferrules above right.

Pictured to the left is the reel seat stamping "Winchester –Trade Mark- 6100".

And pictured to the right is a close up of the welts on the two female ferrules on the rod.

Montague "Rapidan" Combo Rod circa 1930s 6'x2 and 9', 3/2 and 4/1

*T*he Rapidan model by Montague was one grade up from the bottom in the combination rods. The bottom was the "Eel River. The Rapidan sold for $8.50 in 1939. The 1939 Montague catalog describes the configurations of the rod,

> "The Rapidan combination rod will make a 9ft. fly rod with the reel below hand, or you can reverse the butt for still fishing with reel above hand. You can also make a 6'6" light fly rod, a 6 ft. bait casting or light trolling rod, and a 31/2 ft. bait casting or light trolling rod."

*T*he grip is reversible and is made of 1/2" cork rings. The reel seat and ferrules are NiS plated. And in the photos you will notice the cracked male ferrule, which was a common problem of the cheap low quality plated ferrules made by Montague and used on their low priced rods. The rod is wrapped in yellow silk with red trim wraps and full yellow intermediate wraps.

*T*his rod is from the private collection of John Oppenlander.

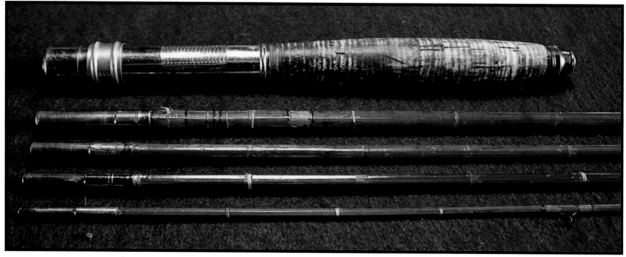

Pictured above is the reversible grip and reel seat. Note the cracked male ferrule on the second section below the grip.

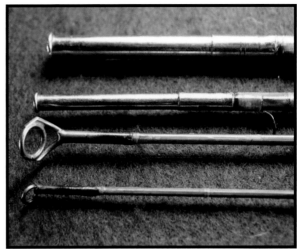

Male Montague ferrules. Note the cracked one. Female ferrules and tiptops from the "Rapidan".

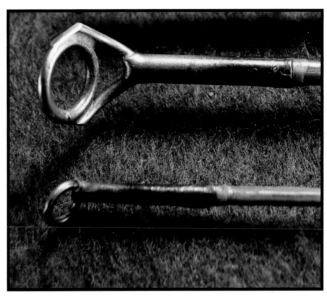

Snake guides and Mildrum style casting guides pictured above left and a close up of the tiptops above right.

Frost type reel seat as described in the ad in the 1939 Montague catalog. How many times have you seen rods with a remnant of a Montague acetate sticker like the one above right? Most stickers self-destruct over time with just a little bit of misuse and improper care.

E.W.Edwards & Sons "Special" Fly Rod 8'6" 3/2 circa 1930s

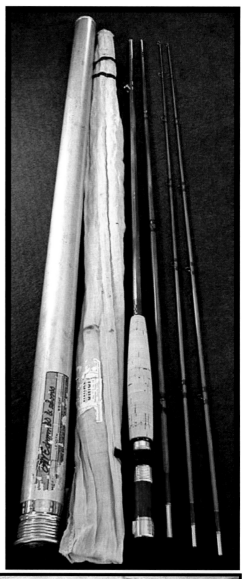

*T*he Horton Mfg. Co. turned out this rod after they purchased the Edwards & Sons Rod Company. It is a Bristol, Connecticut built rod. It has its original cloth bag and aluminum tube. The reel seat is the typical two part walnut barreled seat used by the Edwards. The grip is made of ½ inch cork rings in a cigar style. The stripping guide is an agatine. The snake guides are American twist blued THS. The ferrules are NiS with the Edwards gold trim and deep incised grooves at the base. The rod is wrapped in cinnamon brown silk and has gold trim wraps at the ferrules only and no intermediate wraps.

*T*his rod is from the Harmon Leonard collection and is now in the private collection of John Oppenlander.

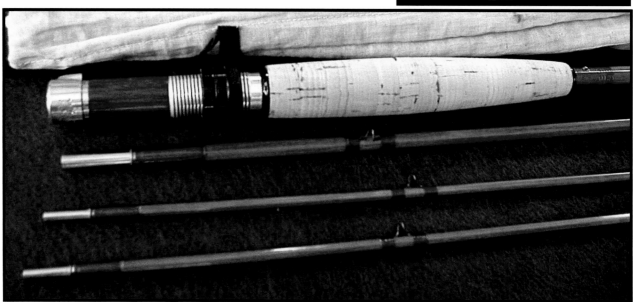

Grip, reel seat, male ferrules and snake guides used on the Bristol Conn. Horton built Edwards special pictured below.

Male and female ferrules used on the "Edwards Special". Agate stripping guide and snakes used by the Edwards on the Special.

Pictured above are the signature "Edwards Special" and the label on the aluminum tube.

To the left is the reel seat and male Edwards's male ferrules.

Bill Edwards,
Bristol Built F-12 Fly Rod
8'6" 3/2 circa 1930s

*T*his is a medium grade rod built by Edwards for Horton of Bristol, Conn. This rod is complete down to its hanging tag, cloth bag and aluminum tube. The reel seat is a cedar insert cap and ring. It has a mild half Wells grip made out of ½" cork rings. The rod is wrapped in black and white jasper silk trimmed with red silk. The rod has no intermediate wraps. The wraps look like black and yellow jasper because of the aging and yellowing of the varnish. The ferrules are NiS and the guides are THS snake guides with a Mildrum stripping guide. The tiptops are perfection tiptops from the Perfection Co from Denver Colorado. At some point a smart owner has shrink-wrapped the hanging tag to protect it and preserve it. I am not sure that it was such a good Idea because if the shrink-wrap goes brittle it may cause injury to the tag inside.

*T*his rod is from the private collection of Richard Collar, D.D.S.

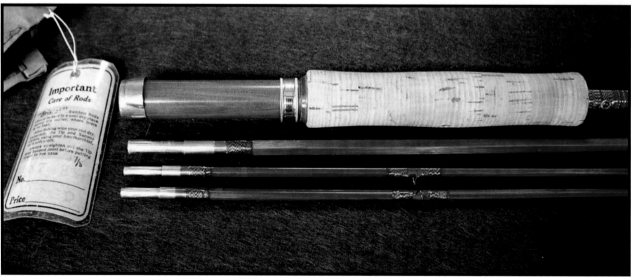

Pictured above are the cedar barreled cap and ring reel seat, the mild half wells grip and hanging tag from the "Bristol F-12".

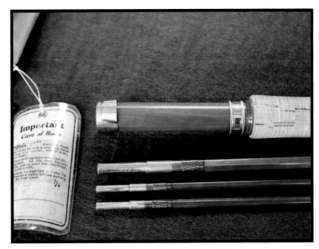

Male and female ferrules from the "F-12" pictured above left. Cedar barreled cap and ring reel seat. Note the similarities to the Divine turned cherry wood reel seats. The turned grip check is an integral part of the reel seat.

Mildrum stripping guide and snakes used on the Bristol 'F-12" above left. The Perfection tiptops are pictured above right.

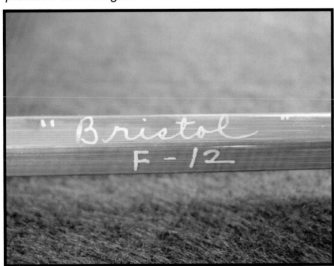

Pictured to the left are the shaft markings.

To the right is some good advice from the hanging tag.

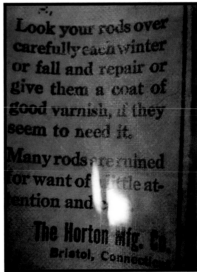

Look your rods over carefully each winter or fall and repair or give them a coat of good varnish, if they seem to need it.

Many rods are ruined for want of a little attention and a

The Horton Mfg. Co.
Bristol, Connecticut

Jay Harvey
Circa 1930's
Lincoln #1 7 ft. 2/1
Heddon Trade Rod.

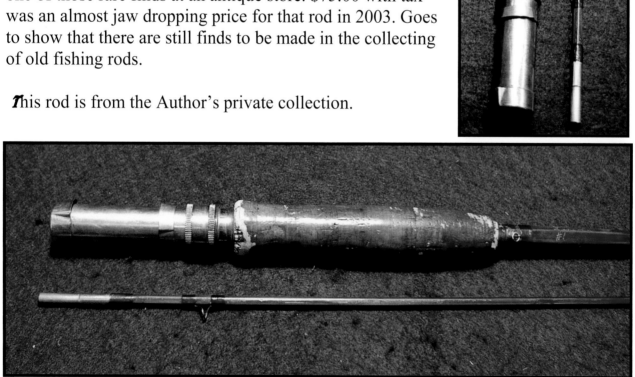

*T*his is another of those odd rods that you cannot find in the Heddon company records. It was probably a special order featherweight trade rod for The Edward K. Tryon Co. of Philadelphia. The Lincoln was the lowest grade sold. It was the equivalent of a Heddon #10 Blue Waters. This rod was at the very bottom of the production line by Heddon. It has non-waterproof rolled welt ferrules and a NiS plated reel seat. Mildrum stripping guide and THS snakes, a round loop tiptop. The rod is wrapped in red silk. It comes with its original cloth bag and is missing one of its tips. This rod was one of those rare finds at an antique store. $75.00 with tax was an almost jaw dropping price for that rod in 2003. Goes to show that there are still finds to be made in the collecting of old fishing rods.

*T*his rod is from the Author's private collection.

Pictured above are the grip and full NiS plated reel seat on the "Jay Harvey, Lincoln # 1 " by Heddon.

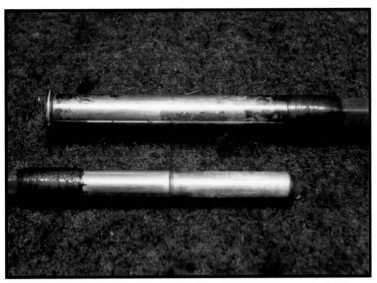

Male and female ferrule from the Jay Harvey rod. Note the condition of the varnish in the photo above right; it has been subjected to too much heat at some point causing the varnish to melt.

Stripping guide and a snake guide above left and the stripping guide and the tiptop above right.

Shaft markings pictured to the left is the Jay Harvey signature and to the right is the Lincoln #1.

South Bend, Fly Rod Cross Double Built 8' 3/2 circa 1930s

*T*his rod is an example of the higher quality rods produced by South Bend Bait & Tackle co. after their acquisition of the Cross Rod & Tackle Co. in 1927. The best part of that merger was South Bend gaining the services of Wes Jordan as their master rod maker. This rod has the aluminum and black bakelite Lite-Lock reel seat with a ½ inch cork ring full Wells grip. The ferrules are the higher quality modified ferrules introduced to by Wes Jordan. The rod is wrapped in white silk with red trim wraps and has full intermediates of white silk. The guides are THS snakes with an agatine stripping guide and the tiptops are Perfection style. The rod has had its shaft markings removed and is in need of a full restoration.

*T*his rod is from the private collection of John Oppenlander.

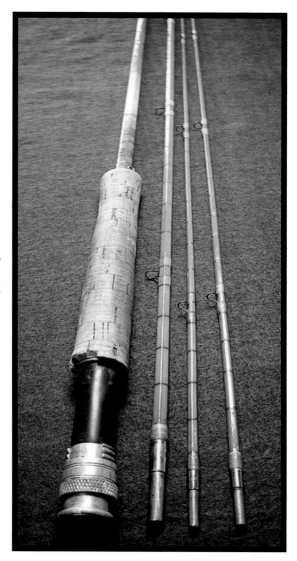

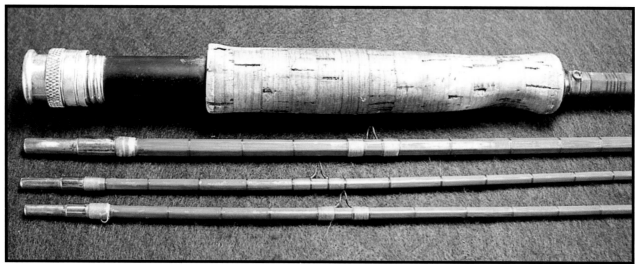

Pictured above is the "Lite-Lock" reel seat, guides, and wrap pattern and male ferrules used on the South Bend Cross Double Built Rod.

South Bend/Cross male ferrules.

South Bend/Cross female ferrules.

Guides used on the S.B. Cross double built.

Close up of the agatine guide.

Cross stampings on the screw band on the reel seat pictured to the left and right. The stamping wrapping around the screw band.

South Bend, Fly Rod Cross Single Built 8' 6" 3/2 circa late 1930s

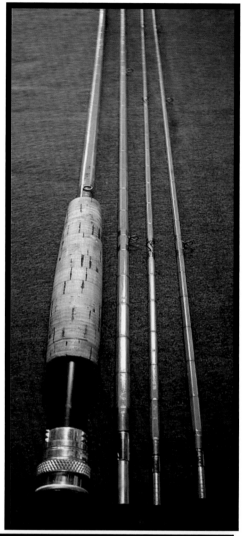

This rod has the typical features of the higher quality rods sold by South Bend. It was competitively priced with the mid to upper grades of such noted makers as Goodwin Granger, James Heddon, and even as competition to Gene Edwards and F.E. Thomas in their lower grades of rods.

This rod has ferrules and a Hardy influenced reel seat that were so prevalent in the twenties and thirties. The rod has snake guides and has perfection style tiptops and a Mildrum stripping guide. The silk is yellow with yellow intermediates and has trim wraps at the ferrules but not on the main wraps. This rod's varnish is soft and tacky and will need a full restoration.

This rod is from the private collection of John Oppenlander.

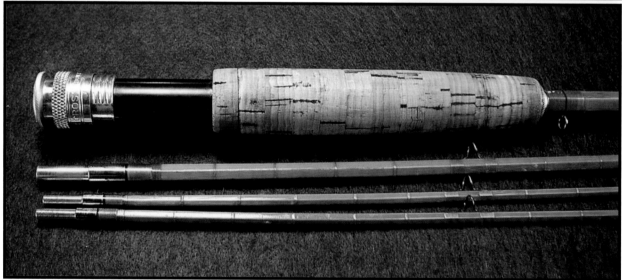

Pictured above is the Hardy style up-locking reel seat used on the "Cross" single built by South Bend Bait and Tackle Co. along with the 1" cork ring cigar grip, snake guides and its characteristic wrap pattern.

Male Cross Ferrules.

Female Cross ferrules and tiptops.

Mildrum stripping guide and snake guides pictured above left. Above right as was the custom at that time the rod is signed by the original owner "JWR '36 ". This is a likely date of manufacture for this rod.

The above set of three photos show the "Single Cross Built" stamping on the screw band of the reel.

South Bend, Casting Rod Cross Double Built 5'6" 2/2 circa late 1930s

*T*his is a casting rod produced by South Bend under the Cross name. The quality of workmanship on this rod is quite high, in keeping with the influences of Wes Jordan. The rod has his Feb. 15th, 1927-patented reel seat. It was assigned the patent number 1,617,951. The rod has Mildrum style guides and is in original condition but is missing its original tube. The cloth bag has survived and the Cross label has worn off, showing the early era South Bend label on the bag underneath the Cross label. The rod is wrapped in red silk and has olive trim wraps. The rod has full intermediate wraps of olive silk. The ferrules are the typical S.B./Cross ferrules of NiS denoting a higher quality rod. The butt cap is a NiS flat round plate screwed into the butt section. The grip is made of ½ inch cork rings. The rod has a fairly elaborate signature wrap.

*T*his rod is from the private collection of John Oppenlander.

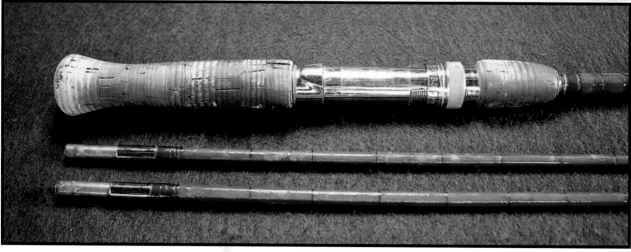

Wes Jordan patented reel seat on the Cross Double built casting rod.

Male Cross Ferrules.

Close up of the welt on the female ferrule.

6861 serial number on the shaft.

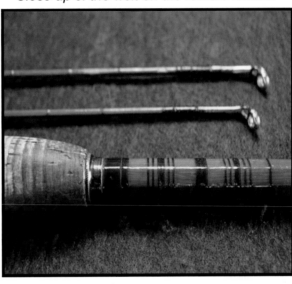

Close up of the winding check and signature wrap.

Wes Jordan patent date and "Double Cross Built" on the sliding band.

Pezon et Michel "Parabolic" Concours Distance 120Gr. Charles Ritz's Personal Rod. Circa 1930s-1940s

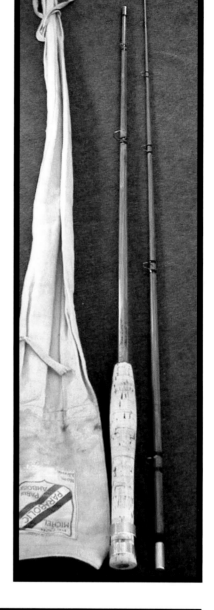

*T*his rod belonged to Charles Ritz, author, and fly fisherman and Motel heir. He was the main benefactor for the Pezon-et Michel rod company of France. This is a competition casting rod that was limited to a weight of not more than 120 grams. The rod shows the efforts that were made to save weight and increase the amount of power fiber within the taper of the rod. The ferrules are a rolled, non-welted, straight and non-waterproof. The slide bands are aluminum and the cork grip was kept to an absolute minimum. This rod is built in the typical short butt, long tip style of a parabolic rod. It has a very large single standing ring for a stripping guide. The rest of the guides are oversize snakes and the tiptop is a classic Perfection style loop tiptop.

*R*ichard Collar, D.D.S. purchased this rod from the Lang,s sporting goods auction in the fall of 2002.

Pictured below is the all cork grip and reel seat with the aluminum sliding bands.

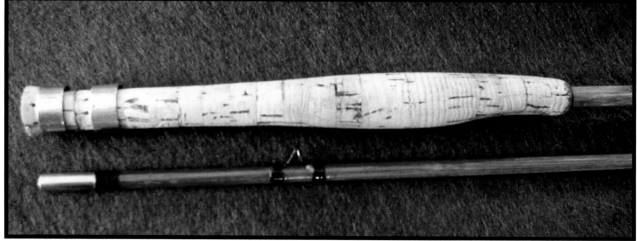

Pezon-Et Michel shaft marking.

Concours Distance 120 gr. Marking.

Oversize stripping guide of wire and the snake guides used on the Ritz Parabolic rod above left and the tiptop and female ferrule above right.

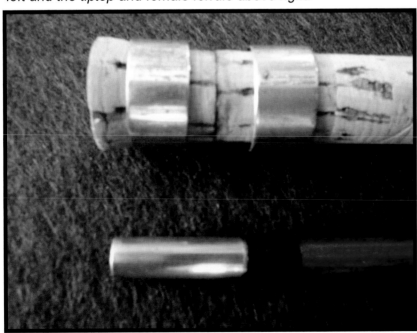

Pictured to the left is a close up of the cork reel seat and the aluminum sliding bands.

Montague Red Wing
9' 3/2
circa 1934 – 1939

*T*he Red Wing and the Manitou were the highest quality rods made by Montague after George I.Varney had left their employment as their head rodmaker. These two models showed the Varney influence until the end of Montague's rod making efforts. Some of those features are a very modern taper in the cane and the high quality NiS components thru out the rod. The ferrules are hand welted and still fit as if they were new. The rod still has its original cloth bag and aluminum tube. Part of the original label is still there. The decal on this rod is one of the most striking ever produced. At that time it was a jab at Heddon's "Rods with Fighting Hearts" logo. The rod is wrapped in red silk with yellow trim wraps. The stripping guide is a Mildrum that is blued. The snake guides are THS and also blued. The rod has its original case and cloth bag.

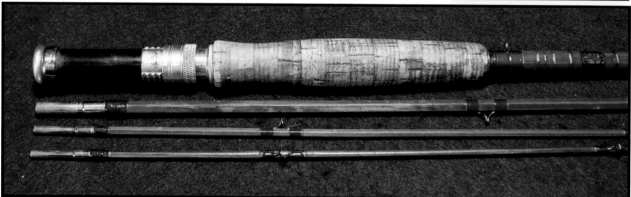

Pictured above is the grip and reel seat and the male ferrules and the snake guides from the 1930s vintage Red Wing by Montague.

Pictured to the right is the hook keeper, the acetate label and the signature wrap on the "Red Wing".

Male ferrules.

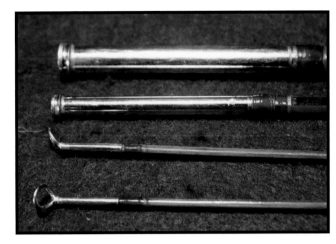

Female ferrules and the tiptops.

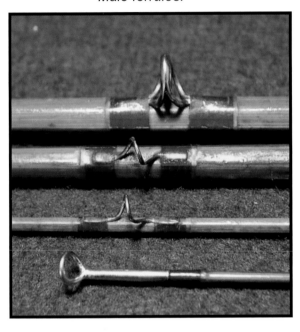

Guides and tiptop.

Close up of the welt on the female ferrule.

Pictured to the left is the winding check and hook keeper and to the right is a close up of the acetate label.

Lyons&Coulson "Captain" Heddon Trade Rod 8'6" 3/2 circa 1936-1953

*T*his L&C Captain is an example of the lowest grade of trade rod made by James Heddon & Sons. Lyons & Coulson was a dealer of fine tackle in Buffalo, N.Y. This rod exhibits classic Heddon traits such as the reel seat, which is the Heddon Hold Tite made of NiS plated brass. The grip is the typical ½ inch cork ring cigar grip equivalent to the grip on the #10 "Blue Waters" model by Heddon. The rod has blued snakes and Perfection style tiptops. The rod is wrapped in black and orange jasper silk and has no trim wraps. The ferrules are NiS plated and straight and with a rolled welt. The stripping guide is an agatine-lined guide. The rod has its original cloth bag. This is a rod that is a very fishable model even today.

*T*his rod is from the private collection of John Oppenlander.

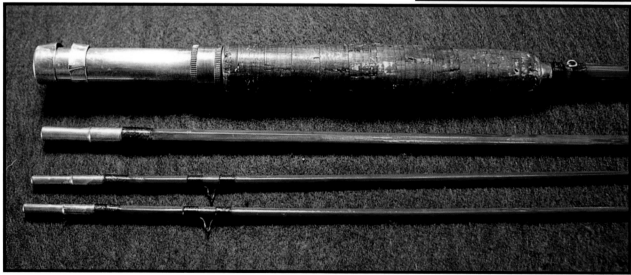

Pictured above are the reel seat and grip, hook keeper, snake guides and male ferrules used on the "L & C Captain #402" trade rod by Heddon & Sons.

Male Heddon trade rod ferrules.　　　　　*Female Heddon ferrules and tiptops.*

Agatine stripping guide and snake guides. Close up of the winding check and hook keeper.

Pictured above are the shaft markings of the "L + C Captain #402" trade rod by Heddon & Sons.

Heddon #20
Bill Stanley's Favorite
8'6" 3/2 Fly Rod
Circa 1938-1939

*T*his was the second model of fly rod introduced by the Heddon Rod Company. It is a fairly easy rod to date due to the down locking pyralin reel seat, the half Wells grip and the fact it is marked #20 and does not say "Bill Stanley's Favorite", which the company added to the signature in the later part of 1939. It is wrapped in maroon and tipped with gold. It has the mid shaft wrap on the butt and no intermediate wraps. This Model 20 was built right in the transition phase of when the model name was added to the spiral rod shaft markings. This dates it to late 1938 or early 1939 quite accurately. The NiS black enameled ferrules also help in the dating of this rod. This rod has its original cloth bag and labeled Heddon rod tube.

*T*his rod is from the Author's collection.

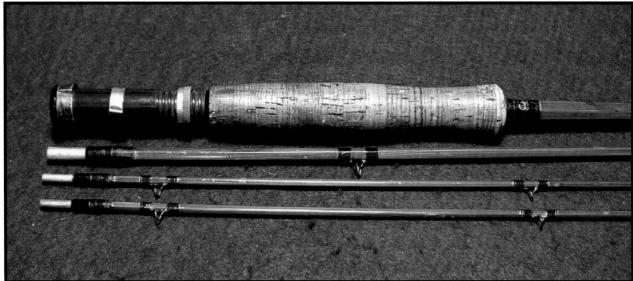

Pictured above is the grip and pyralin reel seat used on the 1930s Heddon # 20 "Bill Stanleys" Favorite.

Male Heddon Ferrules.

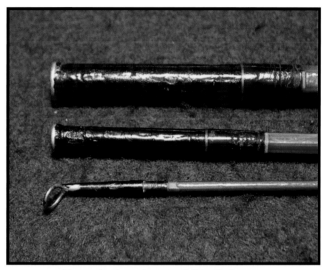

Female ferrules and the tiptop.

Guides and tiptop.   Spiral "Heddon" and the # 20 denoting a manufacture date of the 1930s.

Pictured to the left are the reel seat stampings for the Heddon patented reel seat.

Heddon # 10 Blue Waters
9' 3/2 Fly Rod
circa 1937 – 1947

*T*he Heddon model #10 Blue Waters was introduced in 1934 as a replacement for the #22 Heddon Special. This rod was put into their Complete Fly fishing Outfit's from 1930 to 1934. This rod has the pyralin down locking reel seat in the ivory color, which is not common, and has the heavy cigar grip. The winding check is exposed and the hook keeper is wrapped in the open style. The rod is wrapped in Black and white jasper thread. The ferrules are NiS with a rolled welt.

The guides and tiptops are all Perfection stainless steel. This was Heddon's lowest grade of rod until the introduction of the #8 "The Heddon Fly Rod" in 1951. Bamboo rods were offered for the last time in the 1956 Heddon catalog.

*T*his rod is from the Author's collection.

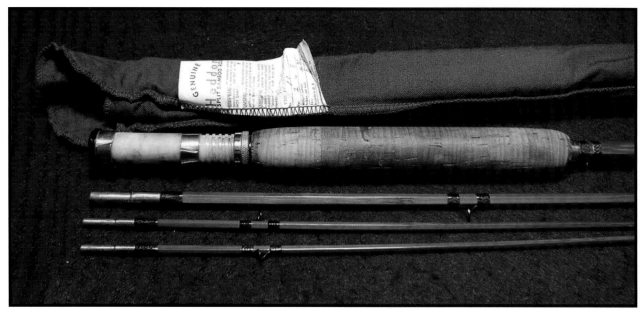

Pictured above are the grip and reel seat and the original cloth bag with its label in immaculate condition.

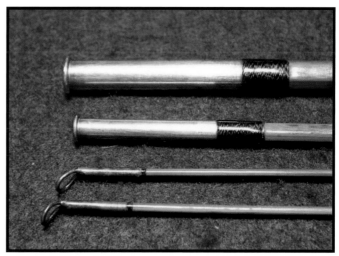

Male ferrules from the Heddon #10 Blue Waters above left and the females and the tiptops above right.

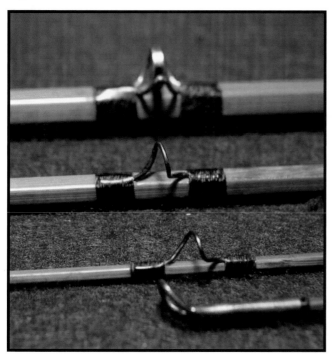

Stripping guide and the snake guides and a tiptop from the Heddon #10 "Blue Waters" {above left}. The two photos above right are the first two of the three sets of shaft markings.

Writing pictured to the left stating "#10-9'-2F-HDH or E" indicating the model number, the ferrule number, and length of rod and the line designation for either a double taper or a level line.

Goodwin Granger "Victory" Denver Co. 9' 3/2 circa 1938-1945

*T*his is the lower grade "Victory" fly rod produced by Goodwin Granger at the end of the company's production era. It has the full NiS Granger patented internal up locking reel seat of 1937. The rod has the classical angular welt on the female NiS ferrules. The rod is wrapped in black and orange jasper silk and has black trim wraps and tip wraps. The rod has no intermediate wraps.

*T*he grip is specie cut ½ inch cork rings in the reversed mild half Wells style that is still one of the most popular grips for 8' to 9' rods of the 5 to 7 weight range to this day. The stripping guide is a chrome plated Mildrum guide. The snake guides are bronze plated the tiptops are Perfection tiptops from the Perfection Co. of Denver Colorado. The rod retains its original cloth bag and its original fiber tube and cap.

*T*his rod is from the Author's collection.

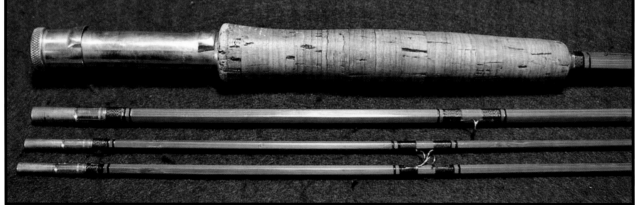

Pictured above are the Granger patented April 12th 1938 pat. No. 2,114,107 reel seat and the reversed mild half Wells grip and the wrap pattern of the Victory fly rod, circa 1938-1945.

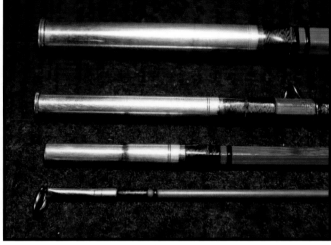

Male ferrules

Female ferrules and the perfection tiptops.

Guides and tiptop are pictured to the left with an ad from 1941 to the right.

To the middle left are the reel seat markings.

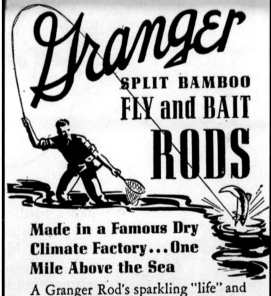

Granger SPLIT BAMBOO FLY and BAIT RODS

Made in a Famous Dry Climate Factory...One Mile Above the Sea

A Granger Rod's sparkling "life" and vibrant action comes from superior construction. Every rod made of finest Tonkin Cane, perfectly seasoned. Built in dry, mile-high air of Colorado. No natural dampness to soften action. Insures tighter joints, longer life. Buy a Granger Rod . . . get a new thrill from fishing. *Write for FREE Catalog.*

GOODWIN GRANGER COMPANY
433 Grant Street, Denver, Colorado

Lower left picture is the label on the fiberboard tube, which states model name and length and weight.

Montague City Rod Co. Splitswitch Casting Rod 5'6" 1/R.G. circa 1939-1949

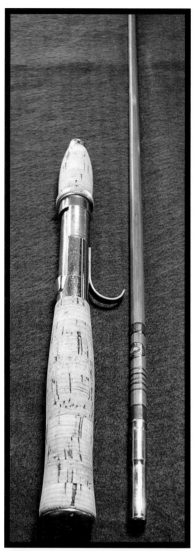

*T*his rod exhibits the most commonly seen Montague decal, and the rods with this decal are the ones you can identify as to model with out the cloth bag and the case. The decal has the model name on it. Note the Wes Jordan 1927 patent style reel seat, which Montague called the scrulock reel seat. This was one level up from the bottom of the single piece rods made by Montague and it originally sold for $7.00. The rod has the typical Montague plated male ferrule. The grip is /2" cork and the rod has a metal butt plate. The rod is wrapped in red silk and has black trim wraps. The guides are Stainless steel and the tiptop is a stainless steel offset tiptop. This rod has seen little use and is in immaculate shape considering that its canvas bag has long since gone away. The sticker on this rod is 100% complete. The finish on the wraps is starting to go and will require a very careful recoat of the wraps. Note the fairly high quality of the cork and the fact it is specie cut. This rod is from the private collection of John Oppenlander.

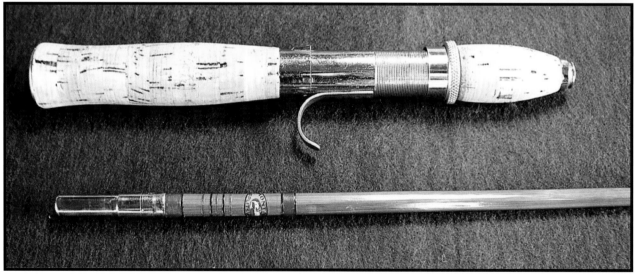

Note the Montague Scrulock reel seat and the signature wraps on the "Splitswitch" pictured above.

Pictured above is the male ferrule from the Splitswitch and to the right is a close up of the female ferrule/ grip check.

Stainless steel casting guide.

Stainless steel offset tiptop.

Montague acetate label with the model name.

Close up of the metal butt plate on the "Splitswitch".

James Heddon & Son's #14 "Thoroughbred" 9' 3/2 circa 1939-1941

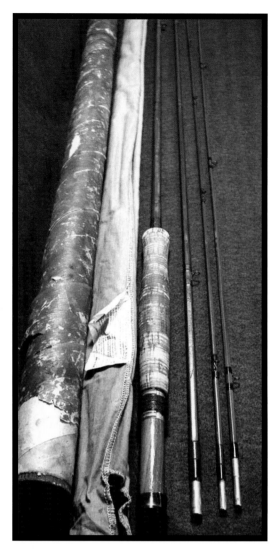

*T*his rod is an example of the Thoroughbred before it evolved into a higher quality rod, as Heddon added lower grades of rods to their line. The markings and quality of components are key features in dating the rod. The spiral Heddon shaft marking along with the rod details written down one flat of the shaft was started in 1939. This rod is marked in that manner. It is wrapped in a deep red silk with black silk trim wraps. The ferrules are the higher-grade darkened ferrules used on the model #17 Black Beauty and higher. The grip is the Heddon half Wells, which also is an aid in dating the rod. Snake guides and Perfection tiptops are used on this rod. This rod was purchased from an online auction where it was listed as a Heddon #10. It was a wonderful surprise to find a model #14 hiding in a model #10 Blue Waters bag.

*T*his rod is from the private collection of John Oppenlander.

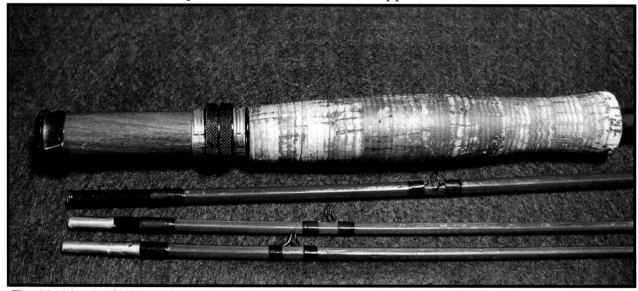

The Heddon half Wells grip, male and female ferrules and the "New Hold Tite" reel seat with the wood insert introduced in 1939.

Male Heddon ferrules.

Female Heddon ferrules.

Stripping guide, snake guide and tiptop.

Spiral Heddon shaft marking.

The "#14 – 9' – 2 ½ F – HCH or D" shaft markings denoting manufacture of 1939 or later.

Lyons & Coulson, Buffalo, N.Y. "Imperial #0241" 7' 2/1 circa 1936-1952 Heddon Trade Rod.

*L*yons & Coulson was one of the many firms that Heddon manufactured rods for. The Imperial was a middle grade rod that was equivalent to a #17 Heddon Black Beauty. The rod has its original tube and bag in excellent condition. This rod was fished a fair amount. It has a slight set in the tip. The rod has blackened ferrules and is wrapped identically to a "Black Beauty" with black wraps tipped with orange. The slide bands for the reel seat are blackened also. It has chrome plated spinning guides and a chrome-plated tiptop. The label on the tube is in outstanding condition. The rod is a classic example of a Heddon trade or private label-spinning rod. The rod is signed in the style of the late classic era Heddon rods. Straight down the shaft on one flat.

*F*rom the private collection Of Mr. John Oppenlander

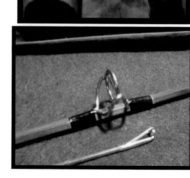

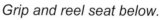

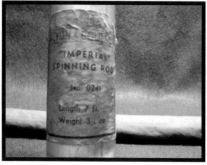
Bag Tag and signature.

Heddon Ferrules.

Spinning guide and tiptop.

Tube label.

Close up of signature.

Grip and reel seat below.

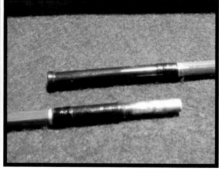

Everret Garrison 209
Q-8-22 7'9" 2/2 Fly rod

Everett Garrison was an engineer by trade and considered himself an amateur rodmaker only. His true place in history is not only well earned but also well deserved as one of the masters of 20th century rod making. The model 209 pictured here was photographed and donated to this project by Mr. Sante L Giuliani 'Fishnbanjo", Many thanks to him for the addition. This rod is built in the classic Garrison style with translucent wraps and the typical Garrison grip and slide band reel seat. This rod is in immaculate condition and is one of the true gems pictured in this book. It has NiS Super Z ferrules. The rod is wrapped in traditional Garrison wraps. The rod making fraternity owes Everett Garrison and Hoagy B. Carmichael a great debt of gratitude for the incredible encouragement and knowledge found in the book that they collaborated on titled " A Masters Guide to Building A Bamboo Fly Rod" Published in 1977 after Mr. Garrison had passed away.

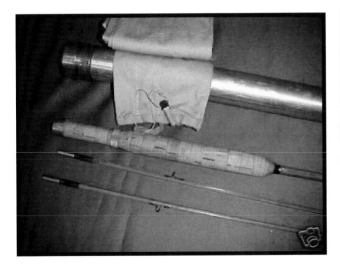

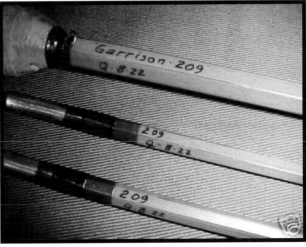

Grip and reel seat and the tube and cloth bag pictured above left and the signature on the butt section and the signature markings on the tips and ferrule wraps above right

Fred DeBell of Denver
Fly/spin Combination Rod
2/1 7' circa1940s-1960s

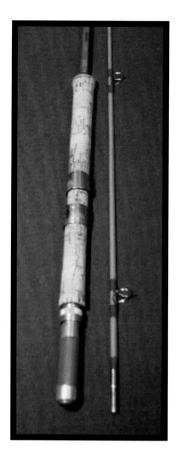

*F*red DeBell was one of the many small time rod makers from Colorado. He made rods for more than 40 years, from slightly before World War II to 1982. It was quite a stretch for a small time maker. He made trade rods. In addition he was a very competent tournament caster and he fished with Bill Phillipson quite a bit. His rods are not known for their cosmetics. His goal was to put a high quality rod in the hands of the fisherman for a very reasonable price. He did this by using as cheap a component as he could find. The rod pictured here is one of the fly-spin combination rods. Not a great spinning rod and it would take a very heavy fly line to load this rod. Like most combination rods, this one was really just adequate for either purpose at best.

DeBell Signature.

Low quality rolled and plated ferrules.

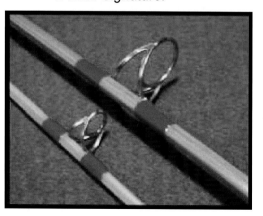

Guides at left

Spinning reel seat slide bands on grip at right.

S.B. # 24 8'6" Fly Rod 3/2 circa 1940s-1950s

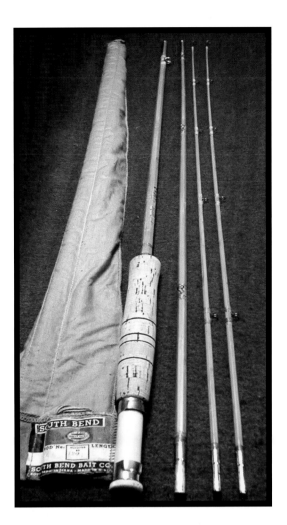

*T*his is the typical South Bend model # 24 in an 8'6" length with its original bag and spare tip. The rod has the South Bend lite lock reel seat in the ivory color, which is fairly uncommon. The rod is wrapped in a red and white jasper thread. It has the South Bend ventilated Comficient grip, which was supposed to be comfortable and efficient all at the same time. It was not a super popular grip but South Bend did put them on rods for 10 plus years.

This rod is from the last period of production cane rods by the South Bend Co. It has plated ferrules with the South Bend rolled welt. It has a Mildrum stripping guide and THS snakes and Perfection tiptops. The bag for this rod is in immaculate shape.

*T*his rod is from the private collection of Mr. John Oppenlander.

Ivory colored plastic lite lock reel seat.

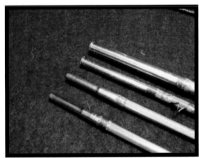
S.B. ferrules.

Hanging tag on the cloth bag.

Model # 24 81/2' shaft marking.

South Bend acetate sticker.

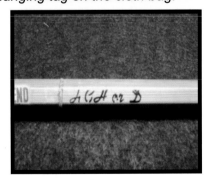
HCH or D line designation.

Heddon "Life Pal"
2030 Steel
Fly Rod 9' 3/2
circa 1940s

Definitely one of the oddest rods you will come across is the Heddon model # 2030. It is made of tubular steel and has NiS ferrules, a pyralin down locking reel seat and the classic Heddon half Wells grip. This rod is in its original cloth bag and aluminum tube. The Hanging tag on the bag is in immaculate condition. A steel rod in this length would have been a real bear to fish because of the weight and tip heaviness of the rod. Talk about a slow-action this rod has it. The shaft of the rod was painted to simulate Bamboo. The rod is signed in gold script towards the grip. It is wrapped in maroon thread. The "Life-Pal Steel" rods were also made in a casting rod.

The steel rods can trace their lineage back to the steel rods by Horton Manufacturing done before 1900.

This rod is from the Author's collection.

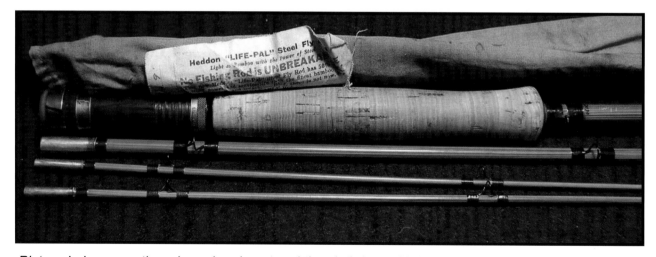

Pictured above are the grip and reel seat and the cloth bag with its tag. Note the red butt cap, which was a feature of Heddon rods during that time frame.

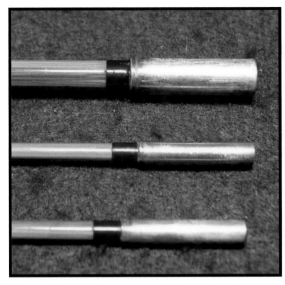

Male ferrules.

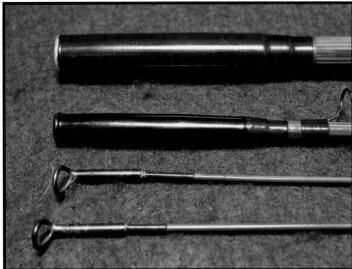

Female ferrules and the tiptops.

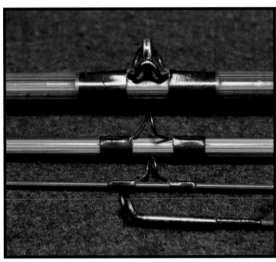

Guides and the tiptop.   Close up of the bottom of the male tip ferrules with one having lost its waterproof cap, which shows the hollow tubular steel construction.

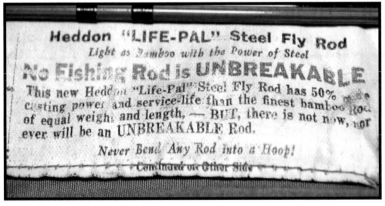

Pictured above are the bag label to the left and the shaft markings " Heddon #2030" and the hook keeper to the right.

Lyle Dickerson, Michigan 8015 Guide Special 8' 2/2 circa 1940s

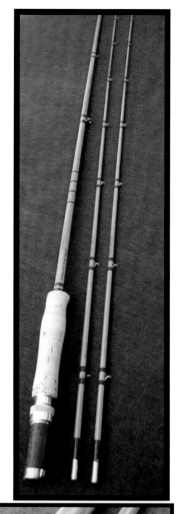

*L*yle Dickerson was one of the Classic era rodmakers who pushed the envelope as far as he possibly could with his rod tapers. Today the Dickerson rods are the epitome of a high quality fast action Fly rod made out of Tonkin cane. His tapers are copied today by many of the modern rodmakers. The 8015 Guide Special was designed as a rod for making long accurate casts under way less than ideal conditions. The rod is a very powerful rod and yet still retains that essence of delicacy that is only available with bamboo.

*T*he rod is wrapped with his typical wrap pattern of the 1940s. The rod has Super Z Style ferrules of NiS. The rod has aluminum down locking reel seat with a wood spacer. The rod has the typical full wells grip that Mr. Dickerson used on his heavier rods.

*T*his rod is from the private collection of Richard Collar, D.D.S.

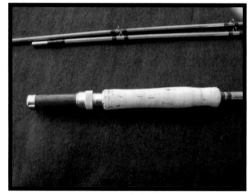

Dickersons full Wells grip.

Stripper and snake guides

Signature and model to the left and the Dickerson ferrules to the right.

E.F. Payne "Parabolic" 7'1" Fly Rod circa 1940s

*T*his is one of the rarest and most coveted of all of the small rods by The E.F.Payne Rod Company. The company traces its lineage as rod makers back to Ed Payne who was one of the true masters of split cane rods. Ed Payne was one of the last makers of the Kosmic and Isaac Walton signatured rods at the turn of 19th to 20th centuries. This rod has its original aluminum tube and cloth bag with its hanging tag and is in mint condition. The butt cap has the Payne stamping on it. The grip and reel seat are all cork. The serial number is 39903 and the rod is 7' 1" and weighs 2 ¾ ounces. The hanging tag on this rod is in very good condition. It is wrapped in the classic Payne colors of brown tipped with gold or tan silk. Abercrombie & Fitch originally sold this rod. Harmon Leonard has honored me greatly by allowing me to photograph his collection for this work.

Male and female ferrules at left.

Grip and reel seat at right.

Pictured below from left to right be the snake and stripping guide, the hanging tag and the hook keeper.

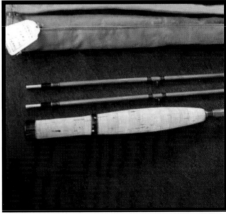

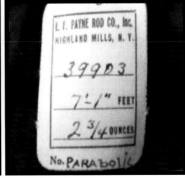

William E. Edwards Quadrate Fly rod 8' 3/2 #34 Circa 1940s

*T*his is the lower grade of the quadrate rod produced by William "Bill" Edwards after he and his son Scott had formed their own company. They left the Bristol rod Company in the late 1930s. The model # 34 was the 8-foot version of the 30 series of quadrate or four-strip rods. Their hardware even included a square grip check and ferrules that transitioned from round to square to fit the square shaft of the cane. The grip and reel seat are ½" cork rings. The reel seat is an aluminum cap and ring. The guides are chrome plated American twist snakes with a Mildrum style-stripping guide. The tiptops are Perfection style tiptops. The ferrules are NiS and are hand made. The rod is wrapped in red silk and has no intermediate wraps or trim wraps. This rod is a true powerhouse of a casting tool and is also very delicate at the same time. I have had the great pleasure of casting this rod, which is from the private collection of Richard Collar, D.D.S.

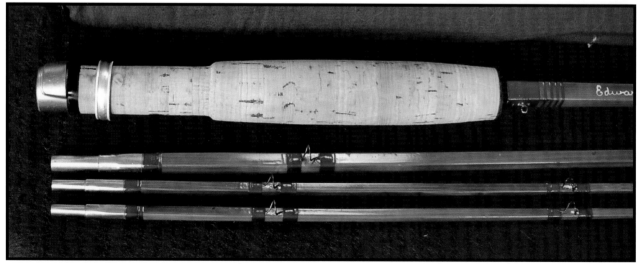

Pictured above are the cap and ring reel seat and grip, male ferrules and snake guides used on the "Edwards Quadrate #34". Note the grip check, which transitions from the round grip to the square rod.

Ferrules used on the Edwards #34 Quadrate rod above left and above right are the snake guides, tiptop and stripping guide from the model #34 quadrate.

Edwards "Quadrate" shaft marking.

#34 shaft marking.

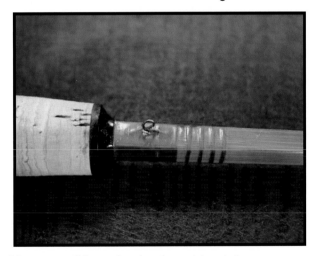

Close up of the cap and ring hardware above left. Close up of the grip check and hook keeper and the signature wrap above right. Note the square shaft of the quadrate rod in the photo above right.

R.L. Winston 8'6" 2/1 Fluted Hollow Built Fly Rod circa 1940s-1950s

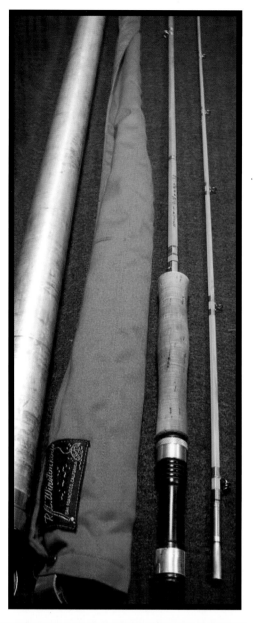

*T*he R.L. Winston Company of San Francisco California made this rod. Their fluted hollow built rods were very light while still retaining a great amount of backbone. This rod has been in one family since it was new. It has a Full wells grip and a typical Winston Screw down locking real seat. The guides are all double wrapped at the end of the guide foot just in front of the beginning twist of the guide for extra strength. It is wrapped in tan and scarlet silk and is serial numbered #8610. It is in immaculate condition. It still has its original rod sock and aluminum tube with the original labels still in great shape. The close-up photos show that even the Winston Company on occasion let a rod out with visible glue seams. This rod is one powerhouse of a casting instrument and quite beautiful. This rod is from the private collection of Mr. Wayne Alfano, given to him by his uncle who was the original owner of the rod.

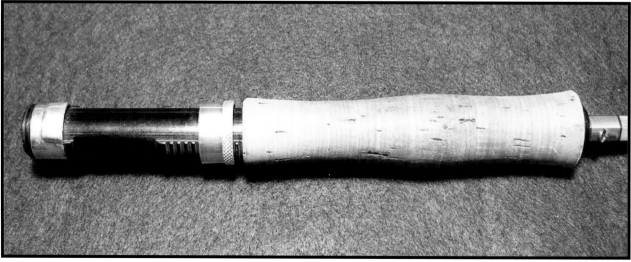

Pictured above are the grip and reel seat from the Winston rod.

Male and female Winston ferrules.

Stripping guide and snake guide.

Shaft signature markings in the above row of pictures including the patent number for the Winston hollow built method.

Pictured to the left is the visible glue seam on the butt section.

Pictured to the right is the serial number and the stripping guides and the wrap pattern.

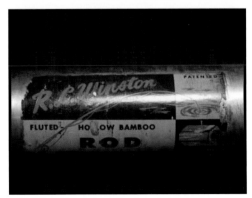

Pictured to the left is the tube label and to the right is the bag label.

Montague City Rod Co.
Fly Rod Rapidan
9' 3/2 circa 1940s-1950s

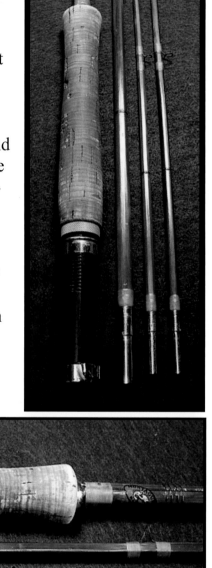

This Rapidan was originally sold for a grand total of $8.00 in the late 1930s. Montague considered the Rapidan as the top of the low priced rods in their line at that time. It has the Montague scrulock reel seat with a half Wells grip made of ½ inch cork rings. The snake guides are tungsten steel with an agatine stripping guide. The tiptops are Perfection style steel. The rod is wrapped in yellow silk and has a single red intermediate wrap between the guides. The ferrules are rolled welt with the Montague-bronzed nickel-plated. The rod has its original cloth bag and cardboard tube, which was described in the 1939 catalog as a "Black leather grain finish fibre case". The Rapidan model was sold in three lengths 8 1/2 ft at 5 1/2oz., 9 ft. at 6 oz. and 9 ½ ft at 6½ oz. As a group the Rapidan fly rods were not light rods and it is no wonder they had ferrule problems on a frequent basis.

This rod is from the private collection of John Oppenlander.

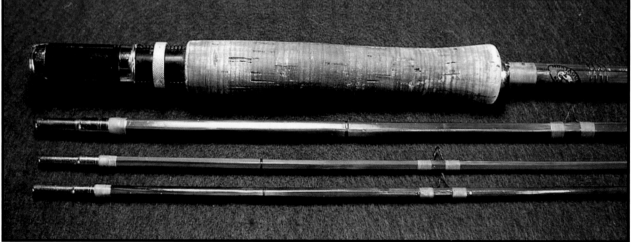

Pictured above are the Montague Scrulock reel seat and half Wells grip, acetate sticker, male ferrules, and the snake guides and wrap pattern.

Male Montague plated ferrules.   Female ferrules showing the classical shape of the Montague ferrule

Montague guides above. Note the rust from improper storage or the rod was put up wet. Signature wraps and acetate sticker pictured above right.

Pictured at the left is a close up of the Montague Scrulock reel seat and the male ferrules.

Goodwin Granger, Granger Deluxe *7' 2/2* Denver, Co. circa 1941

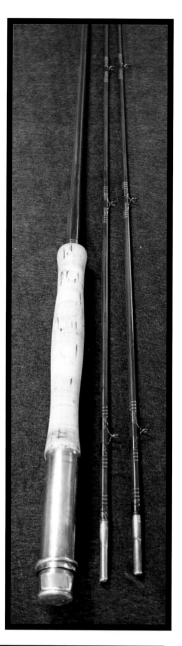

*T*his rod can be dated very accurately by the hardware on the rod. The reel seat in particular dates this rod to 1941. This research material can be found in the great book "Colorado Classic Cane" written by Michael Sinclair and Dick Spurr. The rod has Granger angular welt NiS ferrules that are pinned. The reel seat is a NiS cap and ring that is signed. The rod shaft also has the gum rubber-stamping of the rods grade. The grip is the elliptical half Wells or hammer handle grip of ½" cork rings that was developed by Bill Phillipson while he was shop foreman at the Goodwin Granger Rod co. The rod is wrapped in black and white jasper silk and has yellow silk trim wraps and tip wraps. The stripping guide is a Mildrum and the snake guides are THS that is blued. The rod has Perfection tiptops. It has its original case and cloth bag. This is a fairly rare rod because of the fact that not very many of this length of this model were made in 1941 partly due to material shortages in World War II. This is a rod from the last years of production at the Granger Rod Co. and is truly a pleasure to cast. It has a combination of both power and delicacy. This rod is from the private collection of Richard Collar, D.D.S.

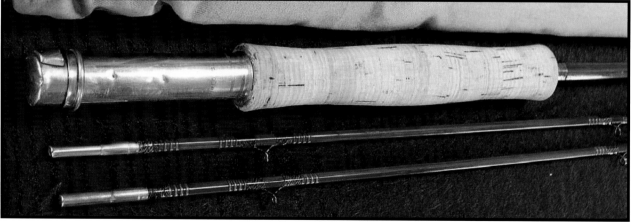

Pictured above is the NiS cap and ring reel seat, Granger/Phillipson elliptical Wells or hammer handle grip, snake guides and male ferrules.

Male and female Goodwin Granger ferrules.

Mildrum stripping guide and THS snakes.

"Granger Deluxe" gum rubber stamp mark.

Reel seat stamping above.

The Goodwin Granger Company was in business from 1918 to 1946 when the Wright & McGill fishing tackle firm of Denver Colorado leased it. Granger Rods and Perfection Tiptops are two of the firms that helped make the state of Colorado into the stronghold of tackle and rod making that it has been for the last eighty plus years. The castability of the Granger rods has become almost legendary, as are the tapers that Goodwin Granger developed. Many small time rod makers are still emulating them today and there has been talk of the Granger Rod Company pulling a Phoenix trick and rising from the ashes. We hope that it does rise from the ashes and that they are able to maintain the quality and integrity of the Granger name because they are truly a pleasure to fish.

Gene Edwards "Deluxe #52" Mount Carmel, Conn. 8' 2/2 circa 1945-1955

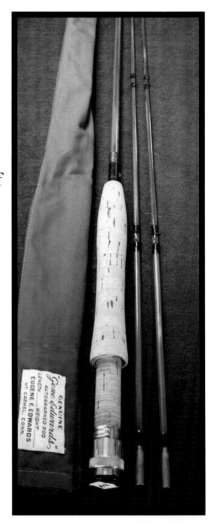

*T*his rod is a classic from the last, of three generations of rodmaking by the Edwards family. Gene Edwards built this rod after he had reacquired the rodmaking tools and equipment from the Bristol Co. in 1945. It is a "Deluxe" #52 in the two-piece configuration. The reel seat is aluminum up-locking with a cork insert with the front hood hidden in the first ring of the cork grip, which is a ½ Wells full taper style. The ferrules are super Z ferrules designed by Lou Fierabend. It is still the standard that all other ferrules are measured against. The rod is wrapped in dark brown with red trim wraps. The snake guides are THS that have been blued. The tiptops are Perfection style tiptops. This rod was obtained at the January 3rd 2004 auction held by Langs Sporting Collectables Inc. and is now in the private collection of Richard Collar, D.D.S.

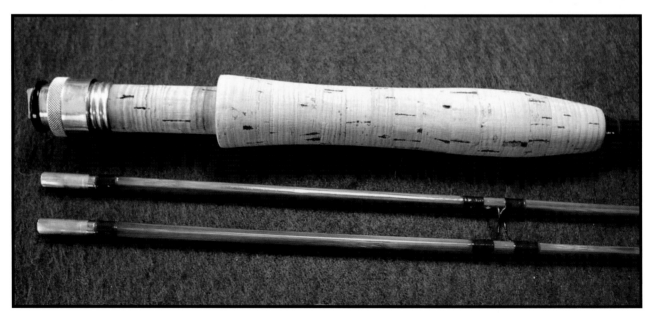

Pictured above are the grip and reel seat, male Super Z ferrules and the snake guides on the Gene Edwards Autographed Deluxe #52 as well as the wrap pattern that was typical to that rod.

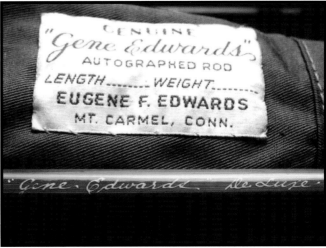

Stripping guide and snake guide and the Perfection tiptop pictured above left and to the above right is the bag label and the signature on the shaft of the butt section.

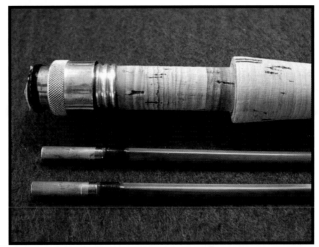

Close up of the Super Z ferrules on the deluxe #52 above left. Cork insert aluminum skeleton reel seat and the male super Z ferrules above right.

Pictured above is the shaft signature " Gene Edwards" Deluxe #52. Note how yellow the signature appears to be due to the aging and yellowing of the varnish over the signature, which is actually white.

Gene Edwards, Fly Rod
Mount Carmel, 1945-1955
7'6" 2/2, Model # 52

*T*his rod is an example of the finest work done by Gene Edwards after World War II. In 1945 he made arrangements with the Bristol Company to acquire the old stocks of equipment and cane left from the Bristol-Edwards production period of 1931-1945. This rod is the epitome of a truly high quality production rod by one of the sons of the old Masters. The rod has the classical features of the high-grade "Gene Edwards Autographed" rods, from the reversed half Wells cork grip to the Edwards ferrules and meticulous wrap and finish work. The reel seat is aluminum up locking with a wood insert. The rod is wrapped in dark brown silk tipped with yellow. The rod has Perfection tiptops and blued THS snake guides. The stripping guide is a blued Mildrum guide. The rod is in its original case and has its original cloth bag and hanging tag. This rod is from the private collection of Richard Collar, D.D.S.

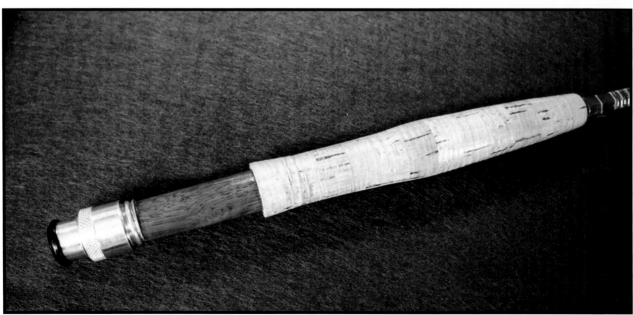

Pictured above are the grip and reel seat of the "Gene Edwards Autographed #52". Note the signature wrap.

Male and female Edwards's ferrules. Mildrum stripping guide with the snake guide and Perfection style tiptop.

Shaft signature markings pictured above left and right.

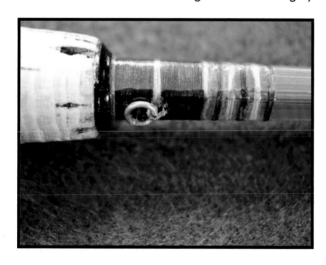
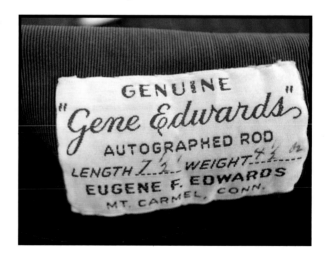

Hook keeper and signature wrap.

Sewn cloth bag label.

Old Faithful Rod Co. Challenger Fly Rod 8' 3/2 circa 1945-1953

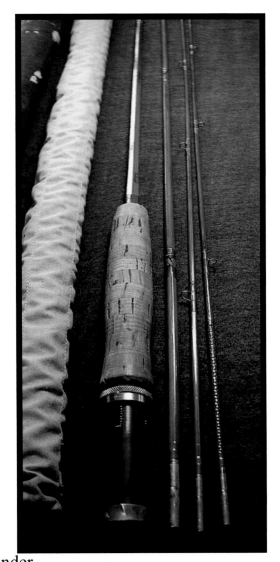

*T*his rod is an example of the trade rods produced by Wright & McGill of Denver Co. for the Old Faithful Rod Co. of 5th and Grant Street, also of Denver, Colorado. This rod has been refinished and is the rod that John Oppenlander's mother grabbed first on their many trips to the upper Fryingpan River during their yearly vacations there. It is a typical example of the quality of rod produced by W&McG as a trade rod I.E. lower quality cane work resulting in the spiral reinforcing wraps that had to be put on to keep the rod fishing {It was an old faithful in many respects and not in some others}. The ferrules are Granger ferrules and are made of NiS with the typical granger welt. The grip is a mild reversed half Wells made of ½ inch cork rings with an aluminum down-locking reel seat. It is wrapped in the original color nylon thread. This rod is from the private collection of John Oppenlander.

Aluminum reel seat and the Granger reversed half Wells grip and the male Granger ferrules. Note the very distinct resorcinol glue lines in the first tip.

Male Granger ferrules.

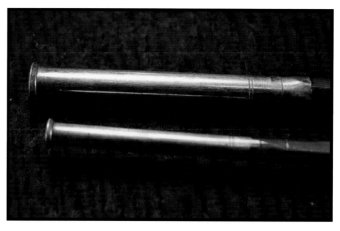

Female Granger ferrules, note the angular welt.

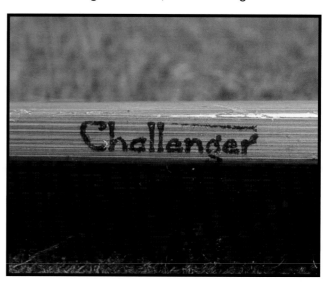

Chrome stripping guide and the snake guides.   *Challenger Butt shaft stamping. Note the similarity to the style of stampings on the Wright & McGill Granger bamboo rods.*

Rod tube label at left.
Close up of the last cork on the grip with the fly dig damage. I was honored to see a couple of the fly's stuck in there by Mom Oppenlander on our visits on the "Pan".

Paul H. Young Rod Co. "Perfectionist" 7'6" 2/2 circa 1945-1970

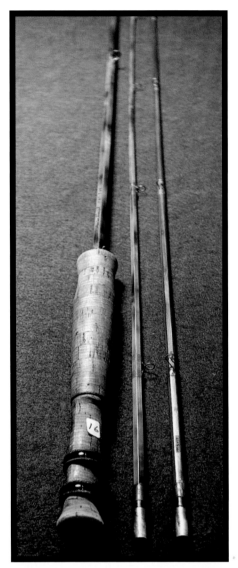

*T*his rod is an example of the work of the Detroit, Michigan Company of Paul Young. This rod has a serial number in the four thousands indicating a date of manufacture to be towards the later part of the 1945 to 1970 time frame. This rod is a true pleasure to cast and is one of the finest rods produced by any of the upper mid west rod makers. The rod has a flame treated shaft with the typical hardware used by the Young Rod Co. The grip and reel seat are made of specie cut ½" cork rings and the guides are American twist snake guides out of THS then blued. The tiptops are Perfection style tiptops. The rod is wrapped in yellow silk and has no intermediate wraps or embellishments of any kind. The reel seat hardware is blackened aluminum slide bands. The ferrules are also blued / blackened.

*T*his rod is from the private collection of Harmon Leonard, DVM.

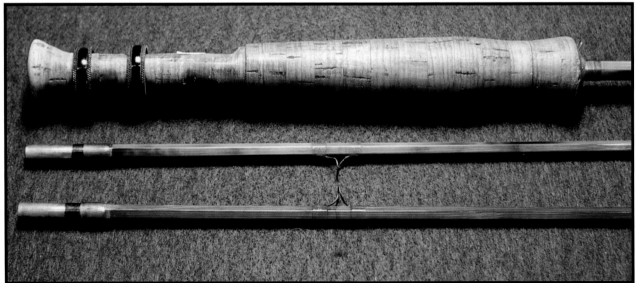

Pictured above are the cork reel seat and grip with the two aluminum slide bands for the reel seat hardware.

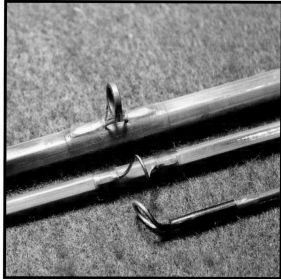

Ferrules from the "Perfectionist" rod.

Guides and tiptop.

Pictured to the left is a close up of the serial numbers on the tips, notice that the one in front has been rewrapped or restored. You can tell this by the edges of dark varnish that are evident in the photograph.

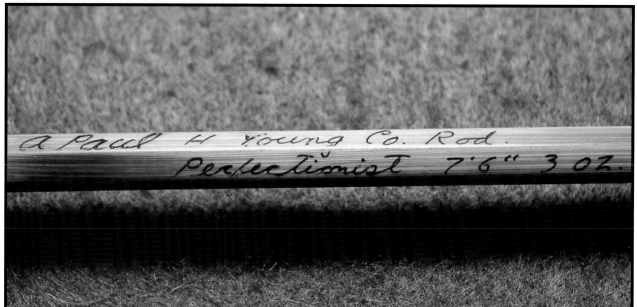

Pictured above are the shaft markings of " A Paul H Young Co. Rod. Perfectionist 7'6" 3 oz."

Lyle Dickerson, Mich.
8013 2/2 8'
Circa 1949

This eight-foot rod the 8013 is one of the less seen models by Lyle Dickerson. The 8012 was the lighter version of this rod and it is documented that he made only two of the 8012. This rod is a classic example of Mr. Dickerson's work from the translucent wraps to the grip, which is a reversed half Wells full taper made out of ½ inch cork rings. The reel seat is a down-locking wood insert with aluminum hardware. The wraps are tipped and are done in silk. The ferrules are Super Z ferrules. The guides are THS snake guides and the tiptops are Perfection tiptops.

The smoothness of the cast with this rod is almost unbelievable. I have had the great pleasure of casting it a couple of times and it is one of the rods by Dickerson that really surprised me with its delicacy and power at the same time. This rod is from the private collection of Richard, Collar D.D.S.

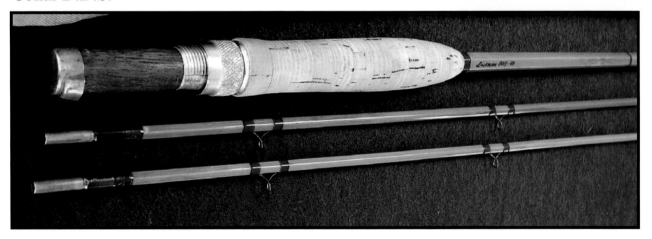

Pictured above are the grip and reel seat, wraps and guides and the male Super Z ferrules used by Lyle Dickerson.

The rods by Lyle Dickerson are some of the most sought after of the Classic Era rods. Their casting and fishing abilities is the equal of the work of almost any other maker of that era. Today Dickerson tapers for faster action bamboo rods are widely used by modern makers.

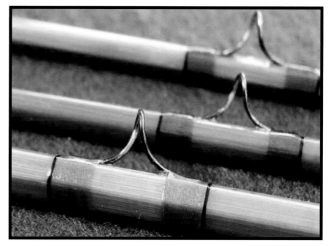

Super Z ferrules used by Dickerson above left and the wraps and guides above right.

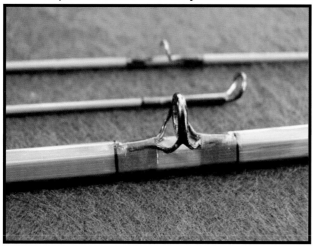

Stripping guide and tiptop.

Signature wraps on the butt section.

"Dickerson 8013-'49" signature on the butt shaft above the grip.

Bill Phillipson, Denver, Co.
Phillipson "Paragon"
8'6" 3/2 now 3/1
circa late 1940s-early1950s

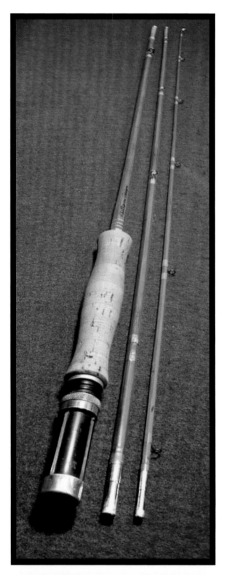

*B*ill Phillipson learned the craft of making bamboo rods under the tutelage of Goodwin Granger, at the end of the Granger rod company's tenure in business he was their head rod maker, and remained as the head rod maker for a short time after the change of ownership from Granger to Wright& McGill. In 1946 Bill Phillipson started the Phillipson rod Co. The "Paragon" was the lowest priced rod sold by Phillipson at $19.75. This rod has a ½ inch cork ring full Wells grip and a plastic reel seat with an aluminum butt cap and down-locking threaded band. The stripping guide is a black Mildrum style with blued American twists snake guides and a Perfection tiptop. The snake guides are THS guides. The rod is wrapped in beige nylon thread.

*T*his rod is from the Author's collection.

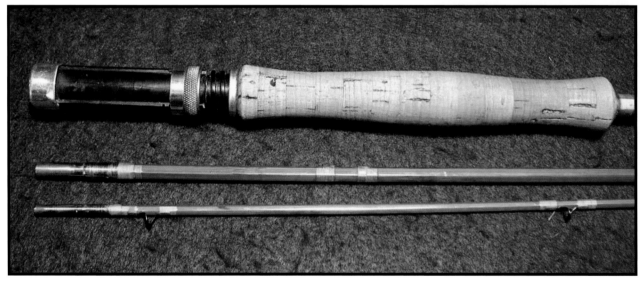

Pictured above are the grip and reel seat from the Phillipson "Paragon".

Male ferrules.

Female ferrules and the Perfection tiptop.

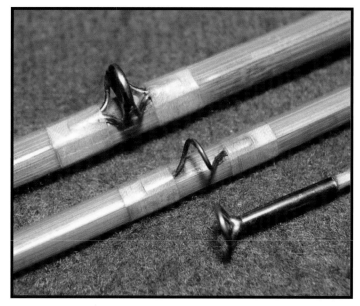

Guides and the Perfection loop tiptop.

Close up of the Phillipson welt on the female ferrule.

Close up of the very low quality plastic and aluminum reel seat on the "Phillipson Paragon" above left and above right is the signature on the blank.

Horrocks & Ibbotsons "Cascade" 8'6" 3/2 circa 1945-1950s

This is an example of the "Hexi-Super cane" rods by H&I. It was a combination of two things that has made these rods the dogs they are. First was the use of a chrome vanadium steel core in the rod similar to what Hardys and the Foster Brothers of England did with some of their rods from around the time frame of 1890-1930. This rod has a plastic reel seat that is an aid in age determination. Post World War 2 due to the plastic. The other thing that H&I did was to impregnate their rods. They did it with a creosote resin that was touted as being clear thru the blank. It was and the resin they used was a horribly heavy addition to the rod's finished weight. The fact that they went ahead and varnished over the impregnated blank, which needed no additional protection also added to the weight. The rod has chrome plated hardware components from the reel seat to the ferrules. The snake guides are THS. The rod is wrapped in dark olive silk thread with black silk trim wraps This rod is very heavy and, is not real fun to fish for a long period of time. The rods last time on the water saw a pretty fair caddis hatch on the lower Gunnison River.

This rod is from the Author's collection.

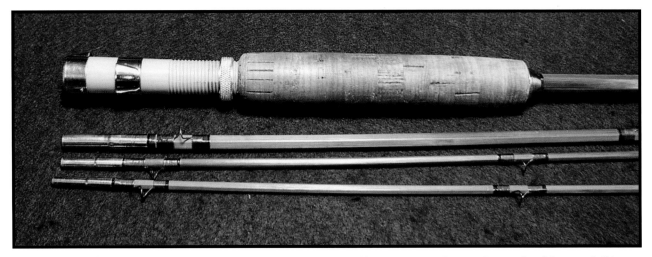

Pictured above are the plastic insert reel seat and the ½" cork ring cigar grip on the "Cascade" by H&I post World War II.

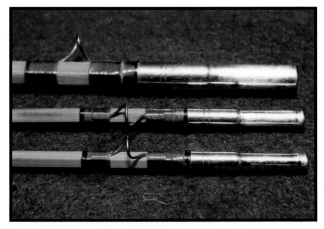

Male ferrules and the snake guides.

Female ferrules and the tiptops.

Pictured to the left is a close up of the guides and the tiptop and the wrap pattern of the Horrocks & Ibbotsons "Cascade" Hexi-Super cane rod from the late 1940s or the early 1950s.

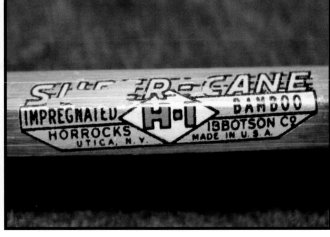

Pictured above are the shaft marking and the acetate label on the "Cascade".

Denverod " Pikes-Peak" Johnson Tackle Denver Co. 9' 3/1 circa 1950s

*T*his is a rod that shows the collusion amongst smalltime Rodmakers and the W & McG Co. If this rod was not made by Johnson tackle, it is a trade rod of W & McG. If Johnson Tackle made it, they used W & McG Granger components. Note the welt on the ferrule and the fact it is not serrated and is a swaged fit. It is identical to the other rods from that time frame in my collection that were produced by W & McG. The ferrules are NiS. The rod is wrapped in silk and has no intermediate wraps but it does have a spiral trim wrap on the guide wraps. The reel seat is all aluminum and is similar to the reel seats used by Bill Phillipson. The rod has a Mildrum style-stripping guide and the snake guides are THS that has been bronzed. The tiptop is a Perfection tiptop. The grip is a full Wells made out of specie cut ½" cork rings. The "Pikes-Peak" was the lowest quality rod that was sold by Johnson Tackle during their brief tenure as a tackle company selling Bamboo rods in the early 1950s. Rods from this company are not seen on a frequent basis but are not really rare. This rod has a serial number just under one million. The serial number is 905,485, which indicates a fairly serious number of Denverods are hiding out there somewhere.

*T*his rod is from the Author's collection.

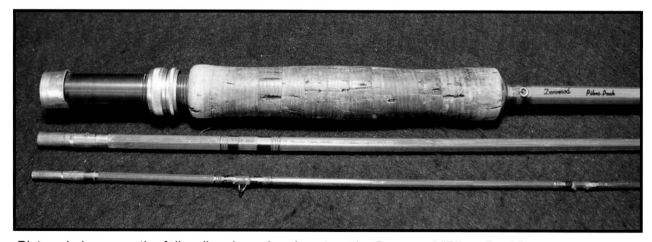

Pictured above are the full wells grip and reel seat on the Denverod "Pikes-Peak".

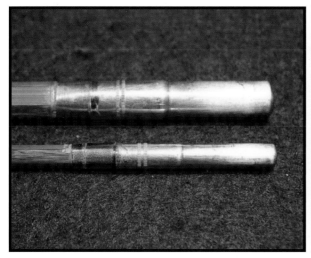

Male ferrules.

Female ferrules and the Perfection tiptop.

Stripping guide and snake guide.

Aluminum reel seat from the "Pikes-Peak".

Pictured above are the shaft markings "Denverod Pikes-Peak" and to the left is a close up of the serial number 905485 on the shaft.

Fiberglass Rods Circa 1950s-1970s H&I, Shakespeare, Heddon

Pictured on these two pages are a representative group of fiberglass rods covering the end of the Classic era the 1950's and up into the modern era to the 1970's. The rods from left to right are a circa 1950's H&I Mohawk fiberglass "Gunnison" model. The next rod is a Shakespeare wonder rod from the 1970s followed by another Wonder rod. The white one is circa 1960s and the last rod in the row is a Heddon Life Pal bass rod is circa 1970s. The Fiberglass rods were the invention of Arthur Howald of the Shakespeare Company right after World War II. The Fiberglass rods held a place of domination within the fishing rod market until they were replaced in the early to mid 1970s by graphite rods.

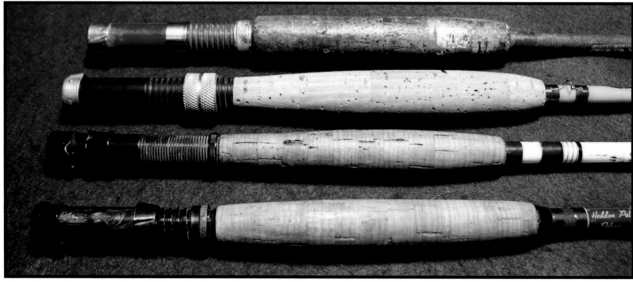

Reel seats and grips pictured above top to bottom are the H&I Gunnison, The 1970s Wonderod then the 1960s Wonderod followed by the 1970's Heddon Deluxe pal rod.

Pictured to the left is the acetate label from the H&I fiberglass rod.

Pictured above are two views of the acetate label on the circa 1970s Shakespeare Wonderod.

Pictured above are two photos of the circa 1960s Wonderod by Shakespeare.

Pictured to the left is the Heddon label on the Heddon Pal Deluxe circa 1970's.

Payne Rod Co.
Model #98, Fly rod
7' 2/2 circa 1951-1970

*T*his rod by Jim Payne is a true powerhouse of a short rod. I have cast this rod and a couple of rods by modern makers based on this taper and they all are consistently fast action rods. Not quite the typical medium to slow action expected of a bamboo rod and it is due mostly to two things, the taper and the heat treatment of the cane. This rod has the typical Payne up-locking wood insert aluminum reel seat with a ½ inch cork ring reversed wells full taper grip. The snake guides and the stripping guide are blued, as are the ferrules. The rod is wrapped in the classic Payne colors of dark brown tipped with gold. The thread used is silk. The tiptops are Perfection tiptops. The rod has its original cloth bag and aluminum tube and the hanging tag is still with the cloth bag.

*T*his rod is from the private collection of Richard Collar, D.D.S.

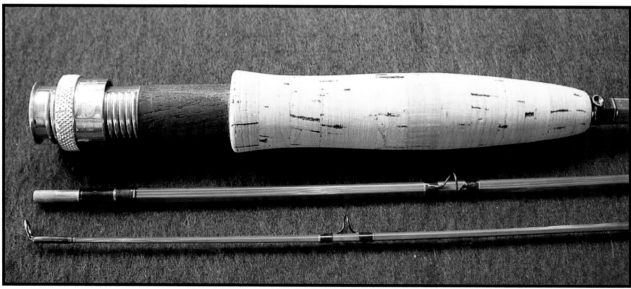

Reel seat, grip and snake guides and the hook keeper used by Jim Payne on the 7' Payne model #98. Note the classical Payne dark brown with gold trim wraps.

Payne male ferrules.

Payne female ferrule.

Stripping guide and snake guides.

Payne stamping on the reel seat.

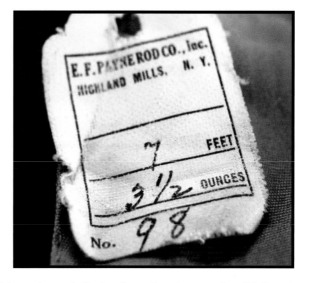

Close up of the male ferrules and the reel seat marking above left, the hanging tag stating "7 feet 3 ½ ounces No. 98" is pictured above right.

Wright & McGill
Granger Favorite 3/2
9 ft. 6 inch 8/9 wt.
circa 1952

*T*his is a rarely seen 9'6" 8/9 wt Granger Favorite by The Wright & McGill Company of Denver, Colorado. In my opinion the Favorite is one of the prettiest of all of the Granger Rods whether made by Goodwin Granger or W&McG.. The Favorite with its intermediate wraps harkens back to an older slower time. This rod has the Granger patent internal up-locking reel seat and the classic granger reversed half Wells grip. The rod is wrapped in black & white Jasper tipped with gold and gold intermediates. The main wraps look like black and yellow jasper because of the aging of the varnish on the thread. It has the classic Granger style of angular welted serrated waterproof NiS Ferrules. The guides are all perfection THS with Perfection tip tops.

*T*his rod is from the Authors collection.

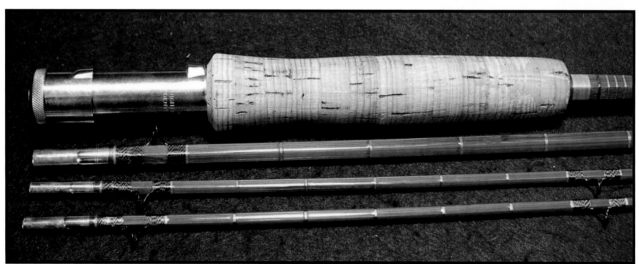

Pictured above are the 1938 patent Granger internal up locking reel seat with the reversed half Wells grip and the snake guides and the wrap pattern of the" Granger Favorite".

Male Granger ferrules.　　　*Female angular welt Granger ferrules and Perfection tiptops.*

Guides and wrap pattern above left. Signature wrap with the three gold bands denoting a manufacture date of after 1951 above right.

Pictured above to the left is the reel seat stampings and above right are the gum rubber stamp shaft markings.

Hardy Brothers, England Palakona Reg. Trade Mark "The Pope" 2/1 10'6" circa1959

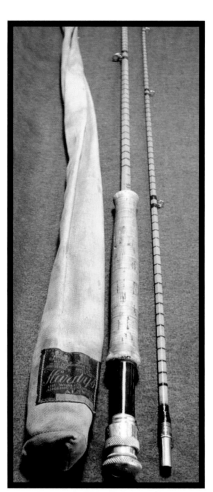

*T*his rod is a classic example of the Hardy brothers of Alnwick, England. This rod has the typical closely spaced intermediate wraps used by the British. It has the Hardy Patented Loc-Fast ferrule. It has the up-locking reel seat that Hardy introduced in 1911 that was eventually copied by notable American makers like Payne and Thomas, even the Cross rods and higher end South Bends also sported very close versions of this reel seat. It is wrapped in silk and has its original canvas bag. The rod has Mildrum style double foot guides the length of the rod and has an agate stripper and tiptop.

*T*his rod is from the Private collection of John Oppenlander.

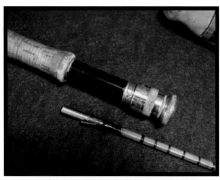

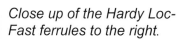
1911 Hardy Up locking reel sea to the left.

Close up of the Hardy Loc-Fast ferrules to the right.

Running guides.

Agate stripper and tiptop.

"The Pope" signature.

Palakona registered trademark.

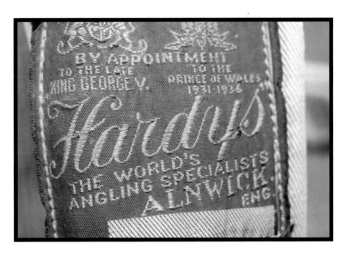

Bag label.

Made by Hardy's England stamping.

The "By appointment" Mark.

Serial number H 20855.

The obverse side "By Appointment" marks.

Lyle Dickerson, Michigan
8' 2/2 D 8014 circa 1969

*T*his rod one of the most sought after of the classic era rods. The Dickerson rods are the epitome of the plain understated look of the classic era. This rod has blued Super Z ferrules and Chrome plated snake guides. The grip is a reversed semi half Wells out of ½" cork rings. The reel seat is aluminum down-locking with a wood insert. The rod has its original cloth bag and aluminum tube. The rod is wrapped in a translucent orange silk and is hand signed by Lyle Dickerson. The number designation used by Dickerson denotes the length and the size of ferrule in 64th's of an inch. This rod is in extremely good condition and is a true pleasure to cast. It was originally made for Phillip M. Wright, who was one of the original founders of Trout Unlimited.

*T*his rod is from the private collection of Richard Collar, D.D.S.

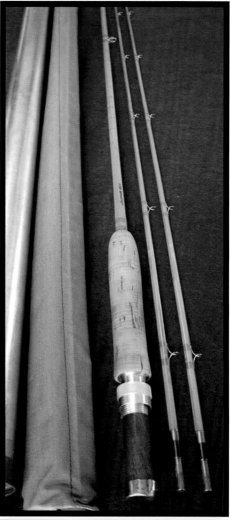

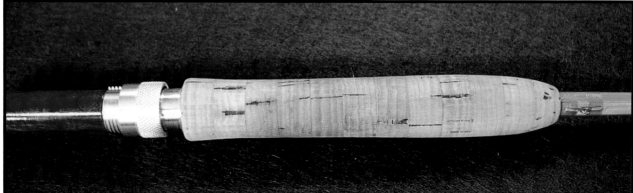

Reversed half Wells grip and the looped hook keeper used by Lyle Dickerson.

*T*his rod was built late in Mr. Dickerson's career as a rodmaker. That is shown first of by the date of manufacture (1969). Secondly, by this point in his career, his eyes were starting to fail and you see a drop in the quality of work done by Mr. Dickerson. The picture on the following page shows the very open seam on the rod. I have this rod listed as a classic even though it was built ten years into the modern era of rods.

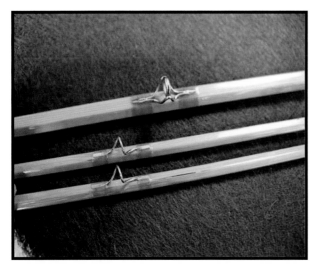
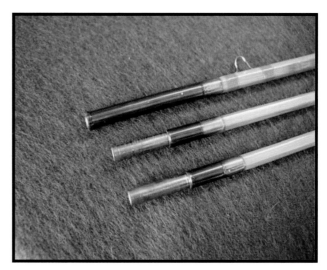

Pictured above left are the stripping guide and snake guides, Note the open seam on the bottom tip to the right of the guide. Blued Super Z ferrules above right.

Rod shaft markings are pictured above, Dickerson model number to the left and the original owners name to the right.

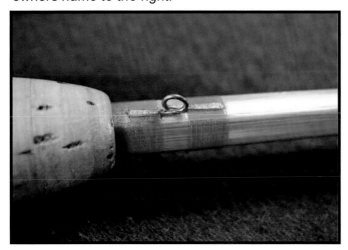

Pictured above left is a close up of the hook keeper used by Dickerson and above right is a close up of the open seam on the shaft, a definite sign of a rod made in the later stages of Lyle Dickerson's career.

Hoagy B. Carmichael, N.Y. Tonkin Cane 206E 7'6" 2/2 circa 1970s

*T*his rod was custom built for Charlie Berry of Denver Co. and it is now in the hands of its second owner. The rod has the typical Garrison style reel seat and grip that are common to the work of Hoagy Carmichael. The rod has NiS super Z ferrules and the stripping guide is a chrome plated Mildrum style guide. The snake guides are THS that have been blued and the tiptops are Perfection style tiptops. The rod is wrapped in a medium cinnamon brown silk that has been allowed to go translucent. The wraps on the guides are not tipped but the ferrule wraps are tipped with a black trim wrap. The reel seat hardware is aluminum with a cork insert.

This rod is based upon the Garrison 209E taper.

This rod is from the private collection of Richard Collar, D.D.S.

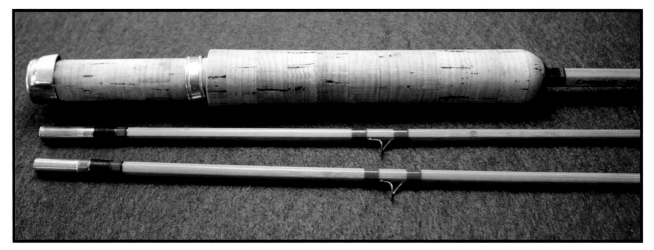

Pictured above are the reel seat and grip and guides and ferrules favored by Hoagy B. Carmichael.

*T*he opportunity that Hoagy had to learn at the side of Everett Garrison was priceless and we all owe him a debt of thanks for making sure that the "Masters Guide" was published and the knowledge was not lost.

Male Super Z ferrules.

Female Super Z ferrule and ferrule plug.

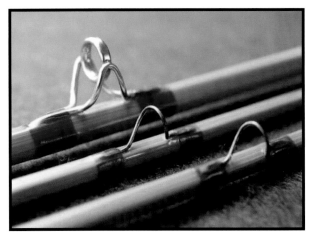

Stripping guide and snake guides above left and the signature on blank "Carmichael – 206 E" and in the shadow is "C-76-2" indicating it was the second of that model made in 1976.

Pictured to the left are the signature markings on the tips.

*H*oagie's father was Hoagy "Star duster" Carmichael who was a very famous jazz musician from the middle of the 1900's. One of my favorite works of his is the soundtrack to the John Wayne / Howard Hawks movie "Hatari". I have this rod listed as a classic even though it was built in the modern era out of respect for Hoagy Carmichael.

Merritt Hawes Blank
Sam Carlson finished for
Harmon Leonard, D.V.M.
8' 3/2 circa early 1970s

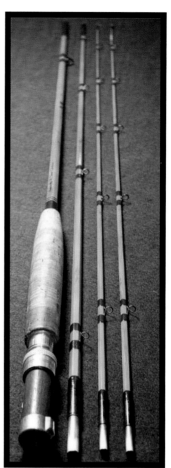

*T*his is a true one of a kind rod with a pedigree that is absolutely impeccable. Shortly before her death, Cora Hawes gave this blank made by her son Merritt Hawes, the son of Hiram Hawes, who was the nephew of Hiram L. Leonard, to Dr. Harmon Leonard, who is the grand nephew of Hiram L. Leonard. Her goal was to make sure that some of the remaining H.L. Leonard relics stayed in the Leonard family. In the early nineteen fifties Cora answered an ad placed by Harmon looking for H.L. Leonard guns or rods and found a branch of the family that was not known before. She took a great liking to Harmon and passed on to him Hiram L. Leonard's personal wicker creel, his tin fly box with a partial label with writing in his hand, his Nottingham reel and a couple of pistols by Hiram as well as a double rifle By Hiram L. Leonard. In addition was his personal game bag. There was also a rifle by Hiram Hawes and a pistol as well involved in that inheritance.

*T*he work performed by Sam Carlson on this rod is absolutely impeccable from the wrap work to the varnish, which is near flawless. Sam and Dr. Leonard were close friends and Sam insisted on finishing the Hawes blank for him.

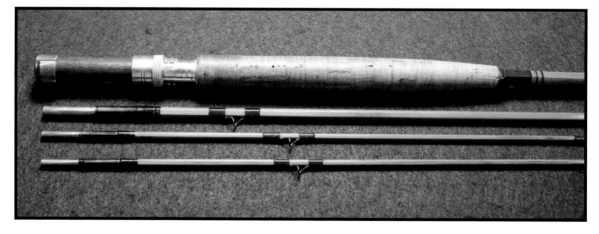

Pictured above are the grip and reel seat used by Sam Carlson on the Merritt Hawes blank. Note the wraps and also the quality of the bluing on the ferrules that is extremely well done.

Male ferrules on the Hawes/Carlson rod.

Female ferrules and tiptops.

Guides and tiptop.

"Rod by Merritt Hawes" signature by Sam Carlson.

Pictured to the left is a close up of shaft markings by Sam Carlson on the Hawes blank.

Sam Carlson is most well known for the "Carlson Four" quadrate rods he made over a 15 plus year career making rods.

Partridge of Redditch.
Single piece 5'10"
Fly rod. Circa 1950-1970

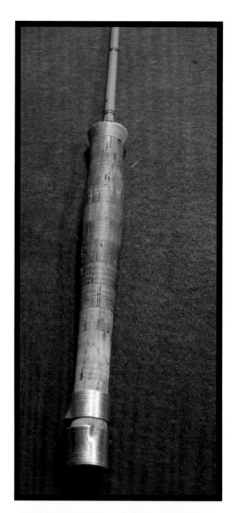

*T*his is a single piece midge rod by Partridge of Redditch, England. The rod is a very slow action lightweight rod. It has an aluminum cap and ring reel seat on the ½ inch cork ring grip and reel seat. The guides are oversize English twist snake guides. It is wrapped with a green silk tipped with black and has a round tiptop. This rod was the model sold by Partridge as an answer to the Wulff Midge and Ultimate sold by Charles Farlow & Co.

*T*he rod being a single piece is very smooth and consistent in its action. The biggest drawback is the length of the rod, which is problematic to modern travel.

*T*his rod is from the private collection of Jerry Schaeffer.

Aluminum and cork Cap and ring reel seat.

Partridge of Redditch, shaft markings.

Stripping guide.

English twist snake.

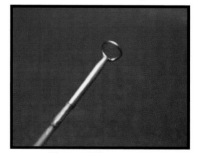

Round tiptop.

Bibliography

The following books are the reference works used to identify and date the rods listed in this book. And are recommended reading for the novice collector and angler.

Bradford, Charles. *Anglers Guide: Nassau press 1908*

Bradford, Charles. *Anglers Guide: The Field and Stream Publishing Co. 1909*

Brooks, Lake. *Science of Fishing: A.R.Harding 1912*

Brooke, R. MD. *Art of Angling: 1799*

Campbell A.J. *Classic & Antique Fly-Fishing Tackle: Lyons&Burford 1997*

Cholmondeley-Pennel, H. *Fishing, Pike and other coarse fish: Longmans, Green, and Co. 3rd edition 1887*

Cholmondeley-Pennel, H. *Fishing, Salmon and Trout: Longmans, Green, and Co. 4th edition 1888*

Chubb, T.H. *9th edition 1891 Retail Catalog: Reprinted by Tom Kerr 2002*

Garrison, Everett. *A Masters Guide to Building a Bamboo Fly Rod: Martha's Glen Publishing 1977*

Hardy, John J. *Salmon Fishing: Country Life Ltd. 1907*

Herbert, Henry William. *Frank Forester's Fish & Fishing: Stringer&Townsend 1850*

Hofland, T.C. *British Anglers Manual: WhiteHead & Co. 1839*

Holden, George Parker, M.D., F.A.C.S. *The Idyll of the Split Bamboo: DerryDale Press 1993 Ltd. Edition*

Keane, Martin J. *Classic Rods and Rodmakers: Winchester Press 1976*

Kelly, Mary Kefover. *U.S. Fishing Rod Patents and other tackle: Thomas B. Reel Co. 1990*

Kerr, Tom. *Patents Plus 1838 to 1900: Tom Kerr 2002 {Cd-Rom}*

Mather, Fred. *Men I have Fished with: Forest and Stream Publishing 1897*

McClane, A.J. *The Wise Fisherman's Encyclopedia: Wm.H.Wise & Co., Inc.*

McGrath, Brian J. Editor *Fishing Collectables Magazine: 1990 V1 #3, 1993 V1 #4, 1993 V5 #2, 1994 V6 #2, 1995 V6 #4, 1996 V8 #2, 1997 V9 #2, 1997 V8 #3*

Melner, Samuel. And Herman Kessler. *Great Fishing Tackle catalogs of the Golden Age: Crown Publishing 1972*

Montague Rods. *Montague Rods. Reprint of the 1939 retail Catalog: Centennial Publications*

Netherton, Cliff. *History of the Sport of Casting: American Casting Education Foundation, Inc. 1981*

Norris, Thaddeus. *American Anglers Book: E.H.Butler & Co. 1865*

Oppian. *Halieuticks of the Nature of Fishes and Fishing of the Ancients: 1st English translation by Diaper Imprimatur Rob. Shippen, Vice-Can. Oxon. Feb 6, 1722*

Prouty, Lorenzo. *Fish their Habits and Haunts: Cupples, Upham and Co. 1887*

Prime, W.C. *I Go A-Fishing: Harper & Brothers 1873*

Radcliffe, William. *Fishing from the Earliest Times: John Murray Pub. 1921*

Schmelzer, J.F.&Sons Arms Co. *Retail/Wholesale Catalog 1906*

Schullery, Paul. *American Fly Fishing a history: Nick Lyons Books 1987*

Schwiebert, Ernest. *Trout, Volume 2 second edition: Truman Talley Books 1984*

Scott, Genio C. *Fishing in American Waters: Harper&Brothers Pub. 1869*

Sheets, K.A. *American fishing books 1743-1993: Sheets 1993*

Sinclair, Michael. *Bamboo Rod Restoration Manual: Centennial Pub. 1994*

Sinclair, Michael. *Fishing Rods by Divine: Centennial Pub. 1993*

Sinclair, Michael. *Heddon The rod with the Fighting Heart: Centennial Pub. 1997*

Spurr, Dick. *Classic Bamboo Rodmakers Past and Present: Centennial Pub. 1992*

Stoddard, Thomas Tod. *The Anglers Guide to the rivers and lochs of Scotland: William Blackwood and Sons 1847*

Waterman, Charles F. *A History of Angling: Winchester Press 1981*

Wells, Henry P. *Fly-Rods and Fly-Tackle: Harper & Brothers 1885*

Wilkinson, A.G. *Notes on Salmon fishing, Scribner's Monthly Vol. 12 #6 October 1876*

Index

Index *Continued*

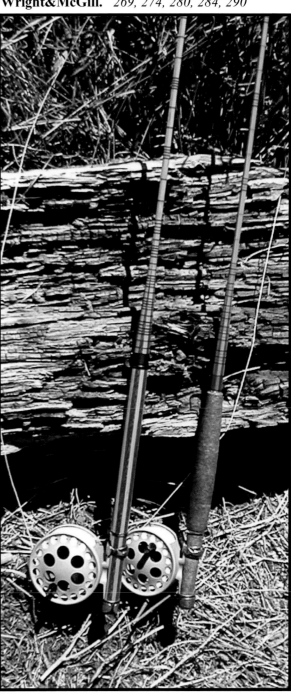

A pair of Mortised rods by the Author, The one to the left is mortised with Leopard wood and the one to the right is mortised with Shedua {African Olivewood}.

Photo Credits/ Finis

This book has been a collaboration of several different photographers and Credit is due to the following for their aid in making this work possible. And also one more thank you to the following people is in order.

Tom Kerr Photographed all the rods in his collection that are featured here in this book with the exception of the Leonard rod on page #34 and the "Bassett" rod on page #136 which were photographed by the Author.

Carla List-Handley photographed the J.B. Daniels rod on page # 44.

Bob Carolan photographed the Dame Stoddard "High Grade" by B.F. Nichols on page # 80.

Erica Gooding photographed the G.W. Boyd rod that is on page # 46.

Sante Giuliani photographed the Garrison rod on page # 255

Craig Lynch, Scott Davis and several others submitted photographs of rods that just did not quite make the cut. Sorry, guys, but I do appreciate the effort.

All other photographs are by the Author.

In Finis

This has been a labor of love and I hope that it enables people to identify rods that they have wondered about and were not quite sure of. And also I hope it shows how obsessed we have been with our efforts to chase the finny tribe. From the wood rods of the 1800's to the glass rods of the mid 1900s and all of the other odd materials used to make fishing rods. I wish that I could say that I have examples of all of the makers in this book but that is not possible at this point in time. Phillipe, Sam and Solon, E.A. Green and Sedgwick are just a few names of a long list that is not represented here in this work.

As I sit here at 4:20 in the afternoon with a single malt scotch and a Flugemocker it is late spring 2004 and it is time to go chase "Old wood" and wild fish now that this project is finished.

The Author   Paonia, Colorado May 2004

Contacts for Old Tackle

Bob Corsetti
Rods & Reels
17 Massasoit Road
Nashua, NH 03063
603-886-0411

Len Codella
Sporting Heritage Collectibles
2201 S. Carnegie Drive
Inverness, Fl. 34450
352-637-5454

Martin J. Keane
Classic Rods & Tackle Inc.
P.O. Box 288
Ashley Falls, Mass. 01222
413-229-7988

Richard Collar
Richards Rods
www.antiquetackle.net
970-921-6474

Langs Sporting Collectibles Inc.
Auction service
John & Debbie Ganung
663 Pleasant Valley Road
Waterville, NY 13480
315-841-4623

Jordan-Mills Rod Co.
Carmine Lisella
11 Wesley Road
Congers, NY 10920

J.L. Hatton
Appraisals / New Bamboo rods
P.O. Box 594
Paonia Co. 81428
970-527-3406

Museums and Organizations

National Fishing Lure Collectors
Club
P.O. Box 13
Grove city, OH 43123

Old Reel Collectors Association

American Museum of Fly Fishing
P.O. Box 42
Manchester, Vt. 05254

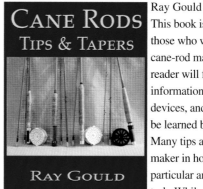

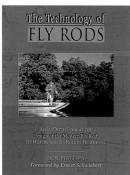